Minnesota Diary,
1942–46

Minnesota Diary, 1942–46

SINCLAIR LEWIS

George Killough, Editor

UNIVERSITY OF IDAHO PRESS
Moscow, Idaho
2000

Published by the University of Idaho Press
Moscow, Idaho 83844-1107
Printed in the United States of America

04 03 02 01 00 5 4 3 2 1

Library of Congress Cataloging-in-Publication Data
Lewis, Sinclair, 1885–1951.
Minnesota diary, 1942–46 / Sinclair Lewis ; George Killough, editor.
p. cm.
Includes index.
ISBN 0-89301-219-X- (hc : alk. paper)
1. Lewis, Sinclair, 1885–1951—Diaries. 2. Lewis, Sinclair, 1885–1951—Homes and haunts—Minnesota. 3. Novelists, American—20th century—Diaries. 4. Minnesota—Intellectual life—20th century. I. Killough, George. II. Title.

PS3523.E94 Z47 2000
818'.5203—dc21
[B] 99-055769

Design by Trina Stahl

COMMITTEE ON
SCHOLARLY EDITIONS
AN APPROVED EDITION
MODERN LANGUAGE
ASSOCIATION OF AMERICA

The emblem of the Committee on Scholarly Editions indicates that this volume is based on an examination of all available relevant textual sources, that it is edited according to principles articulated in the volume, that the source texts and any deviation of edited texts from them are fully described, that the editorial principles, the text, and the apparatus have undergone a peer review, that a rigorous schedule of verification and proofreading was followed to insure a high degree of accuracy in the presentation of the edition, and that the text is accompanied by appropriate textual and historical contextual information.

For

A. Boyd Killough,

my father,

who inspired my devotion to scholarship

Contents

Illustrations

Acknowledgments

THE EDITOR THANKS the University of Idaho Press staff for supporting this project and seeing it through.

The editor thanks the Sinclair Lewis Estate, particularly the executor, the late Paul Gitlin, for granting permission for the publication of the "Minnesota Diary" and quotations from other unpublished Lewis documents. Thanks are due also for permission from the Yale Collection of American Literature, and its curator Patricia Willis, at the Beinecke Rare Book and Manuscript Library where the "Minnesota Diary" is housed along with numerous other Lewis documents including the diary of his youth ("Diary, Nov. 10, 1900–July 4, 1908").

Another institution providing valuable support was the St. Cloud State University Archive, with Archivist Patricia Schenk, where the Lewis Family Papers Collection contains the Marcella Powers Correspondence and numerous photographs.

Additional archives and libraries instrumental for this study were the Northeast Minnesota Historical Center, with Archivist Patricia Maus, sponsored by the St. Louis County Historical Society and housed at the library of the University of Minnesota at Duluth; the Duluth Public Library, especially its newspaper clippings files; the Minnesota Historical Society Library in St. Paul, especially its biography card files, its collection of state newspapers on microfilm, and its photo collection; Bryant Library in Sauk Centre; Wilson Library at the University of Minnesota in Minneapolis; the Minneapolis Institute of Arts; the in-house library at the

Minneapolis *Star Tribune;* the Bancroft Library at the University of California in Berkeley; and the library at the College of St. Scholastica.

Thanks are due as well to the following people, some of them now deceased, who remembered Lewis from the era of the "Minnesota Diary" and reported their observations in interviews: Elsa Anneke, Ann Buck Dalton, Billie Nolan Franey, Harriet Starin Fredin, Mary Banning Friedlander, Evelyn Glendenning, Edward F. Greve, Mary Hugo, Harold Kittleson, Frances McGiffert, Margaret Mitchell, Ann Nolan, Dorothy Tart Putman, Kathleen Ridder, Virginia Fryberger Sellwood, Jane Coulter Spencer, and Marjorie Kelley Wilkins. Thanks also to two Duluthians who met Lewis but wish to remain anonymous.

Among the people contributing further understanding about Duluth, Lewis, Minnesota, or the 1940s were Betty Anneke, Carol Bly, Sr. Mary Richard Boo, Alan and Mary Brain, Donald Cameron, Eddie Crawford, Harry Davis, Josiah Fuller, Pearl Fuller, Peter Gujer, Virginia Hyvarinen, Patrick Labadie, Sr. Margaret James Laughlin, Mary Roberts, Sr. Ann Edward Scanlon, Mrs. George Solon, Sam Solon, Vlasie Solon, Francis C. Sullivan, William and Mary Van Evera, Julius Fred Wolff, Jr., and Linnea Yonkers.

Among the people contributing knowledge of the Lewis family and Sauk Centre, some of whom had known Lewis, were Isabel Lewis Agrell, Faye Besser, Kay Beuning, Art Borgmann, Katie Bromen, David DuBois, Pat DuBois, Bob Freeman, Linda Frumkin, Dave Jacobson, Joyce Lyng, Roberta Olson, and Al Tingley.

Further thanks are due for advice and criticism from fellow scholars of American literature, diaries, or documentary editing, particularly Patrick Coleman, Roger Forseth, James Hutchisson, John Koblas, James Lundquist, Robert McLaughlin, Sally Parry, Stephen Pastore, and Keith Peterson.

In 1989 the project was awarded a Blandin Faculty Fellowship, which funded travel to libraries and the help of a summer research assistant, Heidi Nicholson Bohlmann. The College of St. Scholastica Faculty Development Fund supported further travel to libraries. In 1990 the project had the benefit of a consultation with Don L. Cook, representing the MLA Committee for Scholarly Editions. Two organizations that have provided encouragement are the Sinclair Lewis Society and the Sinclair Lewis Foundation.

The editor is grateful for support from his family, from all the people and institutions named above, and from many people who are not named.

Any errors in this work are completely the responsibility of the editor and him alone.

Minnesota Diary, 1942–46

Introduction

QUIET DIGNITY IS not what people usually remember about Sinclair Lewis. Witnesses recall instead eruptions of rudeness, pranks, long performances of oral mimicry, erratic treatment of friends. His novels teem with caricature, melodrama, vaudevillian tricks of style. Rarely has his public image seemed quiet.

In direct contrast is the image found in his private papers, especially the diaries, which until now have been available only to the occasional scholar journeying to Yale, where they reside in the Beinecke Library. The first of these diaries Lewis began in 1900 at age fifteen in his home in Sauk Centre, Minnesota, and continued through his undergraduate years at Yale until 1908. That diary still remains unpublished. The "Minnesota Diary" dates from the 1940s, when the middle-aged Lewis returned to his home state to try to put down roots.[1] Both diaries provide surprising insight into the private Lewis, who was reflective, lyrical, and self-aware. Passage after passage reveals the quiet dignity that seemed so absent in Lewis's public persona.

He began the "Minnesota Diary" in April 1942 to chronicle an experiment in Minnesota living. Wealthy, famous, somewhat jaded as a world-traveler, and forever restless, he was pursuing two old dreams. One was to find the peace and vitality that Thoreau found at Walden Pond. The other was to revitalize his provincial identity, restore connections to Minnesota roots. The return at age fifty-seven to the old custom of diary-keeping marked the deliberateness in this experiment. He titled the diary accordingly "Minnesota Diary," and during the years the experiment lasted,

1942–46, he wrote entries almost exclusively during time spent in the state, adding only a handful of notes for the many months spent elsewhere. The focus falls mostly on the landscapes and people of Minnesota, for which Lewis had deep affection.

His admiration for Thoreau was longstanding. As a temporary Yale dropout trying to earn a living in the magazine world in New York in 1907, he read *Walden* on his lunch hour, sitting in a park. He imagined the vitality and freedom that Thoreau felt.[2] In the 1930s in his "Book Week" column in *Newsweek,* he portrayed Thoreau as the quintessence of American freedom, the standard to hold up against the native-born Babbittry of Dale Carnegie and the foreign menace of Italy, Germany, and Japan.[3]

In May 1943, a *Time* magazine reporter questioned Lewis about his determination to live in Minnesota, and Lewis pointed to Thoreau as the reason. Unfortunately, an invitation from Hollywood to write a screenplay there put the Minnesota experiment on hold during summer 1943, but not before Lewis had declared his Thoreauvian goal quite clearly. The *Time* report, appearing in the "People" section, was as follows:

> *Bolstered by the complete works of Henry David Thoreau, newly bought, novelist Sinclair Lewis abandoned his Manhattan duplex for rustic life in his home state, Minnesota. He told a reporter that a reading of Thoreau would explain all, but admitted: "I don't mean I want to go around in a sheet like Ghandi." Next fall, he will do some public debating on rusticity, said he.*[4]

Here the public Lewis, wise to the ways of gossip columnists, makes a joke about private aspiration. The purpose is not to destroy the dream but to protect it. He exaggerates the ideal to indicate he knows better than to attempt a utopian objective with rigid purism. At age fifty-eight with less than robust health and with an inescapable celebrity status, he is aware that a Thoreauvian experiment will involve compromise, especially if he continues to write novels. Not only would it be ridiculous for him to go around in a sheet like Ghandi, it would just not be feasible. He had no intention of building a hut on some remote lake in Minnesota and living there on a diet of beans.

The devotion to Thoreau depended on deeper principles. In agreement with ideas in *Walden,* he had always pursued his dreams, always tried to dig through the mud and slush of opinion and prejudice in search of rock bottom reality, and now he was about to pay closer attention than usual to the natural landscape. He was going to chronicle the changing surface of his own equivalent of Walden Pond. The "Minnesota Diary," much of which he had written already during the exploratory summer and fall of 1942, is in fact the record of this observation.

His convictions about Thoreau continued strong even after he bought and settled into his neo-Tudor mansion in Duluth. Although he could accept compromise, he could not abide a deliberate ignoring of Thoreauvian truths. Writing in Duluth during summer 1945, he denounced Louis Bromfield's book about country living, *Pleasant Valley.* Bromfield's tragedy, wrote Lewis, was that instead of making "an enduring book, a true *Walden,* he . . . cluttered and botched it with all the pert vanities of the money-grabbing, socially-climbing, Paris-Broadway-Hollywood literary gent. He did not listen to the quiet of his own fields and of his own heart."[5]

A desire to listen more carefully to the quiet of his own fields had been in Lewis's mind for a long time. He had made other efforts to put down roots in country settings. In 1928 he and second wife Dorothy Thompson, just married, bought an estate near Barnard, Vermont, which they called Twin Farms. In the "Self-Portrait" Lewis wrote for the Nobel Foundation in 1930, he described himself as having recently settled down there in "my first authentic home—a farm in the pastoral state of Vermont."[6] Over a decade later, in spring 1941, long after separating from Dorothy, he looked for a country home in Connecticut, land of his paternal ancestors. He found a house in Lakeville, where he spent much of the summer. At the time he fancied northwestern Connecticut as a permanent place to live, for he wrote that summer in an autobiographical essay, fictionally presented as his own obituary, that the writer Sinclair Lewis had settled there at a small country place in 1952 where he lived "immovably" until his death nineteen years later.[7]

The return to Minnesota in 1942 resulted from an even more concentrated effort to put down roots in provincial soil. Rural Minnesota, after all, was his birthplace. As sensitive readers of *Main Street* have recognized, the criticism of small-town life in that book represents the troubled view of someone who belongs, not the supercilious scorn of an urban sophisticate. Lewis knew he belonged and wanted to belong even more. In two essays, he had already explained his friendly relation to Minnesota. The first, "Minnesota, the Norse State," published originally in

1923, holds the state up as a mystery, the understanding of which would illumine all America: "To understand America, it is merely necessary to understand Minnesota. But to understand Minnesota, you must be an historian, an ethnologist, a poet, a cynic, and a graduate prophet all in one."[8] The other essay, solicited for the fiftieth anniversary issue of the Sauk Centre high school yearbook in 1931, was "The Long Arm of the Small Town." Here Lewis observes that his criticism of prairie villages has been no harsher than his criticism of New York or Paris, and he concludes that the Sauk Centre of his boyhood was for him "a good time, a good place, and a good preparation for life."[9]

The diary of his youth confirms the sincerity of this assertion. Far from being a record of adolescent complaints, this diary emphasizes aspirations and achievements while it also chronicles details of daily life. The writer seems a likable kid, reasonably well adjusted, interested sometimes in mischief, sometimes in serious ideas, sometimes in a girl named Myra Hendryx. Though life in Sauk Centre has bumps, it is remarkably happy. The likable kid has a huge desire to gain entrance to a fine university in the great world beyond. He dreams constantly of this goal, but not because life at home oppresses him. In fact, one would never guess from this diary that the diarist would grow up to write *Main Street*. His dream of the great world seems like any talented boy's dream of achievement. Thinking about home, he can express affection with the same adolescent hyperbole he applies to his dream. He hears Sauk Centre church bells on Wednesday, April 9, 1902, and writes that "in a still evening they make me feel that the world and its riches are not worth a tithe of home and its surroundings."[10]

On top of the desire to live more like Thoreau and to strengthen rural roots, there was also a professional motive for returning to Minnesota in the 1940s: novel-writing. This was an all-absorbing enterprise during Lewis's whole adult life. It was not just a matter of concentrating at the typewriter. It was plunging into experiences so as to absorb the subject.[11] This was Lewis's calling, and he labored hard and fast. When he arrived in Minneapolis in April 1942, he was already working on *Gideon Planish* (1943), the satire on philanthropic fund-raising. He had other projects in the back of his mind. By the time he got to Duluth in 1944, he had a solid vision of *Cass Timberlane* (1945), the novel about December-May marriage, and he moved very quickly after that into work on *Kingsblood Royal* (1947), the protest book on northern race prejudice. During the four years of the Minnesota experiment, he was also reading history and digging into archives in preparation for *The God-Seeker* (1949), the historical novel about the white settlement of Minnesota in the nineteenth century.

Since he had let novel-writing impinge on two marriages already and on his role as a parent, it is no surprise that he would let it encroach as well on his dream of Walden and rural rootedness. The mansion he purchased in Duluth may seem a far cry from Thoreau's hut, and the deliberate entry into Duluth social life an even further barrier to simple living. But in order to write *Cass Timberlane* and *Kingsblood Royal,* both set in a city north of Minneapolis with a population of 85,000 and an economic base of iron ore, lumber, and wheat, Lewis had to know Duluth. So he plunged in. There was some benefit, of course, for his personal goals. Lake Superior provided great natural scenery, and the north woods were very close. Duluth was also not the urban East; it was quite definitely a Minnesota town. He could continue to chronicle the changing appearance of lake and sky in his diary, but he must have known that his work compromised the dream more than he had intended.

THE BROAD OUTLINE of Harry Sinclair Lewis's life may sound like the kind of cliché that he loved to expose: ability and diligence rising from modest beginnings into fame and fortune. He was born in Sauk Centre in 1885 to a physician father, who already had two sons. The first, Fred, who grew up to be a Sauk Centre miller and farmer, was ten years older than young Harry. The second son, Claude, who followed his father into medicine and practiced in St. Cloud, was older than Harry by seven years. Their mother died of tuberculosis when Harry was only six, and a year later their father married the woman who became their kind stepmother.

Graduating from high school in Sauk Centre in 1902, Harry went off to spend two terms at Oberlin Academy in Ohio as preparation for Yale, where he subsequently began his undergraduate career in fall 1903. During the Oberlin period, he had a religious awakening and vowed to become a missionary. Concentrated study of Latin and Greek in Sauk Centre, at Oberlin, and later at Yale inspired him also to imagine a career as a scholar. He had a powerful mind and an intense drive to learn, though not always according to the schedules of his teachers. His father, recognizing both the talent and the drive, provided support. All these things—the religious experience, the interest in scholarship, the intense devotion to ideas, even his father's support—are apparent in the youthful diary. That the diary of his middle age should reveal a quietly reflective dimension in his character is completely consistent with this picture from his youth.

Nor should it be surprising that Lewis as an adult wanted to have so many adventures, live in so many places. He had always had many enthusiasms, and he plunged into them impulsively. Reading his youthful diary, one pictures his parents in the background trying to hold him on course. Before graduating from Yale in 1908, he had been to England twice during summer vacations working on cattle boats, he had dropped out of school to join Upton Sinclair's experimental commune called Helicon Hall, he had gone to Panama to look for employment on the canal, and he had worked as a writer-translator for a magazine in New York City.

His boldness in adventure did not diminish his discipline as a writer. From the Yale years, when the writing bug bit him hard, until the end of his life, he churned out material constantly. Before the extraordinary success of *Main Street,* he had written six books. During the 1920s, the peak decade, he wrote five blockbuster novels: *Main Street* (1920), *Babbitt* (1922), *Arrowsmith* (1925), *Elmer Gantry* (1927), and *Dodsworth* (1929), plus two more of lesser quality.

Intense enthusiasms and intense work, however, took a toll, especially on domestic life. His first wife was Grace Hegger, a New Yorker born to English immigrant parents, her father an art dealer. She was working for *Vogue,* and Lewis for the Frederick Stokes publishing company, when they met in 1912. They married in 1914, had a son in 1917 named Wells, separated in 1927, and divorced in 1928. Her account of the marriage suggests that the feverish pace of Lewis's work and travel was not compatible with domestic life and parenthood.[12]

Lewis's second wife was famous newspaper columnist Dorothy Thompson, a brilliant analyst of international affairs. She and Lewis met in Berlin in 1927, married in 1928, had in 1930 a son named Michael, separated in 1937, and divorced in 1942. She, like Grace, considered him not very devoted to fatherhood, but she resisted divorce. He felt the efforts to domesticate him diminished the quality of his work, and the marriage ended at his behest.

He was at the peak of his fame when he married Dorothy Thompson, and his star shone even brighter in 1930 when he won the Nobel Prize for literature, the first American ever to receive this award. From then on he continued famous and wealthy for the rest of his life. Though he never quite achieved again the creative fire of the 1920s, he still sought experiences on which to base novels and he kept publishing them every two or three years until he died. One data-gathering adventure was in theater. In the late 1930s, he dived in, writing plays, bankrolling plays, acting in plays. The resultant novel was *Bethel Merriday* (1940), which features a traveling theater troupe. The details derive from a traveling production of Lewis's play *Angela Is Twenty-Two,* that ran from December 30, 1938 to April 1, 1939, with Lewis playing a major role during the first month.

Later in 1939, still in the middle of his theater phase, he met Marcella Powers, the girlfriend for whom he felt an extraordinary affection during the years of the "Minnesota Diary." That August he was playing in Eugene O'Neill's *Ah, Wilderness!* in Provincetown. Marcella, an eighteen-year-old apprentice who had graduated from high school in South Orange, New Jersey just a year earlier, was assigned the job of helping the distinguished author learn his lines. They hit it off. Soon they were weekending together. In September he took her back to New York and rented an apartment for her in the same building where his was. When he finished *Bethel Merriday* in October, they went together on a long odyssey south and west.[13] This involved some play acting in Paul Vincent Carroll's *Shadow and Substance* in New Orleans in January 1940 and residence in Hollywood until spring. In summer 1940 they were both playing summer theaters again in New England.

After theater, the next venue for Lewis to explore was the world of teaching. During fall 1940 he spent a little more than a month teaching creative writing at the University of Wisconsin in Madison and then conducted a four-day workshop in December at the University of Iowa. He had already been on the lecture circuit, including an extensive fall-winter tour in 1937–38, but he went out again in November 1941 with his friend Rabbi Lewis Browne, a popular writer on religion and history. They staged debates on such subjects as the Country Versus the City, with Sinclair Lewis taking the side of the country. This tour lasted into January 1942. All these experiences, coupled with the long association with a political commentator wife, enabled Lewis to write *Gideon Planish* (1943), which features a college professor whose gift for public speaking leads him into the disingenuous, wordy world of politics and philanthropy. Characteristically, Lewis threw himself into these experiences beyond need. He started to teach a course at the University of Minnesota in fall 1942 after he had already written most of *Gideon Planish*. He did two more tours with Lewis Browne after *Gideon Planish* was already in print. His life was busy.

The Minnesota experiment itself, as chronicled in the diary, began in April 1942. Lewis found a big house outside Minneapolis on Lake Minnetonka to rent for the summer, which he used as a base from which to explore Minnesota in long trips by car. He wrote most of *Gideon Planish* there. A research assistant named James Hart worked with him for part of the summer. Twelve-year-old son Michael visited for two weeks in August. During the move to a house in Minneapolis for the fall, Lewis took a brief trip east, visiting his son Wells in Illinois, now a second lieutenant in the army, and Marcella Powers at a summer theater in Peterborough, New Hampshire. Back in Minneapolis in late September, he began the creative writing class at the university. In early December he finished the academic term and a final draft of *Gideon Planish,* and he left for New York. During this period of vigorous writing, teaching, and exploring, Lewis also had great enthusiasm for diary-keeping. The largest part of the "Minnesota Diary," fols. 4–106, covers summer-fall 1942 in the Twin Cities area.

He did not return to Minnesota for a concentrated stay until 1944, though there were two short visits, one in February 1943 and another in May when he was thinking of staying. He spent summer 1943 in Hollywood working on a screenplay with Dore Schary called *Storm in the West.* Meeting a score of movie celebrities, he wrote excitedly to Marcella back in New York. There he returned in September but was off again on a lecture tour with Lewis Browne from early October to mid-December 1943.

In New York in winter 1944 he started planning *Cass Timberlane* and the move to Duluth. By May 6, 1944, he was in Minneapolis and on May 27 he took up residence as a renter in the Duluth mansion that he would eventually purchase. That summer he acquainted himself with Duluth society and worked diligently on *Cass Timberlane* until the end of August when he returned to New York. Motoring around the state less than he did in 1942, he had less to write in the diary but he still made faithful entries. Spring and summer 1944 in Duluth occupy fols. 113–148, a sizable portion of the diary.

Most of fall and winter 1944–45 he spent in New York, except for a month-long lecture tour with Lewis Browne in November, during which the news arrived that son Wells had died in action in Europe. In January 1945 he bought the Duluth house, invested in elaborate redecorating, and moved there from New York in April. Marcella Powers's mother, who had helped with the move, kept him company until early July. During June, son Michael, now fifteen, came for a five-day visit.

Lewis's main project in summer 1945 was to learn about race relations to prepare for *Kingsblood Royal.* In addition, he worked on a series of articles for *Esquire,* delivered the commencement address at Duluth State Teachers College, provided weekly lectures there in the summer school until the end of July, and gave a talk at distant teachers' colleges in Moorhead and Bemidji. He stayed on in Duluth until the beginning of September, spent two months in New York, then in mid-November headed south with his Duluth driver Asa Lyons for a view of race prejudice in South Carolina, Mississippi, and Louisiana. He returned to Duluth in early December to spend the winter. His brother Fred died in Sauk Centre in January. Completing the plan for *Kingsblood Royal* at the end of March 1946, he ended the Minnesota experiment and the diary and went east. The diary received practically no attention during spring-summer 1945, the only period during the Minnesota experiment when Lewis was not actually drafting a novel or a novel plan, but entries pick up again in winter 1945–46, as if diary-writing for Lewis worked best during periods of intense professional writing.

Continuing the effort to put down roots in a country setting, he moved into an estate called Thorvale Farm near Williamstown, Massachusetts, in April 1946 and bought the place in June. This was to be his main American home until his death. Extended trips, however, continued—a working winter in Hollywood starting January 1947, a two-month excursion to Minnesota in fall 1947 to research Minnesota history for *The God-Seeker* (his last trip to Minnesota), a trip to Italy for winter 1948–49, and the final trip to Europe in fall 1949. He stayed on in Italy and died of heart failure, complicated by alcoholism, on January 10, 1951.

HEAVY DRINKING IS one of the reasons for the decline in Lewis's reputation. Many people interviewed for Mark Schorer's exhaustive biography, *Sinclair Lewis: An American Life* (1961) reported erratic behavior.[14] Added to stories of heavy consumption were reports that Lewis was restless, depressive, given to fits of rage, unreliable as a friend, husband, or father—all suggesting alcoholism.[15] The reports must be true, for there were numerous witnesses and some still alive to be interviewed for the present study.[16] But Schorer made Lewis seem even worse than he was, allowing the evidence of adult alcoholism to cast a shadow over Lewis's youth. The total picture in that book is of a soul forlorn and maladjusted from cradle to grave, an obnoxious misfit whose success at charming people must have been a fluke. Committed to this view, Schorer found himself puzzled by the evidence of Lewis's virtues, his friendliness, generosity, tolerance, and discipline. To the sensitive reader, the combinations of positives and negatives make Lewis interesting, but Schorer took the low road and suggested that so many opposite qualities might mean there was no essential Sinclair Lewis whatever, just "a large hole in the center."[17]

Part of Lewis's reputation for obnoxiousness resulted from deliberate choices. Having experience with promotion in a publishing house, he knew how to gain attention. This was certainly one of the reasons he refused the Pulitzer Prize for *Arrowsmith* in 1926. That same year while researching for *Elmer Gantry* in Kansas City, he must have been angling for publicity when in a church he defied God to strike him dead, a dramatic way to prove that God would not seek personal revenge. The reputation of his novels was for debunking American life, and even though his attacks were calibrated precisely to be neither too hard nor too soft but just right for the reading audience, the author could not avoid being perceived as a noisy malcontent.[18]

Still, his personal reputation has sunk below any intention he might have had. Other writers besides Schorer have found him distasteful. Brendan Gill, in *Here at the New Yorker,* pictured Lewis as "a man riddled by the disease of himself."[19] Even worse was the image suggested by Hemingway in *Across the River and Into the Trees,* in which the protagonist spots a "caricature of an American" drooling in a bar in Italy, a writer with a "face like an over-enlarged, disappointed weasel," a "pock-marked jerk," "who has never worked at his trade" and "is presumptuous in some annoying way."[20] Although this is fiction and Lewis's name is not mentioned, and the protagonist may not be a reliable observer, the characterization is regularly recognized as an attack on Lewis.[21] Lewis's ravaged face impressed all observers in the 1940s, Hemingway included, who made an unfortunate chronic skin ailment into a symbol of decadence.

Lewis's reputation as a writer has suffered more from judgments about personal character than have the artistic reputations of other heavy drinkers such as Fitzgerald, Faulkner, or Hemingway himself. For nearly three decades after Schorer's 1961 biography, interest in Lewis's novels was in decline. Today many literate Americans under forty have not read him at all. Schorer's most famous critical blow was struck at the end of his book: "He [Lewis] was one of the worst writers in modern American literature, but without his writing one cannot imagine modern American literature."[22] The negative side of this summation, with the phrase "one of the worst writers," carried more weight than the positive side, especially given the devastating impression left by the book as a whole about Lewis as an artist. Schorer claimed Lewis had no ability to feel or express lyric joy, had little subjective understanding, and lacked introspection and self-knowledge.[23]

Even among fans of Lewis, the perception remains that his fictional voice lacks subtlety. James Lundquist, whose short critical monograph sought to counteract the negative excesses of Schorer, thought Lewis had a "garish" fictional style that made "the presence of his abrasive personality felt."[24] Lundquist connected this style to the blare of American pop culture, with its gadgets, automobiles, and movies, that came into its own in the 1920s. And certainly there is an aggressive voice in the novels, often edged with satire, reaching hard to keep the reader's attention.

LEWIS'S PRIVATE PAPERS show a different voice from the voice of the novels and a different personality from the man remembered by so many acquaintances of the 1930s and 1940s. In his letters to Marcella Powers, for example, though still working to hold attention, he is intensely friendly. He charms and amuses. Her collection of his letters, long in private hands, was acquired by the St. Cloud State University Archive in 1996.[25] They make for happy reading. Here, for example, are two paragraphs from the letter dated 23 May 1942 showing Lewis in high spirits. He had recently returned to Lake Minnetonka from Sauk Centre where he helped celebrate the seventy-fifth anniversary of the Congregational Church. He thought the speech went well, and then he reported:

> *After S.C., Hart and I motored on north and found a charming range of hills, the Leaf Mountains, of which the highest looks across many miles*

> *of fields and dozens (literally) of lakes, like sequins on an old tapestry.....I shall never leave Minnesota. You might just as well make up your mind to coming out here at least twelve (12) times every year.*
>
> *So as to get it in while it's still cool, and to avoid any risk of there being gas rationing here--no signs of that yet, but youneverknow--I may make another five day motor trip next week, which would take me up to within two or three days of your arrival. So if you happened to wire, you might not get an answer. But I'll be at the station, with a butterscotch sundae in one hand and a Kodiak bear cub, speaking Finnish and Burmese, in the other, I will, I will, I williwilliwilliwill--darling.*

Hyperbole ("never leave Minnesota") and fictionalizing ("Kodiak bear cub") have a high enough presence here to cause the reader to recognize them as such yet feel delight at the richness of vision being added to the message. Enthusiasm increases pleasantly through fiction.

Also pleasant are the rhymes that Lewis spins out for Marcella's amusement. Here is one from the beginning of the letter dated 4 November 1942 when Lewis was teaching at the University of Minnesota and completing his draft of *Gideon Planish*. He was again in good humor.

> *Heigh ho, h. ho, now to work we'll go, teedle lum tee tee, etc." Classday today--I shall face 54 studlums, of whom 10 are over 40, that leaves 44; 10 are men, lvs 34; 10 are dumb, that leaves 24 pretty nice gals, of whom 8 Or 9 can really write. I shall, today, lecture to them on / Pretty Silly Milly Powers // of whom I sing for hours & hours // altho the tempest glares and glowers // we huddle in our summery bowers // protected by the thought of Powers //.*

As sweet-nothings go, this is charming. The romance-world clichés, the tempests and the bowers, surround the subject with such cornball obviousness that the reader knows she has become a joke, but the joke is constructed just for her and the writer really is devoted. This is high-grade, affectionate kidding.

Equally adept at the other end of the romantic spectrum, Lewis could also be earnest and sincere. A notable example is the letter Lewis wrote late at night the day Japan surrendered and ended the war, 14 August 1945:

> *Darling, my darling, almost four years ago, on a certain Sunday, December 7, 1941, I telephoned to you from Cleveland, being then a lecturer, and was the first, thus, to tell you that we were at war. Tonight, just now, I telephoned--I tried to telephone again, not exactly to tell you that the war was over, but to rejoice with you in the fact. But this time--with, probably, hundreds of thousands of service men and their people trying to telephone, I was told there would be a one to three hour delay--which would make it late even for an agent like you.....And I wanted to tell you that, war on or peace come, after all this time, I love you just as I did then--as I did six immense years ago, this month, when I first saw you--that is, first saw in lovely flesh the idea that I had always had of the you that somewhere must exist. War come or peace returned, New York or Hollywood or little shanty theater in Connecticut, I love you.....This news is immeasurably great, yet not too great for me to think of you, first of all and immediately, when I heard it.*
>
> *me*

Given Lewis's ability as a writer and his need for a companion, one might dismiss this outpouring, and the wit too, as romantic salesmanship, but there seems to have been a genuine shared friendship as well. He dedicated three novels to Marcella: *Gideon Planish* (1943), *Cass Timberlane* (1945), and *Kingsblood Royal* (1947).[26] She inspired him to write about young women, for there are important young-woman roles in the first two of these novels, and she may have influenced the characterization of Bethel Merriday as well. The rocky but enduring marriage of middle-aged Cass Timberlane and young Jinny Marshland suggests a conviction in Lewis's mind that romance with Marcella would work in the end, despite the bad odds represented by vignettes of failed marriage in "An Assemblage of Husbands and Wives" that serve as backdrop for the main story in that novel.

Lewis told friends that he hoped to marry Marcella and his letters show a constant, eager affection. He also recognized her need to develop a career and he encouraged her to see men her own age. In New York they maintained separate apartments, and when he began the effort to put down roots in the Midwest, she stayed in New York to pursue her career. After she gave up on theater, his influence helped land her an assistant editor's job at *Good Housekeeping* in spring 1943. In 1945, he helped establish her as a literary agent. During the Minnesota experiment, she visited him three times, once at Lake Minnetonka in June 1942 and twice in Duluth, July 1944 and Christmas 1945. When she told him on a visit to Thorvale Farm in fall 1946 that she was going to marry someone else, he was deeply disappointed. He continued, however, his friendship with her mother, who had helped him with the move to Duluth and the return move back East. The will he drew up in fall 1948 included bequests for both Marcella and her mother.

The fact that many letters contain long enthusiastic accounts of Lewis's experiences suggests that he felt as if he could share his life with her. In Hollywood during summer 1943, he wrote her excitedly about lunching at George Cukor's estate, dining with Kate Hepburn and Spencer Tracy, meeting Mickey Rooney in the commissary at MGM, and having a dinner-party conversation with a mysterious look-alike of Greta Garbo, who was in fact Greta Garbo.[27] As the ultimate bunk-detector, Lewis was no more seduced by Hollywood than by lords of industry, but exploration regularly inspired wonder. In spring 1944, he wrote with equal wonder about the scenes and people he was getting to know in Duluth.

Excerpts from letters to Marcella appear in the diary in the form of carbon copies that he inserted because they describe the new Minnesota experiences so well. In a dual-purpose letter-and-diary entry for June 24, 1944, he has a moment of self-awareness that reveals the peculiarly upbeat core in his sensibility. Reconsidering his famous novels, he notes shortcomings but in such a way as to show that the reality he was trying to capture has not been exhausted, still offers more. He describes with admiration the upper-middle-class businessmen who take him on a boat ride in the Duluth bay.

> *These men are halfway between a Babbitt and a Dodsworth . . . I think that if one lived among them ten years, one would like them rather better than all our War Correspondents . . . I think they are peculiar to America, and in Babbitt I just began to paint them.* (fol. 138)

This is honesty and optimism. The artist-explorer who has roamed the American heartlands still envisions rich frontiers in the distance, just waiting to be discovered.

AS A TEXT by itself, the "Minnesota Diary" offers an inside view of a very public person. Here is the ultimate verbal performer not performing. Except for the inserted carbon excerpts of letters to Marcella, the main audience is Lewis himself. As a famous writer, he must be aware that posterity may look in on him, but he is not writing to impress, at least not in his characteristic way. He sounds strangely quiet and factual. He keeps meticulous notes on weather, writes appreciative descriptions of scenery, mentions hundreds of people he is meeting, and chronicles exploratory trips around Minnesota. The main emphasis is on the external world, not on the self. Details about Minnesota pile up—names of villages, mileage measurements, the progress of crops, speech habits, the salvage rubber accumulating at filling stations for the war. As a snapshot of Minnesota during World War II, the diary has value for social history.

Diaries sometimes induce dismay in readers unfamiliar with the genre. Depending on the degree of finish, and every degree is possible, the stream of details about daily life and the idiosyncratic gaps and fragmentations and habit-worn thought can leave the impression of a skewed mind at work or a mind lacking depth. This is the nature of the genre. A diary is not an autobiography. In fact, the value of diaries often lies in their lack of polished coherence, their lack of spin and controlled suggestion. One sometimes finds the diarist unmasked. The peculiar combination of fact, feeling, and silence in the "Minnesota Diary" reveals a private Sinclair Lewis of remarkable sensitivity and restraint.

This private Lewis has a refined desire for natural beauty, and he constantly seeks to capture the unique appeal of each landscape in his view; for example: "The earth, just the earth itself, in Southern Minn so black, is very beautiful, striped in long curving lines with young corn across low knolls--like the bubbles in boiling water suddenly fixed . . ." (fol. 61); or: ". . . a small old log cabin without windows, abandoned in a field. Like a Roman Remain in England" (fol. 65).

Some paragraphs in the early part look more like minimalist nature poems than work by Sinclair Lewis. A reader wonders whether what is not said may be as important as what is, as in the following paragraph from fol. 10: "Horses, springtime, loafing in pasture, joy after winter. Cows lie about really dissolutely."

Sometimes the voice is exuberant, struck with awe. About a spring afternoon on Lake Minnetonka, Lewis exults, "And boats on the lake flying too, and small boys, at baseball, shouting. Everything ALIVE" (fol. 40).

Lyrical description of scenery occupies much of the space. Lewis himself may have considered his scenery notes excessive, for he put many of them in a separate twenty-leaf text, which he labeled "Minnesota Hills & Valleys," presently located just after the "Minnesota Diary" in the same ring binder in the Yale Collection (not included in the present edition). Perhaps he thought his multiple-day automobile trips around Minnesota had netted more scenery notes than would be appropriate for a diary.

Modulating the diary's exuberance of description are suggestions of self-awareness and reflection. About himself as a note-taker Lewis writes, "The writer, loving or thinking he loves, the hills busy taking notes about them instead of looking at them" (fol. 64). Again later he wonders whether note-keeping is "interfering with seeing the very country of which make notes" (fol. 74). Regarding native sons who return home, he asks a surprising question about motivation: "Grownup, returning, may care much more to learn all about a district than did as child. Often he also has a much more affectionate attitude. Is this more normal--or more beaten?" (fol. 62). Another doubt he is willing to consider about his own motives is whether it is "only as one grows older that he loves 'scenery' --an escape from human involvements" (fol. 77).

Writing in a dual-purpose letter-and-diary entry, he mocks the exaggerated pine-cone decor of Gateway Lodge at Hungry Jack Lake, then thoughtfully applies the lesson of this mockery to himself:

> *It's interesting, all this earnest effort for no very particular purpose. I suppose all vigorous people do it, an innocence worthy of a wise two-year-old child; you busily perfect a line which you are sure is going to raise the entire standard of the theater, and me--like those home-made-pine-coners--I set up my little table and write like hell in the innocent (and quite home-made) belief that I shall impress you!* (fol. 83)

Of course the diary contains glib self-mockery, too. For example, in complaining about his garrulous twelve-year-old son, he says, "Mick talks as much as either his father or mother, which Christ knows is twice too much" (fol. 81). Interestingly, this tone does not dominate the instances of self-awareness.

Even satiric observations about Minnesota occur as occasional bits of criticism, not as the dominant mode of description. Sprinkled as they are throughout the diary, they preserve the general enthusiasm from sounding blindly boosterish, and they show Lewis's talent for humor, which was always a main reason why his novels sold.[28] Engaging a shoe salesman in a discussion of the difference in styles between the East and the Midwest, Lewis discovers, "Clerk claims feet longer here" (fol. 11). Or later in the diary, he attends "the glorious, free, melodic crook church of the Christian Temple" where the two officiating ministers who "hate each other" manage to take *three* collections, a phenomenon "new to me in the glorious world of Gantryism" (fol. 91). This satiric humor sounds appreciative. And in a diary, without the formal constraints of a satiric novel, such occasional satiric observations open the horizons instead of seeming to limit them.

About Lewis's motives for returning to Minnesota, the diary, just by itself without exterior evidence, offers a range of private reflections. He wanted to see how the Minnesota of his childhood compared with the Minnesota of his middle age: "Remember how as a boy, viewing Sauk Centre from the cemetery, admired how it stretched out surely a full mile --a very considerable city!" (fol. 25). He wanted to check the level of progress in the prairie village: "These Main Streets have improved so much in solidity of architecture....Did the complaining Carol Kennicott help?" (fol. 42). He tried to understand the character of the Midwest by measuring it against the East: "Is there more heavy banter--'kidding'--in Minnesota than in NY?" (fol. 12). He questioned his own lonely love of place: "Can love of land--and perhaps animals--take place of all love of human beings?" (fol. 8). He looked for his roots, seizing upon facts about grandparents as he surveyed their graves in the Elysian cemetery (fol. 21).

As the diary of a practicing novelist, it includes occasional notes on ideas for fiction—the life of Jay Hormel (fol. 10), the Fairmont polo players of the 1870s (fol. 22), Judge Mark Nolan in Duluth who was to be a prototype for the character Cass Timberlane (fol. 127). Lewis went out of his way to meet people from all walks of life in his constant hunger for experience that might serve art. But the diary's goals were as personal as they were professional. Lewis wanted to keep track of his own daily history, the weather, the dinner guests, the date of finishing the "first draft of novel GIDEON PLANISH" (fol. 96). And he was chronicling his search for a home, whether at a fantasized spot like the St. Croix River (fol. 94) or in the eventually chosen Duluth (fol. 115ff). In his own peculiar way, he was trying to understand who he was, where he came from, and what direction he should take.

Amid the prevailing affection for landscapes, one may detect a considerable range of other emotions. For example, he is cowed by the unrelieved openness of Minnesota heartland, the "almost treeless prairie--steppes--could heap FEAR on a sensitive person. No place to hide" (fol. 4). On occasion he is homesick for other places, like New York City (fol. 71). He feels sorrow as he contemplates the grave of a nineteen-year-old bride from Minnesota's pioneer past, and he fends off from his mind the hard wit of the sophisticated city that might ridicule the homely sentiment on the gravestone, which reads: "Rest thee, loved one, where we laid thee, / Where the wild wood maketh sigh. / Tears perfume the bed we made thee, / Where the withered foliage lie" (fol. 22). Worries Lewis, "Probably Lucius Beebee, Mencken, and the New Yorker would find this all very funny."

There is also happy anticipation of visits by loved ones—by son Micky (fol. 80), by girlfriend Marcella Powers (fol. 140). There is the sense of well-being associated with proprietorship: "Return to Lake Minnetonka. The house so spacious, yet so private; so much cooler than prairies in car; shining, belonging to me" (fol. 66). And there is the delight of the imagination, which pictures a Minnesota town as if it were a "hilltop mediaeval village" (fol. 66) and which enables the imaginer to believe he "is able to live in a romantic novel for a day or two" (fol. 129).

One interesting suggestion emerging from the diary's private view of Lewis is the provincial character of the writer. In his own terms, he is Midwestern and rural.[29] Explaining his interest in chronicling the weather, he twice asserts his rural identity (fols. 16, 68), observing that urbanites like Marcella Powers pay little heed to measurements of temperature and moisture, whereas he and his forefathers have considered these details crucial: "To real urbanite, weather doesn't exist. To the rustic, all important, chief topic of talk, exasperatingly human in its moods" (fol. 68). In reporting a discussion on "What is a Provincial?" he declares resoundingly, "I am" (fol. 16).

Thinking with rural sensitivity about the nature of cosmopolitanism, the Lewis of the diary is capable of finding refinement in a real village person in almost the same way that fictional village-dweller Dr. Will Kennicott finds Gopher Prairie to contain some of "the best people on earth."[30] Says Lewis about his friend the Sauk Centre real estate agent and municipal judge William Parker:

> *You find a sleek, urbane person like Billy Parker who has little travelled, who knows no known language; you find rustic, awkward, American-toned people like Norman Davis, Cordell Hull, Col. House, who have been in every strange land, dined with kings and professors, may also know no languages or may know a dozen. Travel does* <u>*what*</u>*?* (fol. 97)

Like *Main Street*'s Carol Kennicott, Lewis had been to the national capital and found there such a "thick streak of Main Street" that he could return to the prairie village with appreciation for its people.[31] That he continued to be concerned with this issue shows how close in spirit he was with all of small-town America that self-consciously asserts its own value against the city.

A further indication of Lewis's Midwestern provincial character is the degree of silence in the diary about personal loss. Of the death of beloved son Wells, a casualty of the war, there is no mention at all. About the death of elder brother Fred back in Sauk Centre, there is but the barest mention, the bleak details of winter weather on the trip to the funeral serving as the exclusive conveyance of emotion (fol. 155). The diary says little about Lewis's most recent wife, Dorothy Thompson, and it records the severing of ties with friends and servants with cryptic brevity, giving little or no account of Lewis's grievance, expressing no regret, no pain (see the parting with Jim Hart, fol. 43; the departure of Lillian the cook, fol. 154; the end of the friendship with the Ridders, fol. 142).

This rigorous laconism about loss may be explained in part as a characteristic lifetime response for someone who has suffered a childhood blow, in this case the loss of his mother to tuberculosis when he was just six. However, the village atmosphere among middle-class Protestants with a Calvinist heritage certainly played a role. Lewis's stoical physician father would have regarded breast-beating with suspicion.[32] Although Sauk Centre at the turn of the century recognized the brute facts of loss and published them in the newspaper, the prevailing culture discouraged emotional display.[33] Sometimes in the diary Lewis writes as if he fears he has gushed too much. Note how the following awestruck description ends: "At 9:45, when already dark on shore, the still lake half silver, half rosy, and against it the trees silhouetted, every twig, every shrub, clear. So beautiful--and a sound of distant singing--Edelkitsch [grandly pretentious kitsch]" (fol. 67).

The checks and balances in Lewis's village-born sensibility govern his search for beauty, enable him to dig in his own way for Thoreauvian reality and detect sometimes a hint of rock bottom and sometimes the shifting sands of a cliché. That he avoided discussing deep personal loss must mean that discussion was no reliable avenue in his world for detecting rock-bottom value, serious words often being inadequate for serious meaning.[34] This distrust of words may explain why Lewis's diary, founded on a Thoreauvian desire, lacks the ever-expanding ideation of Thoreau's journals: Thoreau had more faith in language.

Distrust of words also helps explain the connection between the private Lewis and the public one. The public Lewis often played the role of noisy verbal performer, joyfully exposing words. He especially loved clichés, using them in pranks, in oral mimicry, in novels. From the widow Bogart's gossip in *Main Street,* to Babbitt's booster speech for the Zenith Real Estate Board, to Elmer Gantry's sermons, to the topics and terms bandied by New York liberals at parties in *Ann Vickers,* to the letters of philanthrobbers in *Gideon Planish,* Lewis lovingly recorded familiar words that, deliberately or obliviously, miss the truth.[35] One might call these words the fictions of real life. Displaying them in a novel exposes the fictional quality of real-life discourse and amuses the reader by suggesting the contrary reality underneath.

That Lewis was consciously suspicious of the adequacy of serious words is demonstrated by the conclusion of *The God-Seeker.* Aaron Gadd turns his back on frontier missionaries in nineteenth-century Minnesota and all their theology. He decides he will keep his core beliefs but says, "Let's try not to use the *words* [italics Lewis's]!"[36] For the middle-aged Lewis to construct a serious diary, using many facts, avoiding inflation and cliché, and concentrating on the natural landscape is for him to implement this imagined pioneer principle of not mucking things up with too many words. He is also approximating the rural laconic standard against which he had been measuring the inflations and formulas of public discourse all his life.

Given the rural brevity, the silence about loss, and the self-consciousness about provincialism, the diary reinforces the view that Lewis was not just the critic of the prairie village but also very often its voice. Left to himself, he sounds strangely quiet, reflective, even dignified. In many passages, one sees no more than the word-wary rural diarist jotting down a note or two after listening to the quiet of his own fields.

This word-wary rural persona increases the interest of the text as an addendum to *Main Street*. In that novel of 1920, Lewis made himself into one of the premier definers of the American landscape in the twentieth century. He helped formulate the idea of the American heartland as it stood in the generation after the era of the frontier.[37] The "Minnesota Diary" shows the great definer re-examining his subject two decades later, avid to capture its significant details during World War II. Some objectionable provincialisms still annoy him, for example, the misguided import of commercial urban tawdriness in greeting cards and figurines (fol. 31), but he also discovers improvements, like the addition of trees and gardens and more solid architecture (fol. 42). Written straight and rough, without Lewis's characteristic verbal performing, these new observations open up the old definition and call attention to its provisional quality. In addition, the way these observations identify Lewis himself as rural reminds the reader that the description of Main Street had its main origin in a prairie-village sensibility.[38]

Comprehensive biographical statements about Lewis are difficult. Right now, private papers offer the most hope for new insight, but they also increase the challenge of summing up such a man. External sources like news records, memoirs, and witnesses have combined with the evidence of his novels to construct a sense of him as social historian, satirist, moralist, busy consumer of experience, impulsive adventurer, boisterous publicist, prank-loving oral mimic, alcoholic, and lonely misfit. His political sympathies comprise a range of interests from socialism and labor to the American capitalist middle class to a romantic yearning for the aristocratic.[39] The "Minnesota Diary," with its inside view, shows how he could also be a Thoreauvian idealist, a buoyant artist-explorer, a laconic rural observer who distrusts words, and a self-aware reflective examiner of his origins. Although these revelations increase the difficulty of producing a unified picture, the inside view still seems promising as a way by which to understand eventually his public character and his art. The hope of this edition is that new thinking, based on the inside view, will lead to a deeper picture. If Lewis thought he had just *begun* to capture a uniquely American character in Babbitt, this diary should provide enough glimpses of the private Lewis to allow readers to feel the same optimism for discovery about this significant American author.

Notes for the Introduction

1. The "Minnesota Diary" is housed in the Yale Collection of American Literature, Beinecke Rare Book and Manuscript Library, New Haven, Connecticut, catalogue number Za Lewis 520. References will be identified by folio number within the text. A small excerpt was once edited and published by Mark Schorer: Sinclair Lewis, "A Minnesota Diary," *Esquire,* October 1958, 160–62.

2. Lewis penciled on the front pastedown of his copy: "NY. Aug '07 / Read in noon hours of freedom from the semi-bondage of 'Tales'; on benches in Bryant Park; my Walden 2 feet of bench, my pond a drinking fountain, my forest a few elms and maples, where sparrow twittered. S. L." This is quoted in Julian Mason, "Sinclair Lewis' Copy of *Walden,*" *Thoreau Society Bulletin* 173 (fall 1985): 7. Mason found it quoted in a sale catalogue of rare books: Serendipity Books of Berkeley, CA (#43, July 1985) offering Lewis's copy of *Walden* (item 345) for sale at $900. This edition of *Walden,* with an introduction by G. D. Roberts, was published by Crowell, 1899, in the Handy Volume Classics series.

3. Sinclair Lewis, "One Man Revolution," *Newsweek,* 22 November 1937, 33.

4. "People," *Time,* 24 May 1943, 82.

5. Sinclair Lewis, "The Boxers of M. Voltaire," review of *Pleasant Valley,* by Louis Bromfield, and of *Plainesville, U.S.A.,* by James West, *Esquire,* October 1945, 79. Although this review was published in October, it is clear from the Powers letters that Lewis completed it while in Duluth. See Lewis to Powers, 29 July 1945, Marcella Powers Correspondence, Lewis Family Papers, St. Cloud State University Archive, St. Cloud, Minnesota.

6. Sinclair Lewis, "Self-Portrait (Nobel Foundation)," in *The Man from Main Street: Selected Essays and Other Writings, 1904–1950,* eds. Harry E. Maule and Melville H. Cane (New York: Random House, 1953), 55.

7. Sinclair Lewis, "The Death of Arrowsmith," in *The Man from Main Street,* 106; first published in *Coronet,* July 1941.

8. Sinclair Lewis, "Minnesota, the Norse State," in *The Man from Main Street,* 283; first published in *The Nation,* 30 May 1923.

9. Sinclair Lewis, "The Long Arm of the Small Town," in *The Man from Main Street,* 272; first published in *O-Sa-Ge* [Sauk Centre high school yearbook], 1931.

10. This is from Mark Schorer's typewritten transcription of Sinclair Lewis's "Diary, Nov. 10, 1900–July 4, 1908," autograph ms., 5 vols., catalogue number Za Lewis 315, Yale Collection of American Literature, Beinecke Rare Book and Manuscript Library, New Haven, Connecticut. A copy of Schorer's transcript is also at the Beinecke, catalogued as Za Lewis 316. The quoted passage is from vol. 1, p. 64, the entry for Wednesday, 9 April 1902.

11. The best coverage of Lewis's disciplined method as an author is James M. Hutchisson, *The Rise of Sinclair Lewis, 1920–1930* (University Park, Pa.: Pennsylvania

State University Press, 1996). Mark Schorer's long biography also describes the process: *Sinclair Lewis: An American Life* (New York: McGraw-Hill, 1961).

12. Grace Hegger Lewis published the story of the marriage twice; the first time as fiction *Half a Loaf* (New York: Horace Liveright, 1931), and the second time as a nonfiction memoir *With Love from Gracie* (New York: Harcourt Brace, 1955).

13. If Schorer's facts are accurate, Lewis must have had a nearly complete vision of Bethel Merriday before he met Marcella Powers. He began work on the novel in May 1939, met Marcella Powers on August 14, and sent a finished draft to the publisher in mid-October. See Schorer, *Sinclair Lewis: An American Life,* 645, 646, 652.

14. Because Schorer interviewed dozens of witnesses and also had access to all the main Lewis documents, his biography *Sinclair Lewis: An American Life* is indispensable as a source for the facts of Lewis's life. The present study is deeply indebted to Schorer's systematic fact-digging and to some of his insights as well.

15. The most revealing discussion of Lewis's alcoholism is Roger Forseth, "'Alcoholite at the Altar': Lewis, Drink, and the Literary Imagination," *Modern Fiction Studies* 31 (fall 1985): 581–607.

16. For example Edward F. Greve, interview by the author, Duluth, Minnesota, 18 April 1990, second interview by phone, 19 August 1993. While Greve (1923–97) was a student at Duluth State Teachers College, he worked as part-time secretary-researcher for Lewis at 2601 East Second Street in Duluth, later had a career as a librarian at the University of Wisconsin in Superior. Many people in Duluth who observed erratic behavior in Lewis thought he was dry, but Greve, who had a closer view, discovered otherwise.

17. Schorer, *Sinclair Lewis: An American Life,* 810.

18. See Hutchisson, *The Rise of Sinclair Lewis, 1920–1930* for a revealing discussion of the care with which Lewis adjusted his texts for the audience.

19. Brendan Gill, *Here at the New Yorker* (New York: Random House, 1975; reprint New York: Berkley Publishing, 1976), 72.

20. Ernest Hemingway, *Across the River and Into the Trees* (New York: Scribners, 1950), 87–88, 97.

21. See for example Roger Forseth, "Can You Go Home Again? Sinclair Lewis: Main Street and Paris," in *Sinclair Lewis: New Essays in Criticism,* ed. James M. Hutchisson (Troy, N.Y.: Whitston, 1997).

22. Schorer, *Sinclair Lewis: An American Life,* 813.

23. Schorer, *Sinclair Lewis: An American Life,* 685, 809, 813. New interest in Lewis in the 1990s has stimulated discussion of Schorer and the nature of literary reputation. See especially the following three articles in *Sinclair Lewis: New Essays in Criticism:* Paula Marantz Cohen, "Return to *Main Street*: Sinclair Lewis and the Politics of Literary Reputation"; Robert L. McLaughlin, "Mark Schorer, Dialogic Discourse, and *It Can't Happen Here*"; Roger Forseth, "Can You Go Home Again? Sinclair Lewis: Main Street and Paris."

24. James Lundquist, *Sinclair Lewis* (New York: Frederick Ungar, 1973), 128.

25. Also at the St. Cloud State University Archive are some letters from Lewis to his father, to his brother Claude and members of Claude's family, and to Ida Kay Compton (Lewis's young friend whom he met at Thorvale Farm in spring 1947). Lewis's total surviving correspondence, scattered in several archives, is substantial. Two publications have collected a small portion. Correspondence with editors at Harcourt, Brace, his publisher in the 1920s, is collected in Harrison Smith, ed., *From Main Street to Stockholm: Letters of Sinclair Lewis, 1919–1930* (New York: Harcourt, Brace, 1952). Various letters to Lewis's father, to brother Claude and family, to actress Kitty Carlisle, and to author August Derleth are collected in John J. Koblas and Dave Page, eds., *Selected Letters of Sinclair Lewis* (Madison, Wis.: Main Street Press, 1985).

26. The dedication to *Gideon Planish* (New York: Random House, 1943) spells out Marcella's name, but the other two dedications are cryptic. *Cass Timberlane* (New York: Random House, 1945) is "To P. M. R.," a rearrangement of the initials of Rosemary Marcella Powers. *Kingsblood Roya*l (New York: Random House, 1947) is "To S. S., who first heard this story." These initials appear as a term of endearment in the Powers correspondence, translated variously as "Small Size Spies," or "Sweeter than Sugar or Saccharine." See Lewis to Powers, 25 February 1946, Marcella Powers Correspondence, St. Cloud State University Archive.

27. See Lewis to Powers, 6 July 1943, 17 July 1943, 24 July 1943, and 25 July 1943, Marcella Powers Correspondence, St. Cloud State University Archive.

28. Mark Schorer, afterword to *Main Street,* by Sinclair Lewis (New York: Signet-NAL, 1961), 437.

29. Although the self-awareness of rural identity in the diary is clear, Lewis is on record earlier making a denial. In a pique at an interview in 1939, Lewis told reporters that he hated the word "folksy" and the legend that made him "just a bouncing prairie boy." See "Note for Main Street: Lewis Hasn't Changed His Mind," *St. Paul Pioneer Press,* 18 January 1939. He was on tour at the time with his production of *Angela Is Twenty-Two* and reacting to the perception that "the regular fellow is the one from the small town." Lewis did not want to be judged that way, nor did he ever want small towns to be idealized as little paradises.

30. Sinclair Lewis, *Main Street* (New York: Harcourt, Brace, 1920), 17.

31. Sinclair Lewis, *Main Street,* (New York: Harcourt, Brace, 1920), 427.

32. See Schorer, *Sinclair Lewis: An American Life,* 13–22. Lewis's father, Edwin J. Lewis, was descended from New England Congregationalists, and the Lewises' church affiliation in Sauk Centre was Congregational.

33. Cf. James Lundquist, "The Sauk Centre Lewis Didn't Write About," *Critical Essays on Sinclair Lewis,* ed. Martin Bucco (Boston: G. K. Hall, 1986).

34. This idea is developed more fully in George Killough, "*Elmer Gantry,* Chaucer's Pardoner, and the Limits of Serious Words," in *Sinclair Lewis: New Essays in Criticism.*

35. For the less well-known of these examples, see Sinclair Lewis, *Ann Vickers* (Garden City, N.Y.: Doubleday, Doran, 1933; reprint Lincoln: University of Nebraska Press, 1994), 421–25; *Gideon Planish*, 216–17.

36. Sinclair Lewis, *The God-Seeker* (New York: Random House, 1949), 379.

37. Useful for this theme is David D. Anderson, "Sinclair Lewis and the Midwestern Tradition," in *Sinclair Lewis at 100: Papers Presented at a Centennial Conference,* ed. Michael Connaughton (St. Cloud, Minn.: St. Cloud State University, 1985).

38. The overall sensibility in *Main Street* is Lewis's, even though in formulating Carol Kennicott's view of Gopher Prairie, he had the benefit of imagining how his stepmother and his wife Grace, both of whom came from cities, saw Sauk Centre. Carol Kennicott's limited viewpoint in the book represents a side of Lewis as well, by his own admission. See Hutchisson, "*Main Street,* 1905–1920," chap. 1 in *The Rise of Sinclair Lewis, 1920–1930,* and Charles Breasted, "The 'Sauk-Centricities' of Sinclair Lewis," *The Saturday Review,* 14 August 1954, 7–8, 33–36.

39. A full recent analysis is Christopher P. Wilson, "Sinclair Lewis and the Passing of Capitalism," chap. 6 in *White Collar Fictions: Class and Social Representation in American Literature, 1885–1925* (Athens, Ga.: University of Georgia Press, 1992). Dorothy Thompson described Lewis as "basically apolitical" but with the general views of "an old-fashioned populist American radical"; she also thought he yearned for aristocratic culture; see "The Boy and the Man from Sauk Centre," *The Atlantic Monthly,* November 1960, 39–48.

The Text and Its Treatment

Lewis left the "Minnesota Diary" among his papers at Yale, which now reside in the Beinecke Library, not yet completely catalogued. The diary occupies the first 159 leaves of a three-ring loose-leaf notebook, which contains also his travel notes titled "Minnesota Hills & Valleys" (fols. 161–180) and a collection of miscellaneous notes and scrapbook items (fols. 181–220). The leaves of the notebook are numbered in pencil. The diary and "Minnesota Hills & Valleys" are, for the most part, single-spaced pica typescripts on 8½ by 11 white unlined paper.

That Lewis considered his "Minnesota Diary" a text all by itself is clear from the way he gave separate titles to it and to the companion text "Minnesota Hills & Valleys." He also divided notes on the same trips between the diary and "Hills & Valleys" as if the two texts had distinct purposes. Whether the distinction was that "Hills & Valleys" collected overflow so the diary could remain more readable or whether "Hills & Valleys" was to be a narrow record of vista locations on trips as opposed to the wider record of the diary is not certain. What is certain is that he intended the "Minnesota Diary" and "Hills & Valleys" to be distinct texts, each with its own peculiar focus and title to separate the one from the other and from the untitled miscellany occupying the last forty leaves of the notebook.

Among the materials within the diary are carbons of pages from letters, labeled to indicate that Lewis intended them to do double duty as diary entries. All these letters were written to Marcella Powers, as shown by comparison with the originals in the St. Cloud State University library archive. Also included in the diary are various scrapbook items, some mounted on diary leaves and some just punched to fit into the loose-leaf binder. Most scrapbook items are mounted newspaper clippings but there are also occasional pieces such as a menu and after-dinner program, two mimeographed pages of songs used by a literary fraternity, a letter found on Red Lake Reservation, a travel brochure on the Lake Superior north shore, and a calling card.

Lewis kept the diary diligently in the first year, the Minneapolis period. The first two-thirds of the text (fols. 4–106) are devoted to 1942, spring, summer, and fall. Of the remaining third of the text, there are just a few notes on February and May 1943 (fols. 107–9), some jottings on winter 1944 in New York City (fols. 110–112), a sizable portion for spring and summer 1944 when Lewis moved to Duluth (fols. 113–148), some irregular notes on 1945 (fols. 149–154), and a last gasp of daily entries for January to March 1946 (fols. 154–159).

Given Lewis's well-known speed as a writer, he must have composed some entries directly on the typewriter, but the document shows he often typed entries from handwritten notes. He says as much in a typed entry for February 9, 1946 on fol. 156: "probably end of the world by this PM, but I'll have these notes copied from scrawled memoes, anyway." The reader can observe one step of this method in process in the seven holograph leaves on which there is no typing: fols. 107, 110, 111, 112, 114, 149, and 159. Generally less orderly in construction than typed entries, the entries on these leaves must be the sort of notes Lewis wrote before typing.

As confirmation that this was in fact his practice, contents of the handwritten entries for May 15 and 16, 1944 on fol. 114 are partly duplicated in the typed entry for May 15 and 16, 1944 on fol. 113. The typed version is very different. Whether the two versions represent the normal difference between Lewis's "scrawled memoes" and typed entries or whether the "scrawled memoes" were saved in this case only because they were *uncharacteristically* different in content cannot be determined without more instances. What is clear at least is that Lewis did write in two steps as he claimed, first by hand, then on the typewriter.

That the typewritten entries were often delayed and constructed in batches is shown by other features of the document. For one thing, left margins are often regular and the spaces between paragraphs even, as if to indicate that the page was not pulled out and reinserted in the typewriter after each date but filled up all in one sitting. For example, fol. 141, which contains a short paragraph entry for each of thirteen dates, July 10–22, 1944, has no deviation in the left margin, no change in darkness of ink, and regular double-spacing between paragraphs.

The other indication of batch-typing is found in summary comments preceding daily entries. On fol. 20, for example, Lewis summarizes a five-day motor trip, including the daily mileage totals and some details of weather and food. Then follow sizable entries for each day of the trip, extending to fol. 31. Clearly the whole twelve leaves were typed *after* the trip was over. The document shows other summary instances like this, in which facts in an introductory summary could not have been known until after events in the subsequent paragraphs had taken place. One of these has to do with summarized weather data for September 22–26, 1942 on fol. 90.

Although Lewis cared enough about the diary to make it orderly and intelligible—to title it, to try to preserve focus by relegating some travel notes to a different text, to type smoother entries from "scrawled memoes," and to feed entries into it in summarized batches—he very likely did not regard the document left at Yale as a final copy. Many uncorrected typographical errors testify to this fact, as well as numerous cancellations made during the process of typing and the few additions and corrections made by hand after the typing.

Probably he never intended to produce a finished copy. Despite a likely awareness that the diary would be published for posterity, he was not inclined to do the final preparation himself. Even in the early stages of high enthusiasm for diary-keeping, he allowed himself to type entries with leap-frogging dates. On fol. 11, a sequence of paragraphs from 1942 begins with the following labels in this order: "APRIL TWENTY-ONE," "APRIL TWENTY-TWO," "NOTES ON THE Jitter-Bug Inn," "Apr 22," "APRIL TWENTY-ONE cont."

The carbons of letter extracts, the first not appearing until halfway through the diary on fol. 83, occasion more leap-frogging of dated entries. Leaves from the Duluth section in 1944, where the letters multiply, show a sequence beginning this way: fol. 115-letter-May 18; fol. 116-letter-May 20; fol. 117-entries-May 19, 20, 21, 22, 23, 24, 25, 26; fol. 118-letter-June 1; fol.

119-entries-May 27, 28, 29, 30, 31, June 1, 2; fol. 120-letter-June 3-plus-entries-June 3, 4, 5.

This spate of interwoven letter carbons and normal entries, continuing to fol. 129 with leap-frogging dates, gives the text a decidedly unfinished aspect, compounded by the incompleteness of the letter extracts which lack salutations and closings. Interestingly enough, salutations are missing in all the original Marcella Powers letters from which the carbons were taken, this absence being a normal feature of that correspondence. However, many originals do contain more typed material than shown in the diary's carbon inserts. The diary reader, not seeing to whom a letter is addressed and finding inconclusive breakoffs, feels a loss of significant material, especially when a carbon leaf ends with a comma instead of a period (fol. 122). If Lewis had been readying the diary for publication, he would almost certainly have left fuller copies of the letters, added more notes to explain them, or woven the letter matter into normal entries in such a way as to diminish disparities of sequence and content. He would also have integrated the scrapbook items more effectively.

Another feature in the diary's lack of finish is the irregularity in daily-entry format. Many entries show Lewis striving for a pattern, with one line for the date, a separate line or two for temperatures, and then a new line on which to start prose description. The fourth paragraph on fol. 96 has this format, with Lewis throwing the carriage for each category but not double-spacing down to indicate a new paragraph. If the diary contents could all fit this format, one can imagine it might be Lewis's choice for a finished presentation, but the contents do not easily lend themselves to this kind of slotted form, nor does Lewis regularly follow such a form even when they do. Sometimes the temperatures come at the end; sometimes there are several dates within a paragraph and no effort to put them in a list format; and very often the heading, temperatures, and prose description are all merged together, as in the last paragraph on fol. 99, no separate carriage throws intervening.

Some paragraph blocks contain clear lists, with a carriage throw for each item. The penultimate paragraph on fol. 106 is a good example, where a series of dated events is each given a separate line. Some paragraphs suggest a list format at the beginning but then after a while take on more than one item in a line, so that the carriage throws no longer correspond to list organization, as for example in the catalogue of features of a typical

Minnesota farm on fol. 23. This merging of layout designs, the list and wrap-around prose, suggests the writer is not yet certain about the way he wants the text to appear.

Still, the diary has integrity as a text that was meant to be a text. Though it lacks final polish, it shows a considerable level of preparation. Because Lewis was a fast writer and because he was working from rough notes already, he turned out respectable copy without having to make large numbers of alterations. On average, based on a check of every fifth leaf, there are just three alterations per page made on the typewriter during the initial inscription. These are usually false-start corrections in mid-sentence, rarely substantive. That Lewis was able to type so cleanly is testimony to his expertise as a writer.

Further alterations made by hand after the initial inscription show that his concern was far more for recording the facts than for polishing the style. The average number of handwritten alterations per page is only one or two (actual average in the check of every fifth leaf—1.5), and two-thirds of the hand alterations are additions while only one-third are corrections. Many of the corrections are simply corrected spellings of names or corrected hours and times. That Lewis strove for a clear accounting of facts in his revisions is quite certain, but rarely do the revisions show him reaching for final stylistic polish.

The Present Edition

TO REPRODUCE IN print the intentions manifest in the document left at Yale, the present edition provides a clear text transcription, using Lewis's corrected typescript as copy-text. This editorial method is the best one for a document that shows a considerable degree of readiness for publication without being completely finished. The purpose is to reflect the state of preparedness of the document, provide an authentic and reliable text for general readers and scholars, and handle the transition from typescript to print with the greatest economy of detail.

Lewis's spelling, punctuation, and capitalization are preserved. For the sake of authenticity, this policy obtains throughout, even in cases where Lewis almost certainly intended to strike one key on the typewriter but struck another instead. The problem for the editor is the difficulty of being sure of Lewis's intention. Lewis was fond of cute coinages and misspellings, as in *thosedaysofold in joy* (page 68, line 13; hereafter indicated as p. --.--), *cold enuff* (p. 166.24), *he dunno why* (p. 183.26), *offnon* for "off and on" (p. 187.17), *two lil darlings* (p. 189.18), and *gl-oo-oom* (p. 226.8). Given this feature of style, it is risky to emend misspellings, especially when they could just as easily represent a stroke of wit as a stroke of the wrong key, as in *Snother* for "Another" (p. 48.10), *hating the hatives* (p. 121.13–14), *musterious* (p. 123.28), or *Locomotive smokem* (p. 226.25). An editor could reason in three of these cases that the offending letter is so close on the keyboard to the correct letter that the misspelling must not have been intended, but emending on these grounds would be inadvisable for a diary sporting cute misspellings. Also, preserving rather than emending misspellings is a better policy for editions of documentary texts, given the goal of reflecting the state of preparedness of the document.

The Textual Record at the back of this edition identifies the following details:

- shifts in the text from journal format to letter format. These shifts are also reported in italics in the text.
- placement of marginalia for which Lewis leaves unspecific indications about where to insert in the text; typed or holographic additions marked clearly for insertion location are inserted silently.
- leaves that are all in Lewis's hand.
- extensive holograph additions (thirty words or more).
- headline, newspaper, and date of clippings—to the extent that Lewis makes these identifications.
- some identifying features of scrapbook materials like travel brochures or unpublished items.
- blank spaces left on a leaf of one-third of the page or more. Lesser blank spaces are not reported, specifically the nine instances of gaps of three-fourths inch to two inches between dated entries, which Lewis may or may not have left as space for additional material. Neither do the notes report the occasional places where left-margin indentation varies on one page. Except for the leaves

containing excerpts from letters, there are only six leaves showing left-margin variation.

- editorial interpretations of some difficult spellings and readings.
- a few rare emendations made to clarify passages that are already clear in the typescript but that become unclear in the process of transcription. An example is the addition of a comma after a marginal note marked for insertion within a list of items in series, as before *Pingree* on p. 128.11.

Not all features of the documentary text can be preserved in print as easily as idiosyncratic spellings, punctuation, and capitalization. One feature not preserved is Lewis's lineation, nor is it reported. Another feature difficult to replicate is Lewis's pagination, which is not preserved but is reported by means of folio numbers inserted in italics in the text. In the transition from typescript to book, changes in page size and print size make any effort to reproduce original lineation and pagination awkward. However, the folio numbers will signal at least the original page breaks and, more important, preserve a location system for a diary that does not structure everything in single-day dated entries all in sequence.

Following Lewis's manifest intentions, his clearly marked, short, typewritten and handwritten alterations (cancellations, substitutions, additions) are incorporated silently. Preserving them as such in the text or reporting them in notes would swell the record of details with little, if any, benefit. As explained above, the facts of alteration largely show Lewis (1) reducing false-start or false-strike errors while typing or (2) inserting additional facts by hand after the typing. There is little evidence of the stylistic upgrading that might be of interest to students of Lewis's art.*

Ten silent emendations are made to carry through corrections where the typescript firmly establishes Lewis's intention to correct. There are two main kinds of errors: (1) the uncanceled false-start error, for example, where Lewis began to type *tn,* then typed *ten* without crossing out the *tn;* this edition silently deletes the *tn;* and (2) the incomplete cancellation,

*For readers with textual curiosity, a record of Lewis's alterations is available through the mail. Please write to the editor, George Killough, English Department, The College of St. Scholastica, Duluth, MN 55811. Include an e-mail address if available.

where a series of letters has been crossed out but one or two remain, for example, where the typescript reads *gMMM grass,* the *M* serving as Lewis's normal method for crossing out mistakes. The present text silently deletes the isolated surviving g.

Another silent emendation is the deletion of hyphens that occur at line-end in Lewis's typescript for the sole purpose of splitting a word so as to fit it on the page. In contrast, line-end hyphens used for word connection are preserved. To illustrate, the word *longer,* split at line-end in the original, is now joined silently without a hyphen on p. 48.17, whereas *bug-squashing*, also split at line-end in the original, keeps its hyphen in this edition, p. 41.13.

Lewis's intention for hyphenated compound words appearing at line-end is difficult to judge because his practice was variable. The compound noun *heat wave,* for example, occurs seven times as two words, once as one word, and once with a hyphen at line-end—in each case as substantive, not modifier. Also, many hyphenated words occur only once. Without evidence of a fixed consistent intention in Lewis's practice, the editor has made his best guesses according to the few parallel instances that exist, the context of the words themselves, and the likelihood that some linkages would never occur as one word, only as two or with a hyphen, for example, *Fargo-Moorhead* or *isle-sheltered*. In such cases, if a hyphen appears at line-end in Lewis's typescript, it would probably appear in mid-line as well.

The present edition includes all hyphens that should be preserved for precise quoting and adds no new ones for the sake of line-justification, the right margin being left uneven for this purpose. Hyphenated words, judged to be intended as such, are brought down to the next line. Only the hyphens Lewis used as dashes appear at line-end. Except for the rare emendation mentioned in the Textual Record, all hyphens are Lewis's.

Lewis's typed double-hyphen dashes (--) are preserved, but his dashes in handwritten additions are represented by the em dash. His occasional typed single-hyphen dashes are preserved and indicated just as he indicated them by spacing, for example *green again - but lumps* on p. 150.11–12. The diary transcription uses no en dashes.

The editor has tried to reflect original paragraphing and headings as closely as possible. The general rule has been to regard a double-space down as the main indicator of a paragraph boundary. In a few rare cases Lewis has used underlinings to designate paragraph boundaries where room was not left for a double-space down. These underlinings are not preserved as such, but instead translated into paragraph or spacing divisions. Underlinings for titles, emphasis, and headings *are* preserved.

Where Lewis threw the carriage early but did not double-space down, this edition normally does not impose a paragraph boundary, unless strong additional clues show that Lewis intended a full break. For examples of early carriage throws, look within the fourth and sixth paragraphs in the facsimile of fol. 104 on p. 167. Such instances usually suggest, as they do here, that Lewis was thinking of subdivisions *within* paragraphs, not breaks between them.

In the case of additions by Lewis that are marked for insertion between paragraphs and might belong to the end of the first or the beginning of the second, or yet might constitute a separate paragraph altogether, the editor again silently tries to follow Lewis's intention. However, the textual notes do report between-paragraph additions where the paragraphs belong to different dates, and the notes also report marginal additions adjacent to a paragraph but not marked for insertion at a definite point in the sequence of words. On three leaves (fols. 88, 95, and 114), Lewis has written separate dated paragraphs further down the page that comment on or add to a paragraph above. These are preserved in their original position in the stream of writing.

Layout *within* paragraphs has been adjusted in most cases to wrap-around prose. In the early stages of transcription the editor experimented with inserting hard returns wherever Lewis threw the carriage before line-end, but in a reproduction that does not preserve original lineation anyway, the result was confusing. It was also impossible to determine whether a sentence ending one-and-a-half inches from the right paper edge represented the end of a line in Lewis's mind or just the end of a sentence within a stream of prose, given the way Lewis's lists so often merge into prose within a paragraph block. The best solution to this problem has been to keep the list format for blocks of copy that are definitely lists (for example, the penultimate paragraph on fol. 106), but to use wrap-around prose for all else, including the paragraphs in the original that suggest an effort to give separate slots respectively to heading, temperature, and description. Lewis's intention is not definite and systematic enough to mandate otherwise.

For consistency with Lewis's typing, two features of his handwritten punctuation are changed. First, the handwritten plus sign (+), his normal hand abbreviation for *and,* is transcribed as ampersand (&), his normal typed abbreviation. Second, the equal sign (=), used in handwritten notes for a hyphen, is transcribed as a hyphen, for Lewis regularly used the hyphen in such cases when typing.

Slashes, which Lewis used in eleven places instead of a period, probably as the result of striking the wrong key, are preserved in the text.

Lewis's pica typewriter indicated the numeral *one* with a letterform looking like lower-case *l,* and the *zero* with a letterform looking like upper-case O. The type design chosen for this edition represents these numerals respectively with old-style figures 1 and 0.

Scrapbook materials are not transcribed within the main text. The ones from published sources such as newspapers are identified but not transcribed in the textual notes. The ones from by-now inaccessible sources (such as travel brochures) are described in the textual notes. The ones from unpublished sources (such as mimeographed fraternity songs) are identified in the textual notes and transcribed in an appendix. All the scrapbook materials mentioned in textual notes are mounted on numbered leaves in the original or are themselves numbered leaves of the diary, as if integral.

One final bit of material relegated to the appendix is the table showing corresponding temperatures in New York, Duluth, and the Twin Cities from December 1944 to early April 1945 on fols. 150–51. This table is different from Lewis's normal diary material. Its continuation on fol. 152, showing temperatures into June 1945, is kept in the text because here the table merges gradually into diary entries.

The text was transcribed, that is, keyed into a computer, from a photocopy provided by the Yale Collection of American Literature, Beinecke Rare Book and Manuscript Library, New Haven, Connecticut. After two complete proofings using the photocopy as exemplar, the editor returned to Yale to verify uncertain readings and check on features in the original that could not be determined from photocopy—for example, whether headings had been cut off in the copies, whether handwritten additions were in ink, pencil, or crayon, whether any material appeared on verso pages, whether Lewis had added any further organizing clues to the notebook. The diary is for the most part a clear typescript that photocopies well, but this second trip to check on particular questions was necessary and useful. A third complete proofing, using as exemplar the photocopy of the original and the notes taken at Yale, took place before the text was submitted in electronic format to the press. For each of the two stages of proofs, the diary text was proofread again against the photocopy of the original.

1942 photo of the house on Lake Minnetonka where Lewis lived in summer 1942. © *1998 STAR TRIBUNE / Minneapolis-St. Paul.*

1998 photo of 1500 Mt. Curve Avenue in Minneapolis where Lewis lived fall 1942.

1989 photo of 2601 East Second Street in Duluth, Lewis's main residence from late May 1944 to late March 1946.

"Head of Sinclair Lewis" in pencil, ink, and red Conté crayon drawn in 1923 by American illustrator Boardman Robinson, 1876–1952. On May 6, 1942, Lewis "Only ½ liked Boardman Robinson's colored drawing of me" (fol. 17). *Courtesy of the Minneapolis Institute of Arts.*

Lewis in the late 1930s, his inscription to Marcella Powers dated less than a month after they met. *Photo by Harold Stein, courtesy of St. Cloud State University Archive.*

Snapshot that belonged to Marcella Powers, who wrote on the back, "Red & I at Ogunquit, Me. 1940." *Courtesy of St. Cloud State University Archive.*

Lewis in Duluth, June 13, 1944. To Marcella he described this photo as "an exact picture of the place and apparati in use at this second, while I write you, and proves that I have I [*sic*] very fine sensitive face" (Lewis to Powers, 6 July 1944, Marcella Powers Correspondence, St. Cloud State University Archive). *Photo ascribed variously to Wayne Bell or Ted Miller, courtesy of the Minnesota Historical Society.*

Sinclair Lewis on June 13, 1944 in his Duluth home, perusing a map of Minnesota's Arrowhead region. *Photo ascribed variously to Wayne Bell or Ted Miller, courtesy of the Minnesota Historical Society.*

(These temperatures, from the Tribune, all for minneapolis only)

M I N N E S O T A   D I A R Y

MINNEAPOLIS, APRIL EIGHTH, 1942 -- arrivedM from New York at seven A.M. Cool bright. 44 degrees at noon, 51 at 6 PM. City grass green, country not. Not snow.

At first sight, Minneapolis is so ugly. Parking lots like scabs. Most buildings are narrow, drab, dirty, flimsy, irregular in relationship to one another -- a set of bad teeth. Window frames either bleak or vv., overonramented. But modern Star-Journal-Trib and Farners & mechanics Bank, gray stone and sleek, yet strong, seem suited to a modern city such as Mpls should be.

No planning in a public mind -- an no "soul," such as a mediaeval city -- or Litchfield -- or NY has -- no style.

Metropolitan Life Insurance Bldg; glass floors about a lightwell, scared me as a child.

APRIL NINE. 48 at noon, 58 at 6 PM.
Country, h grass green only on lawns; but at Osceola, where went with McNally, skunk cabbage green in hollow by spring below bluff. Clear, delicious spring air....Asher Howard kept Kentucky cardinals all winter by feeding them.

APRIL 10: chill and windy; noon, 36; 6 PM, 38. It is now fairly light from 6:15 AM to 8 PM, but that is War Saving Time and by God's time is 5:15 AM to 7 PM)....Little dying moon at 6 AM on the 11th.

Country, heard one meadow lark; liquid, sweet, gay....Toward evening, clouds of blackbirds swooping as though playing. A pheasant by the road -- none been planted in Minn when I was child.

With driver, Mpls, St. Peter, New Ulm (museum in library basement)m Mankato, Owatonna, Faribault, Northfield, Snelling. All thru, very black soil -- been lake bottom -- and level. Bluffs about Minnesota & Cannon rivers.

NEM Plowing, esp corn land with its dead stalks, with tractors; saw man seeding with four-horse team....Miry littered farm yards. ....Houses so often white and L-shaped, with gable facing road.

Tile silos, brown and white often, sometimes cream and gray, with tile-patterns at top -- apparently individual with builder, for they are in maltese crosses, zigzags, squares. Top of silo, when thus elaborate, cement or a bright metal -- steel??

Windy round of great cumulus clouds seen all day across prairie, which is very flat except MMMM at rivers, and till get to line of hills Owatonna to Northfield....Little clouds of blown dark earth.....On a dark day, this round of hillless, almost treeless prairie -- steppes -- could heap FEAR on a sensitive person. No place to hide.

Dogs streaking out to try to bite tires of car, after hiding by rd.

First page of the "Minnesota Diary" (fol. 4). *Yale Collection of American Literature, Beinecke Rare Book and Manuscript Library.*

Minnesota Diary

fol. 4

MINNESOTA DIARY

(These temperatures, from the Tribune, all for Minneapolis only)

MINNEAPOLIS, APRIL EIGHTH, 1942--arrived from New York at seven A.M. Cool bright. 44 degrees at noon, 51 at 6 PM. City grass green, country not. No snow.

At first sight, Minneapolis is so ugly. Parking lots like scabs. Most buildings are narrow, drab, dirty, flimsy, irregular in relationship to one another--a set of bad teeth. Window frames either bleak or vv., overonramented. But modern Star-Journal-Trib and Farners & mechanics Bank, gray stone and sleek, yet strong, seem suited to a modern city such as Mpls should be.

No planning in a public mind--no "soul," such as a mediaeval city--or Litchfield--or NY has--no style.

Metropolitan Life Insurance Bldg; glass floors about a lightwell, scared me as a child.

APRIL NINE. 48 at noon, 58 at 6 PM. Country, grass green only on lawns; but at Osceola, where went with McNally, skunk cabbage green in hollow by spring below bluff. Clear, delicious spring air....Asher Howard kept Kentucky cardinals all winter by feeding them.

APRIL 10: chill and windy; noon, 36; 6 PM, 38. It is now fairly light from 6:15 AM to 8 PM, but that is War Saving Time and by God's time is 5:15 AM to 7 PM)....Little dying moon at 6 AM on the 11th.

Country, heard one meadow lark; liquid, sweet, gay....Toward evening, clouds of blackbirds swooping as though playing. A pheasant by the road--none been planted in Minn when I was child.

With driver, Mpls, St. Peter, New Ulm (museum in library basement) Mankato, Owatonna, Faribault, Northfield, Snelling. All thru, very black soil--been lake bottom--and level. Bluffs about Minnesota & Cannon rivers.

Plowing, esp corn land with its dead stalks, with tractors; saw man seeding with four-horse team....Miry littered farm yards.....Houses so often white and L-shaped, with gable facing road.

Tile silos, brown and white often, sometimes cream and gray, with tile-patterns at top--apparently individual with builder, for they are in maltese crosses, zigzags, squares. Top of silo, when thus elaborate, cement or a bright metal--steel??

Windy <u>round</u> of great cumulus clouds seen all day across prairie, which is very flat except at rivers, and till get to line of hills Owatonna to Northfield....Little clouds of blown dark earth.....On a dark day, this round of hillless, almost treeless prairie--steppes--could heap FEAR on a sensitive person. No place to hide.

Dogs streaking out to try to bite tires of car, after hiding by rd.

fol. 5

APRIL 10, cont.
Remember how in winter, farm houses bank dirt or manure about lower

part of house, after lining with tarpaper....Storm doors, windows, paper strips.

In spring, straw stacks eaten away by cattle, horses.

APRIL 11: bright, cold. Noon, 35. Lilacs have begun to bud...In sheltered lawn at Goodfellow's house, Mpls, crocuses peep out.

APRIL 12, Sunday, with Virginia to St. Cloud. Soft day, warmer: noon, 51, 6 PM, 60. Winter wheat is green. Bluebird, pigeons.

Villages West side of Mississippi: Dayton, with high-placed church with windows "don de Felix X."

ST. MICHAEL, almost opposite Elk River: most of the village the usual dirty white building blocks on flat land, but by the gaunt, very tall yellow brick Catholic Church, the cemetery looks to a low sepia-colored (will be green) hollow of plowed fields rising to small smooth hills. It might have been the hollow from which Jude scared the rooks. The mind nestles in here, secure from the steppes; and beyond, on a hill, is an old schoolhouse with a foolish chunky square tower of two stories and a catwalk--very pleasant to child disliking sameness of prairies. Except for a couple of French names and couple English--one is May--all the names on the chunky granite tombstones are German, with insriptions almost always in German:

Ruhe in Frieden
GRETA BRAUN, geb. Schmidt,
ges. 1907.

Iron cast crosses for stones, many cases, and some cheap wooden ones, in groups--"across the tracks in a graveyard." Large wooden Savior on cross.

HENRY HOMO--sic--keeps the genl store and gas station at HASSAN, MINNESOTA, a hamlet of perhaps 40 population, or less, but on the detail map, lying between St. Michael and Fletcher; and NW of it is the hamlet of HASTY. (Homo once Homeau?)

Burning brush, strawstacks--a high thick white smoke across plains

A silo of gray tile with black tile ornament at top and what looks like a polished steel cap, but scarcely can be; a capsule as "modern" as an aeroplane bomb.

St. Cloud all drab-gray houses, or stucco--equally drab, or a peculiar lifeless yellow Minnesota brick. The elms, maples in the streets pindling. Only three or four models of houses, all harsh.

At the Hotel Nicollet, there actually are some waiters, even men room waiters, who are Americans & speak without accent.

fol. 6

APRIL THIRTEENTH. Noon, 55; 6 PM, 66. Morning, Marine on St. Croix; rocky hilly farms W of it, actually with stones in fields, like New England. CHARLEY BROWN, the real estate man, b. in S. Dak, but his father a Vermonter, and Charley is as Vermont as Coolidge: long face, Amer Gothic spectacles, dry accent; mackinaw, colored flannel shirt, <u>rubbers</u>. Office a one-rm store bldg, heated by Garland stove. Shelf of old cheap bks, mostly novels--they were selling out a country club and he asked for them. No phone because "out so much"--i.e., a real Vermonter. On shelves in store, pictures his family, megaphone for St. Croix regatta.

One comes from New England to Minnesota in 1942 as one did in 1872 and seeks hills and houses as much as possible like the N Eng one has left in disgust. EG, Marine, Carleton Cge.

After a few days here, one's eyes are opened to variations in prairie levels, which seem much less flat; one sees the creeks and small trees; and even sees a beauty in the dark rackety bldgs of Mple near Bridge Square--Gateway.

PM to Carleton College--dark red brick men's dormitories. Terraces to women's dorms. Annual musical spectacle on island in river (Cannon?) facing natural theater slope.

All fields plowed or being plowed....Gophers run across roads. See many jackrabbits killed on road, and see the jacks run across fields, size of small dog.

Add Apr 12th: small patch of snow left in shade at Claude's house.

Burnt grass edge of fields now like black velvet....Scrub oaks in fields.

APRIL FOURTEEN. Very hot: 8 AM, 46; noon 68; 6 PM, 79. Return from Carleton. Government taking over 11,000 acres of farmland for range and ammunition dumps at the roseless and unmounted village of Rosemount, S of Mpls.

APRIL FIFTEEN, very hot: 6 AM, 60; noon 70; 4 PM 79; 8 PM 74. "Club Cafe" is a favorite name for saloons in Mpls. To Minnetonka, Marine--car sunk on gravel driveway. Places Grace Davis, Judge Royal Stone....Return by dusk, first bug-squashing on windshield. All over, grass being burned--fiery scallops in dusk.

APRIL SIXTEEN: gray, humid, warm at 8 AM (51 degrees). But by three PM (65), cool and crystal clear.....Pheasants abt Lake Minnetonka....Take Charles Lane Harris place.

Midwest Democracy: strangers do butt in at your table at a hotel dining-room or bar. But largely they are kind to negroes and take them seriously as human beings.

The instinct that makes rebellious Vermonter seek Vt in Minn is universal: American who thinks he hates America flees to Paris and spends all his time with Americans at Harry's Bar and the Select; English woman in English colony in Florence.

fol. 7

APRIL SIXTEEN CONT: A man like Confer, whose frail body has reached over sixty, will speak with wonder of a stone house only 55 years old as "ancient."

APRIL SEVENTEEN: 8 AM, 36; noon, 44; 6 PM, 56. With Joseph to Frontenac, Winona, Rushford, Rochester: 317 miles. This is the exhilarating blue & crystal spring day Minnesota boasts of; cool and sweet and clear. You feel full of vigor, really want to walk. Not a leaf out yet, but the pastures are very green.

Sky: no clouds, candid blue, not deep shade; much lighter blue at horizon.

Cutover land: pastures with the short wild bright grass I like, with low old stumps.

Great V of geese in early afternoon, along Mississippi--first I've seen in years. They waver, change direction. Tardy pair of geese follow them five miles after.....Muskrat houses edge of pond. (Add Fifteenth: brown octagon house below Stillwater.)

Many country night clubs, for patrons not only from MPls and St.P, but some near Rochester....Somerset, a French town, night clubs, apparently no gambling. Shakopee was full of gambling, now lulled.

Sign in fields between Rushford & Mabel: "Visit the art exhibit--four miles" Later I saw it: a horrible figure of an Indian, a bust of Lincoln, in the yard, with soft drink stand.

Lots of harrowing now, with tractor.

Mpls: Schiek's and Charlie's Exceptionale.

Remember from boyhood: dusty but exciting smell in dark wheat elevator, above bins, and feeling of danger of falling down into that quicksand.

APRIL EIGHTEEN. Noon, 49; six, 58. Another crystal & sapphire day How friendly the people here in shops, except for a few young woman who resent working and believe they are being "kidded."

APRIL NINETEEN, Sunday. Another crystal-saph day, slightly cooler. First Baptist Church, gaunt gray stone, inside drab choir benches behind pulpit and windows meaningless streaks of color. With it, the brisk Tudor Northwestern Bible and Missionary Training School--fundamentalist--called Jackson Hall. Sermon by W.B.RILEY: tall, lean Gillette type of actor, white thick mop of hair at probably 70.....Sermon a dullness about how Philip, filled with the spirit of God, became an orator over night, which is more than WB did.

fol. 8

APRIL NINETEEN CONT
Much fundamentalism and evangelism still everywhere in Mimmesota. Signs on rocks, on small signboards on trees: Prepare to meet thy God." "Christ died for our sins." "Christ or chaos?"

Road to Rochester, in neat farmyard: ecclesiastical stone frame with narrow Gothic side arches, in center in stone frame large printed sign: Believe on the Lord Jesus Christ and thou shalt be saved." Huge roadside sign nr Rochester: "First Baptist Church of Rochester: Ye Must be Born Again."

On back of car parked at Jackson Hall, Mpls, above number, two small plates with "Jesus saves" and "You must be reborn."

Too many women in sloppy slacks in Minneapolis and toothpicks--even women--and hair still clipped above ears and high in back--like plucked chicken (this, men.)

APRIL TWENTY, with Joseph to Lanesboro. Another perfect day, clear; a little hot in early afternoon. Noon, 61; six, 66. Fog in AM, thick, clear by 10:30. Cirrus clouds then. In early afternoon, threat of rain (which never came) in mackerel sky with small dark clouds. This vanished and late in afternoon, cirrus clouds just <u>brushed in</u>.

Huge barn roofs, semi-cylindrical, gothic curve flaring out at eaves, or hip roof.

Drivers wave to one another and to pedestrians all thru here--that automatic gesture always recd with a motionless stare in New Eng.

Heighth of hills don't matter so much as just enough for refuge.

Frost boils on blacktop--Tarvia--roads in spring.

Can love of land--and perhaps animals--take place of all love of human beings?

Fine <u>black</u> soil all thru So. Minn....Rem to see Addison Lewis farm.....Cheese factories, small, all thru.

Dragging fields now--the drag bobs behind tractor, which on rough plowed ground must be seasick-making....Spring, disc, and tooth harrows, or drag.

Cannon Falls
Zumbrota--Zumbro River; origin of name?
Pine Island.

Rolls of snow-fencing on platforms along RR's and on hillocks along road; picket and wire.

You see farm-wives working about yard in trousers, now--never when I was kid, or wd have indicated gt poverty and roughness.

How often this Midwest population moves on. Coming back after 20 years, huge % are gone. Would not be true in East.

fol. 9

APRIL TWENTY CONT

BURMA SHAVE ROAD SIGNS (from memory only)
(all end with Burma Shave)

Trains don't wander
All over the map,
For no one sits
On the engineer's lap.

Broken romance
Stated fully.
She got mad
When he got woolly.

A bar
A car
Gates ajar.

Wild dashes
From byroads
Make crashes
On highroads.

"Shiver my timbers,"
Said Captain Jack,
"It's ten knots out
But I'm turning back."
I forgot my Burma Shave.

Substitutes
Like a tail-chasing pup.
Follow and follow
But never catch up.

You see the new rhymes
Every season.
You've seen the rhymes,
Now try the reason--
Burma Shave

fol. 10

APRIL TWENTY CONT.

Big chicken hawk driven from road by car.

Hunting, fishing--the desire to kill--a sign of primitive barbarism? Yet so common in England.

Always, coming up from river, phenomenon here of rising from valley and gulleys suddenly to flat prairie, the valley forgot, evident how now-quite-small stream has carved valley/

In village cafe, radio on all day.

No leaves yet, but trees budding and willows by Minnesota River, returning to Mpls from south to Lyndale River, are all misty, almost in leaf.....Reedy flats by Minnesota river that way--road to Lakeville.

A few log cabins, must be very old; almost tumbling down, and plaster mostly fallen out from between logs.

How appallingly familiar and permanent and drear becomes roadside scene when car stuck there, and joy of going on--being beside that willow down the road that seemed unattainable

Horses, springtime, loafing in pasture, joy after winter. Cows lie about really dissolutely.

Pigeons abt farm.

Do you like waterfalls and caves, the gt features of souvenir postcards?

Gophers and jackrabbits the gt Minnesota fauna.

Smell cheese factories half a mile away.

Saw one clump pollarded willows.

Semicylindrical portable wooden brooder houses.

"Contour strip cropping."

Children still walk to school with lunch boxes.

On almost treeless prairies there will be a lone Lutheran or Catholic church in a drove of dark pines.....So much Lutheran church, school, hospital, home in Mpls.

How dry gray cement pavement in distance, in sun glare, seems dark and set ahead....When gray is black; when honey is a solid and granite a liquid.

Modern scrapers with vast rubber wheels.

Life of Jay Hormel?....The wives of lesser officials in such a plant as Hormel or Cream of Wheat, socially--country club, golf, NY, music, new houses--small country club of an Austin.

Big blackbirds in damp pasture by road, picking--like rooks.

fol. 11

APRIL TWENTY CONT

New windmills for electric power with blades like aeroplane propellors.

Dust devils dance. Dust where work on gravel road.

I remember the name Blooming Prairie. The town is a Sauk Centre, but with the Mystery of a water tower in a grove; and a Gun Club five miles north.

A GREAT PRAIRIE (name for town) should have some, but few, groves, almost no fences, and should slope gradually toward distant low hills.

When dark, silos of pure cream cement are startling.

At Farmington, long rows of maples either side street--good & big but not well cared for--well in bud.

APRIL TWENTY-ONE 5 AM, 44; noon, 67. 6 PM, 75. Another perfect day. NO RAIN FOR OVER TWO WEEKS NOW. Worry on farms, in northern forests, danger fire

APRIL TWENTY-TWO, another perfect day. But warmer. noon, 69; 6, 76.

NOTES ON THE Jitter-Bug Inn, Nicollet Avenue, round the corner from Washington Ave. Hangout people curious: bar tender in shirt and trousers proves to be woman--looks like man with womanish face. What seems to be proprietor, well-dressed masculine woman with short gray hair. Sitting there, a person one cdn't see whether man or woman. Bartendress like school teacher but plenty cigarettes, beer; another barmaid, anemic hatchet face--something out of wax musee. Girlish woman with one tough slender man; another man comes in, slaps the first, and drags her out, cursing. Snother, quite nice, claims to be English, admits not, son in Amer army in Ireland, "he never knew I was a rounder or went to places like this." Killer with flattened nose and husky woman mate.

Apr 22: high wind very gay on Nicolett misigates a fair HEAT and whisks gkirts about Dayton corners.....Everybody here seems to adore hunting and fishing; shoe clerk dayton's admires Minnetonka only for the fishing....Shoes out here never plain about toe as in East; must have punched holes. Clerk claims feet longer here.

APRIL TWENTY-ONE cont. Minneapolis <u>is</u> ugly. When they want to change residence, do not built up old section as new but just abandon it, and comfortable old middleclass houses become tenements, paintless and staggering and bare of yard; on Portland and Park avenues, magnificent--sometimes ugly--stone and brisk castles become School of Chiropractic, Swedish Institute, Secretarial School, worst of all is car-parking lots

In these smaller cities, the hideous clanking jarring noise of STREET CARS, gone from the larger ones. as bad as elevated, if close to. Accumulates, on nerves.....Mpls, more drunken voices after midnight

fol. 12

April 23. Again a perfect day; cooler at lake but hot in Mpls: 7 AM, 54; noon, 71; 6 PM, 81; midnight, 63.

Settled in Charles Lane Harris house, Edgewood (near Eureka), Excelsior Route One, Lake Minnetonka.

Trees half out.

Trying to identify spots known long ago; often hard; often unexpected clarity--place recalls itself. In Mpls, Johnson's undertaking parlors.....In doctor-locate novel?

APRIL 24, Friday; most variable temperatures: 4 AM, 60; 8, 53; noon, 74; 4 PM, 81; 6, 79. Late in the afternoon, the day turns gray--first time in two weeks, promises rain again, again not realized. At sunset: surely rain; cloud-covered sun is sulphurous yellow.

Constant change in ripples and color of lake....Muskrat swimming, making a V on smooth surface.....Red and gray squirrels, pheasant, woodpeckers. Garter snakes along shore after frogs.

APRIL 25, Saturday. Gray and cool at 7 AM--uneasy wind--rain really coming!--after I've expected it for 5 days. And at 10:15 AM, it does come. But gently. Lake lead-colored in the rain....All over by 11, and sun faintly out...Then gray again, and rain starts again, hard, at four, and continues into the night.

Is there more heavy banter--"kidding"--in Minnesota than in NY? It's very American.

APRIL 26, Sunday: Brenda Ueland, Charles and Ida Harris, Le Roy and Mrs. Arnold, Caroline Hoke. 8 AM, 66; noon, 67; 6, 64. Alternate clear and dark, cool at lake. Leaves much advanced, not full.

3:30 sky slate, with apricot-colored clouds nr horizon, and lake pure silver exception for the reflection of those clouds at one end....Nite of 26th, heavy thunder-shower; I think the first I've heard this year.

APRIL 27, Monday, to Lanesboro and Forestville with Jim Hart, driving 470 miles, staying overnight at Chatfield, Fillmore County.

8 AM, 55; noon, 62; 6, 70. Rain threat at 8 AM but decided to go, and in morning only a few drops, then hard rain for only half an hour at 2 PM at Chatfield.

Farmington, Cannon Falls, Zumbrota, Pine Island, Rochester (dining-rm Hotel Kahler, wood paneled, city menu, nice girl waitresses, corridor below connect with tunnel to clinic?), Chatfield, turn from #52 E on 30, Pilot Mound, Arendahl, Rushford, Lanesboro, Union Prairie, Preston, Fountain, Chatfield, Preston, W on 80, Carimona, Forestville, Cherry Grove, Harmony (lunch Tuesday), Mabel, Spring Grove, Caledonia (Houston County), Hokah, La Crescent, Winona, Wabasha, Lake City, Red Wing, New Trier (German church and like a monastery) and home.

fol. 13

APRIL 27, CONT.

After threat of rain, heavy mist, continued till ten, with dark sky most of the day.

The trees are about two-thirds out.

No more Tom Thumb golf courses, but way to Mpls, a "driving range," to test golf drives. Never seem to be any customers.

GROWTH OF MINNEAPOLIS
1870 -- 13,000
1880 -- 47,000
1890 -- 165,000
1900 -- 203,000
1910 -- 301,000
1920 --- 381,000
1930 -- 464,000
1940 -- 492,000

Degrees of looking each way at RR crossing.

MORE BURMA SHAVE ADS--copied from boards:

If hugging on highways
Is your sport,
Trade in your car
For a davenport.

Approached a crossing
Without looking.
Who will eat
His widow's cooking?

What you hollered
May be true,
But did you hear
What he called you?

Drove too long,
Driver snoozing.
What happened next
Is not amusing.

Pa likes the cream,
Ma likes the jar,
Both like the price,
So there you are.

RELIGIOUS SIGNS BY ROAD

JESUS SAVES

THE GIFT OF GOD IS
ETERNAL LIFE THROUGH
JESUS CHRIST

GOD IS LOVE

REPENT YE and
BE CONVERTED

The way of the Cross
Is the way home

JESUS HEALS (on rwy bridge)

JESUS SAID, "REPENT
AND BELIEVE THE BIBLE
N.W. Bible Institute

fol. 14

APRIL 27--CONT--2

On this darkish and varying day, from a ridge road the prairies and groves are touched by an apricot light from between silver clouds hemmed with dark clouds. The rays like Biblical pictures. The sky beautiful all day, with many low-colored clouds fast changing. Now all is getting green. The pastures will never again be quite so green. The winter wheat is sketched in delicate curving soft-green lines against the black So. Minn. earth.

In less than three weeks--April 8 to 27--I have seen the whole land, trees and fields and grass, turn from gray-brown to young bright green--which will fade a little.

Many silos not tile but cement, some of them with tiles set in at top for ornament.

A low cart for manure, heavy, drawn by three handsome, head-tossing horses.

In Goodhue County, many big white comfortable farmhouses, tend to be square with porches; quite as good as village houses; large barns and often two silos.

Town names, So. Minn:

Wanamingo	Greenleafton	Cherry Grove
Rollingstone	Eyota	Mabel
Mazeppa	Hokah	Lenora
Brush Creek		
Hayfield	Waseca County: Waldorf & Vivian	
	Blue Earth County: Medo & Little Cobb	

Cabin courts the new thing in tourist cabins.

Farmers wear canvas jackets now......In town, they walk and talk so slowly.....Do they still squat on heels on street, talking? Hart says Lancashire miners do same.

Gladys Hart notes out here less rusting machinery in farm yards than in New England....How very few abandoned farmhouses--they, mostly, I think, where farmer nextdoor has taken over this farm.

Some wild violets....Blue patches of bluebells.

A neat white-trimmed red corn-crib.

At six PM, hill horizons very gray

APRIL 28, Tuesday--trip with Hart continued. 8 AM, 48; noon, 60; 6, 72. After raining or being dark all yesterday and a heavy wind last night that made the Chatfield Hotel sign creak--odd that this sign, inviting guests, shd keep them awake!--this morning is cool, clear, the most crystal and delicious day that ever was, at least at 8 AM, and nearly so all day.... Yesterday afternoon, Tornado at Ortonville, western border of state, wiped out a country school house, killed 3 of eight pupils--another tornado once struck schoolhouse in same place.

At Forestville, on Route 80 West from Preston, Joseph Meighen, of 1st Natl Bank, Preston, still owns 2000 out of the 20,000 acres his grandfather bought with the $75,000 he brought from Pennsylvania, after being a 49'er in California. 1500 acres

fol. 15

APRIL 28th CONT:

of the almost-unknown virgin timber: 17 varieties, said Joe: soft maple, hard maple, red oak, white oak, basswood, hickory, white pine, spruce, poplar, birch, elm, et al.

In the midst of the deep valley, wooded hills on either side like Vermont, first a brick farmhouse like New England--heavy stone lintel over door; then the old store, same architecture, but in an ell, with white upper porch on one side, upper porch reached from outside by white-lattice-hid stairs on the other; fine old brick, handmade right here by man imported from Pennsylvania; rather rosy....Across from store, wide barn, ruins of school. Beside it, fine clear stream of the Middle Branch of Root River....The 2000 acres over hills and up again, with several tenant farms and cleared acres; also fishermen's cottages--trout planted.....Meighan claims his valley cool in summer, in re virgin timber with underbrush holding moisture.

Saw scarlet tanager, and what seemed to be rose-breasted grosbeak.

Outside Winona, Townsend Club signs, proclaiming that plan would be needed, and would conquer, after this war.....In Winona, large factory of Watkins patent medicine company/

Note that passers-by in car still wave the hand to strangers and get response, as never in New England.

Route out here usually pronounced Rowt, even by fairly educated.

Rural post boxes furnished by city newspapers.

Hear mourning doves along lake, at home, in morning.

APRIL 29. Mostly gray day. 8 AM, 60; noon, 71; 6, 77.

fol. 16

APRIL 30, Thursday. 8 AM, 68; noon, 72; 6, 71. The moon last night was full, but a thin cloudiness veiled it. The morning damp, rather hot, gray--depressing like a damp day at the seashore, though here one expects the air to be nimble always. Then there was thin sunshine, then a little rain--and suddenly, just at noon, it turned almost as dark as night. The lights had to be put on in the house. And with a crash came a heavy thunderstorm.

Lightning hit near the house, and one could see, in the darkness, columnar shafts of lightning coming down across the lake. Though mostly dark, the sky still held a rosy light low in the East.

The lake was first leaden, with shivers of wind across it, then lost to sight in the thickness of the rain. The young leaves trembled as in fear. Depressions in the lawn were suddenly filled with water--made hairy with grass stalks--and water dripped through the porch roof.

By halfpast twelve, it became fairly light again. The lake was gray, the foliage of trees an almost poison green against gray sky. By 12:40, the rain was ceasing. In the afternoon, dim sunshine, with the lake gray and asleep.

MAY FIRST, Friday. 8 AM, 59; noon 68; 6, 62--going down: midnight, 56.

TREES ARE PRACTICALLY ALL OUT NOW. Very handsome tall elms and maples here at the lake, on Harris place--first growth? Chilly, gray, with threat of rain all day. Wind and heavy rain, lasting about 20 minutes, at 11:30; heavy sudden rain 3:15 to 3:30, then quits on the minute, almost, as if on radio schedule.

Then rain starts again at 4:43, quits 4:52; sulky sky till 4:55, then sun out bright, sky clear and sweet and soft blue with the new green foliage against it. Sun hidden again at 5:20 and dark clouds rising to swallow sky. But no rain this time, and sun again after 6. Rain again, for twenty minutes, at 7:00.

After the whole shore is dark, in evening the lake still holds the light.

MAY 2: (thermometer at lake) 50 at 11 AM, with cold breeze; 1:30 PM, 52; 11 PM, 48. Chilly, sky gray, no sun, all day. For the first time, heat on in furnace all day.

MAY 3, SUNDAY: (ther at lake): 8 AM, 46; 4 PM, 48; midnight, 43. (In Mpls, apparently colder: Tribune figures for same day: 8 AM, 40; 4 PM, 43; midnight, 38. No rain all day, but gray all day till 4:20, when 5 minutes of sun.

Jos and Dagmar Beach, Wm and Lois McNally, Virginia Lewis, Dotty Bennett, Starke and Mrs. Hathaway, Eddie and Marie Ford, the Harts, here for cocktails, stayed (except Beaches) for supper, buffet and emergency....Talk of What is a Provincial? In Minnesota, Carleton Miles was, but disbelieved; I am. Is George Jean Nathan a provincial, in NY?.....Ford on Weather is news. Our fathers kept the daily temperature in dairy. Marcella would never think of doing so, in NY.

Paper speaks of "spring tornado season." Been several--Minn, Oklahoma, Texas, last few days.

fol. 17

MAY FOURTH--Monday. (ther at lake): 8 AM, 44; 1:30 PM, 49; 5, 52; 7, 54. Cold spell seems getting over--tomorrow may be a Christian day. All day, no rain, but gray--“autumnal”--with sun coming out, only 2 minutes at a time, at 4:10, 5, 5:15 and so on, and no cold wind.

Registering for sugar--teachers at small local brick school, (Also is a branch Hennepin County Library.) don’t know the blanks any better than I do--seems inefficient.

(Temperatures here on, unless otherwise given, by thermometer at the lake.)

Gray squirrels chase one another thru branches.

This May 4, first real sunset in several days: sun a naked gold at setting; lake silver, no longer lead; trunks of trees are, on the side facing sunset, pink, in contrast to the deepened black of rest of trunk. Later, afterglow, clinging so long above the dark woods across the lake that you feel this really <u>is</u> The North, solitary and dark and strong, even down here near Mpls.

MAY FIFTH, Tuesday. Today is <u>not</u> a Xian day! At 8:30 AM (by thermometer here at Edgewood, on Minnetonka), 46, and gray. 4:30 PM, 53. Find out from papers late today that at Duluth it has been only 31 degrees, at Winnipeg, 28. It’s gray till 4 PM, then sun comes and goes. Rains at 11:30 PM.

Power mower working on lawn. Grass been too damp, hitherto, tho getting long....By the secluded shore here, a few ducks feed, sheltered by trees submerged by the unusually high water. There are some big woodpeckers. Piliated?

The season rather early this year....Down the road, big lilac bush in full bloom.

Into Minneapolis: In a week or so, the whole aspect of the city has changed, the streets become pretty and friendly and rather village-like, as the trees have come out--and you realize how many trees there are in the city.

Dinner with John Cowles, prest Tribune-Star-Journal Corp. and brother of Des Moines Register and Look. House one of the few still haughty on the degenerating, once grand Park Avenue, where a Touraine chateau becomes Swedish Institute and another mansion a Chiropractic School; house colonial brick, surr by high brick wall; rooms wood-paneled, many books...John Cowles, his wife Betty, Bill & Lois McNally, A.M. and Mrs. Wilson, Mrs., (Rufus) Rand.

MAY SIXTH, Wednesday....9 AM, raining, 48; 3 PM, 56. Rain quits at noon. Been in Minnesota four weeks today. Papers late today say there was snow today at Austin, in Southern Minnesota.

Into Minneapolis....Art Institute; a bad Rembrandt, a fine El Greco, a so-so Gaugin. Liked Oliver Dennett Grover's "Gray Day in Venice." Only ½ liked Boardman Robinson's colored drawing of me--with evening clothes, long cigarette holder, GSB!

fol. 18

May Six, cont:

To house of LeRoy Arnold, head English dept., Hamline University, St. Paul....Arnolds lived here for 3 generations, on Park Ave., couple blocks from Cowles house. Old red brick, shabby, thin and steep-staired, narrow halls....To Hamline, a Methodist school; buildings unrelated and skimpy. 6 O'clock dinner at The Manor House--girls' dormitory, and by edict of the dean of women, a small, pleasant, restrained, powerful lady, no cigarette, not even for the Speaker, between supper and his spiel--on "Environments dont create writers, but vv., witness Shakespeare creating English royalty, Dickens, London, Washn Irving, the Hudson--when will the Mississippi bluffs, Mpls to La Crosse, have their Irving?

Sit beside Pace, President, ex-Methodist preacher, but like a chunky brisk, large-nosed, shrewd, dissembling business executive. I suggested that as even girls are allowed to smoke in the Union, no excuse for not smoking in this dorm. "I'm not making any excuses!" he said with cheerful, cynical firmness, and then I knew he was almost as good a politician as Cowling of Carleton.

Came up after dinner, Margaret Snyder (address, Bass Lake Farm, R 11, Mpls), who's been teaching 20 yrs at St. Mary's School, Faribault. She has discovered and loves Chatfield where, she says, an example of every age of Minnesota from 1840 to today; she's "been writing a novel about it for 20 yrs" and, nervously, will I lay off?.....Pretty Johnson girl, senior, fr Sauk Centre.

To Arnold's house through St. Paul, along Summit Avenue, still as stately as ever; see old Pierce house, and call on Oscar Kalman, just back from Florida, with his Sandra mysteriously remaining there "for a rest." At Arnold's, W.S. Cooper (Minnetonka address, Groveland) who is botanist at Univ of Minn, and lived in Carmel, Calif, in 1911....Arnold was born be protestant preacher--careful.

During the night, says paper next morning, thermometer down to 37.

MAY SEVENTH, Thursday. 7 AM, 50; noon 67; 3:30 69; 6, 68. For first time in two weeks, again "a perfect day," such as had then: sky a lively blue, trees glowing, birches brilliant against the blue water here at the lake; the lake gay, still, mirroring the wooded bluffs across, as it has not done in two restless weeks.

Camilla Wing (Mrs. Dr. Danl Bessenen) 30, neighbor who writes books for children about diet, calls with loaf homemade bread.

A village sound: carpenter driving home a nail, the sound climactic.

SUNDOWN: the sun red and clouded, like a pile of crimson robes, goes down at 8:25 CWT (Central War Time, really 7:25). It's dark at 9:30. But lake is still a round of clear silver, perceptible, for twenty minutes more, after shores dark, with a faint afterglow. Extraordinarily beautiful: the mysterious channels between isles, distant shore lights, including red one on a bridge......

Lights suddenly went out complete, at midnight, just when I was reading a dismayingly frighteening passage from Marcus Goodrich's fine novel "Delilah," and I was certain that burglers were invading at every door.

fol. 19

MAY EIGHT, Friday. Perfect day; cool, bright, sweet. 9:30 AM, 58, during day up to 65....Note that West, at Brownton, trees much less in leaf. With Jim Hart, 300 mile trip, to Chaska, Cologne, Norwood, Plato--all Germans, Glencoe--antinque shop in upstairs of house, Brownton, Stewart, Hector, Bird Island, Olivia, Renville, Granite Falls--irregular streets above river, Montevideo--most of town residences on bluffs overlooking merging valleys of Minnesota and Chippewa Rivers, Cottonwood, Echo, Belview--garageman: "No, that pump don't register when I'm taking from other one,"--trying to find ruins of 19-rm granite castle of Joseph R. Brown, running dirt road along bluffs of wide Minnesota Valley, back to Renville and home.

Note in ten days not motoring that grain thicker, lines of it not so precise. But plenty pre-seed plowing still going on, and more harrowing....This black earth of So. Minnesota--none cd be blacker--the more so when fresh turned, because before that a little gray from dust and stubble and stalks. This anywhere from, say, Bird Island to Cottonwood. Few hills, except Minnesota River bluffs--there, in wide river valley, masses of Archean boulders been exposed.

Dandelions unusually thick on all lawns in villages.....Red wing blackbirds. Many pheasants--the cock with ruby burnished neck, walking placidly, unafraid, on border of road....Killed along road: snakes, rabbits, one pheasant....Saw once a crow consuming killed bird on road....Cheerful small doves

The tillplain--broken by moraines......Sheep just been sheared, very naked in rocky pastures on valley side, G. Falls to Montevideo.

Gophers constantly skittering across road. Does the gopher ever cross the Mississippi? It is unknown, even the name, in the East. Readers called the town in Main St, "Gawfer Prairie."

Tarpaper shacks, still.....Tin-covered gray elevators with the red wooden.....Cherry and crab apple in bloom...Real apple orchard at "House by the Side of the Road," nr Minnetonka.

Roads parallel railroad for miles, on prairie....All day, scattered not-large cumulus clouds, solid, slow-moving.

Remember from boyhood, DUCK HUNTING: blinds, low-gunwale boat, or float, decoys, grass mantels like shock of wheat, 10 and 12 gauge.

Galvanized-iron barn cowl ventilators.....Silhouette of plowman and horses on low plump black plowed hill....Nr Chaska, abandoned brick brick-kilns, with bushes growing in crevices, rusty iron-band brace loose.

MAY NINE, Saturday, another perfday. 9:35 AM, 58; 10:45, 64; cooler in afternoon....Dinner at Addison Lewis's, Long Lake: Harry Piper, investment banker, & wife; Mr. and Mrs. Charles Swett, Honeywell Regulator Co., Helen Rand (husband in army). Five daughters of Cousin Addison, each more beautiful than the next. His wife, a Dorothy.

fol. 20

MAY NINE CONT: Piper, big, dark, soldierly figure, asks aloud what so many here think: Why, after so long away, do I return for considerable stay in Minnesota?....I try to answer: In New York, because of distance from Provinces, one does not return to native heath often--as a Jack Priestley can skip up to Yorkshire in six hours--and one loses contact with roots--a largely rootless folk there. And why does he stay here?

He asserts that--next to California--this is the most beautiful state in the union--especially the swamps!--"Looking at Nature is the one pleasure left, in this crazy world." But, he admits, he must have hunting to take him out to Nature.

Fishing, hunting, they seem enormously important to all the men here, from Piper to Professor Hathaway, who at least likes fishing. VS New York.

MAY TEN, Sunday. Five-year anniversary. A perfect day, cool, clear, in the morning. Tribune temperature for the 10th: 8 AM, 47; noon, 61; 6 PM, 66. Rain late in the afternoon as we approached S.Dakota, however, the beginning of 3½ days of bad weather: wet and chilly.

Five-day trip to:

MINNESOTA: Chaska, Jordan (German with municipal saloon), New Prague, Kilkenny, Elysian, Janesville, Waseca, Albert Lea, west to Blue Earth, Fairmont, Welcome, Jackson, Worthington, Luverne for NIGHT--Manitou Hotel, red granite.

MONDAY: SOUTH DAKOTA: Sious Falls, Mitchell and Dakota Wesleyan University, Huron, Aberdeen for NIGHT, at Sherman Hotel.

TUESDAY: into NORTH DAKOTA, nr Linton--and roast beef lunch--Sterling and eagles, Bismarck, and NIGHT at Prince Hotel.

WEDNESDAY, east again, to Jamestown, Valley City, Fargo, back into Minnesota, Moorhead, Breckenridge, Wahpeton, Fergus Falls. NIGHT at River Inn, Fergus.

THURSDAY back to Minnetonka via Elbow Lake, Kensington, Glenwood, Brooten, Belgrade, Paynesville, Buffalo, Wayzata.

Mileage: Sunday, 288; M, 256; Tue, 218; Wedn, 316; Thur, 195--total, 1273, or only 90 miles less than from New York to Mpls.

Return to May 10:

Jim Hart, before trip is over: most struck by two things, coming West: real extent of prairie--hadn't been able to imagine it; and people, though friendly--e.g., neighbor at lake, finding they have no dressing table, not only lends one but bring it over on back--not intrusively friendly, as had feared. They wait some days before calling.

Plowman accompanied by woolly dog, more than friend of companion--a real Second Self, turning with him in each slightest motion.

Montgomery, settled by Czechs: church with bulbous spire.

Two small birds attack crow in air and make him retreat....Wild canaries.

Minnesota not so many consolidated rural schools as some states? At least, many one-rm school still seen, mostly white. Differ from my day, apparently, only in having play grounds with apparatus like parallel bars. Janesville: preacher going home after church; flowers & book.

fol. 21

MAY TEN, CONT.

CEMETERY AT ELYSIAN, MINNESOTA, near Mankato. Coming out of prairie country, but rolling, this graveyard is on a wooded bluffs overlooking Lake Elysian. It is truly rural. Fresh lilacs, plucked, on a grave, give a sweet odor. Many cedars.

The graves of my paternal grandfather and grandmother--who had a farm here 60 years ago, on which my father worked--and later paid the mortgage!--and where my mother and Fred took refuge while Father was attending Rush Medical College--these graves are humble and hard to find.

There is a pair of little, twin marble headstones, slender and not over a yard high, side by side, with inscriptions:

In memory of		In memory of
John Lewis		E. Lewis
Died	next	Died
Dec. 26, 1884	to it	Nov. 23, 1886
Aged		Aged
70 Years		70 Years

Grandfather--the day after Xmas--44 days before I was born. Grandmother died two years minus two months after her husband, and at the same age. Her full maiden name is not given. I think it was Emma.* Note that there are no religious sentiments on the stones. I don't think they were very churchly.

From Fred's family Bible.
John Lewis, b. Oxford, Conn. Apr. 28, 1815.
* Emeline Johnson, b. Seymour Conn., Apr. 28 1817
E. J. Lewis, b. Westville, Conn. Sept. 18, 1848. d. Aug. 29 1926.
One of Dad's sisters m. Frank Long; one a Mr. Williams.

This whole cemetery, in contrast to the strong German, Scandinavian, Bohemian, or Irish racial flavor of almost all graveyards in Southern Minnesota (and most of the rest of the state) is Yankee-English, indicating the history, and there is no other cemetery nr the village. There are non-British names, a few of them, on the stones--e.g. Vincenc Rocek and Wendelschafer--but so few. Here are some names:

Wood	Jewell	Coffin	Higgins	Brand
Lyon	Warburton	Warner	Clarke	Whitten
Bruce	Beardsley	Simons	Cowles	Popham
Swain	Gifford	Willis	Tooker	Sterling
Brooks	Abbott	Adams	Danbury	Morton
Lundy	Pine	Tobias		

Complete:

Dorothy Surdam Ellins
Jason B. Terrell
Eben T. Holcomb
Ada & Clyde Long
David Jewell
John Ash

Otis Fish
Minerva Carpenter
Elizabeth York
Almeda Culp Casebeer

I think the Beardsleys have some family relationship to me. The Longs have, I know. One of my father's sisters married a Long. And two of my own first cousins are buried here--brother and sister, very rural but ran the little one-room bank in Elysian the one time I ever saw them, when I went with Father to Elysian, in 1919, summer. Here they are now: Albert John Long, 1877-1940; Edna Grace Long, 1880-1930.

fol. 22

MAY TEN, CONT--2

ELYSIAN CEMETERY CONT:

Most of the stones are of polished red or gray granite: the kind that came between Grandfather's marble and the present softly rough granite with chaste letters.

The most touching stone that of a nineteen-year old bride--and remember that when it was set up here, this place really <u>was</u> in the wild woods--it was 3 years before the great Sioux Massacre. (This copy does not exactly follow spelling or spacing)

Sarah
Wife of Hiram M. Fish
Died Jan. 14, 1859
Aged 19 years, 5 mos, 12 days

Gone to Her Rest
(below this, a marble hand
pointing to it. Then this
poem, probably original)

Rest thee, loved one, where we laid thee,
Where the wild wood maketh sigh.
Tears perfume the bed we made thee,
Where the withered foliage lie.

Probably Lucius Beebee, Mencken, and the New Yorker would find this all very funny. What became of Hiram, the young husband? I did not see his headstone in the cemetery. Did he wander on West? Did he marry again? Had he raven locks, like a steel engraving? Or was he young, at all, this husband of poor little Sarah, aged 19 years, 5 months, 12 days?

****

Like all the Middlewest, Southern Minnesota has racial districts, close together and slowly united, but still with a lot of cleveage--ably assisted by the pastors, whose jobs lie in keeping up such nationalistic churches as the Lutheran and, to some extent, the Catholic.....Here in So. Minnesota are such districts as: Swedish, Norwegian, Bohemian, Polish--or last 2 combined, German, and Irish (vge of Kilkenny) with, in other parts of the-state, Welsh, Finnish, Icelandic.....and even Yankee! The blending of these communities and elements, through marriage, business, politics, schools, would make an epic novel....Not many Jews, and they usually men's & women's clothes, in the larger towns....Don't some Jews pass here as Pure Austrian?

How suddenly roads change in surface at county lines.

Mexicans are imported for the hard work of sugar beet farming to village of Blue Earth.....Remem the English colony, the "Fairmont Sportsmen," at Fairmont, riding to hounds after rabbits or wolves, circ 1875, in red coats made by vge tailor<u>ess</u>, fighting grasshopper plague, taking the show away from President Hayes at State fair in 1878 by riding hurdles; of them, Ward, bank prest, left money and son.....Any connection with them and the fact that Worthington, pop. 3900, 60 miles away, has a polo team? A novel!

fol. 23

MAY TEN, CONT--3

Typical farmhouse

Here is a typical farmhouse & buildings as you approach them, in fat rich Southern Minnesota--but no one would have <u>all</u> these features.

A willow or dark pine grove, with at least one windmill sticking up above it, and maybe two--the second usually for electric power. It is often on a low knoll....RFD box. Whitehouse, huge red barn, perhaps with white trim, red stable. Dooryard, small lawn, shrubs, maybe flowers. Corncrib. Garage. Milkhouse. Machine shed. One or two tall silos. Granary. Fenced pasture nr house with Holsteins, pigs, horses. Chicken house and run--

usually white chickens. Brooder houses. Crabapple tree, now in bloom. Lilac bush. Sometimes ornamental iron fence and gate before house. Woodlot, with stumps; usually oaks. Sometimes crisp pasture grass in woodlot. Pile of cut wood. Small sparkling pond with ducks. And old log cabin, left from earlier days, leaning. Eaten away strawstack in barnyard. Black and white pigs. Pigeons. Swing for the children. (Tire) A dog, very barking collie & a smaller dog, and a cat. Sometimes sheep. Tractor, harrow, sometimes combine, old Ford.

You still, in 1942, see Model T Fords, some with top completely gone, on the road. The last was made in ?

Waseca garageman--opp the great Catholic church and parochial school--on how they "kid" man from New York for saying "frahg" for "frawg."

GIRLS IN SLACKS, on streets, even going to school--slacks gray, blue, lilac, yellow, even in beer joint in evening at Luverne--all along this trip, Minn & Dakotas.

Albert Lea courthouse. rough granite, above it, red brick, with oriel and turrets......Many real apple trees, now in blossom, west of Albert Lea......Plover by pond.

NAMES IN SOUTHERN MINNESOTA--(town names)
Guckeen
Imogene
Leota

Sunday, farmers and wives out fishing, on every brookside, from every brook bridge, with cars parked.

See guide book for the delightful marble log-cabin momument of Moses Sailor in Blue Earth--logs and door and chimney.

Near Fairmont, the Bethel Free Church of that metropolis advertises righteousness in separated roadsigns imitative of the

(to next page)

fol. 24

MAY TEN, CONT--4

exclusive Burma Shave advertisements:

We preach
  Christ
   Crucified
      Risen
       Coming Again.

******

In many villages, near the depot, are the large Ever Normal Granary tanks of the government.

Many barns have outstretched peak at gable of roof, to attach hay-hoist.

West from Fairmont on 16, you really get flat prairie, except for the Des Moines River valley at Jackson. You can see long distances--but not as far as They say. It takes a church steeple to be seen over five miles.

In the country, nr a road junction, a unit of general store with nothing else but backhouse. The store carries gasoline, soda, coke--as every one here calls Coca Cola--groceries. Also a speakeasy? A solid man, like an army sergeant, soldier-looking in gas company's uniform of gray shirt and lettered gray cap, runs it--King of the Prairies, an adventurer, an individualist, and a whole novel!

******

Late in the afternoon, rain clouds threaten for an hour, and then RAIN, at 6:20, after the virginal seductive promises of the morning...In the rain, the wide prairie has a misty horizon; the scattered groves are blurred. It is all melancholy, but not harsh.

Caught in the heavy rain, which makes you a little uneasy on narrow blacktop roads with deep ditch on either side, Jim Hart and I stop at the

Manitou House, Luverne, for the night...Both here and Aberdeen, we can gets rooms with baths, but no cafe in the hotel, no food, though both sell drinks--the Manitou only beer.

A town like this, Luverne, 2600, is much more sporting than Sauk Centre when I was a boy. The hotel basement is a beer joint, open till 12, even on Sunday--in S.C. then, the town would have been dead by ten. It's a dreary place: cement floor, drab plaster walls, pipes strung across ceiling, lights dim and, in effort to be romantic rose probably, just rusty. The young farmers and girls--one a fat one in slacks--just walk, for dancing, and don't walk very well. They ostensibly drink only beer and soft drinks; some do "spike their coke with hootch," but only one or two drunks and not objectionable. Just dull! No advance on SC in thosedaysofold in joy, certainly....And flip girl waitresses in cafe, with its invariable booths.

In the morning, the 11th, when I send out for coffee, the "bell boy" who brings it is a young farm lout, who walks right into the room with cap on, in canvas windbreaker; a milk bottle full of coffee only ten cents .....Night of tenth, cars lv town till 1 AM.

fol. 25

MAY ELEVEN, MONDAY

In Luverne at 8 AM, 55 and gray. (Mpls Tribune for temperature, Monday: 8 AM, 49; noon, 48; 6,54.

Under the gray sky, the prairie seems wider, more mysterious. At 10:30, the sun is out, just as we cross border into SOUTH DAKOTA, then it deceitfully vanishes again.

One always expects an immediate change when one crosses a national, even a state, border, but here is the same rolling prairie, same quite black soil, same red barns. Sign at border:

Welcome to South Dakota
Home of Midwest Oil Co.

Town etc. names in South Dakota:

Pumpkin Center
Bonilla
Pukwana
Spink County
Bon Homme "
Washabaugh "
Ziebach "
Punished Woman Lake

All these little plains villages, so humble, so flimsily built, so planlessly scattered, open to the prairie and naked in the snowstorm, the August duststorm, yet so small are the one and two story buildings, so large are the dooryards, that they cover an unexpected amount of ground; and seen from a mile away, a vge of 300, with its spires and trees so stretches out that you think it will be one of 700 or 1000....Remember how as a boy, viewing Sauk Centre from the cemetery, admired how it stretched out surely a full mile--a very considerable city!

Sioux Falls:

First Baptist Church
Sermon: Vitamins for the Soul
August M. Hintz, pastor.

Roadside sign:

I'm for Joe
The best man for the job
BOTTUM FOR GOVERNOR

And Herbert Agar would teach us democracy!

Blackbirds, yellow neck and red wing.

There is real splendor in a day of intermittent sunshine like this: the masses of cumulus clouds, with flitting shadows, and the width of the plains--which, vs prairie, begin here, perhaps.

How a Sauk Centre can be the center of the universe. Brenda Ueland's story of the man fr Podunk, "I don't see much future for Chicago--it's too far away. New York or Pekin, symphonies or Corning glass,

fol. 26

MAY ELEVEN, CONT.

a University class in Sanskrit or a German-English war--what have they for a man in Sauk Centre, he unconsciously asks himself. And there is Everything there: friends, enemies, work, love, home, bed, cigars, ham, fishing and fishing tackle, shoes, pencils, music--once in Eastern Star recital and now on radio, church and hence God, and a railroad station at which he <u>could</u> take train for steamers to Rome--if he wanted to.

Title: Windmill Against the Sky.

Sioux Falls to Mitchell:

Small Dakota Wesleyan Univ. Mitchell. 6 buildings. Harvey Dunn picture pioneer S. Dak woman. Prest Jos. H Edge; profs J. Almus Russell & Van Kirk.

Many less towns than in Minnesota....Vge of Bridgewater, pop 808, shabbier, more Western than vge of same size in Minnesota, which comes now to seem like Massachusetts. Dirt side streets, very muddy and with no sidewalks. It all seems lost.

A new (to me) feature in all these towns is the water tower, silvered, painted with name of town, on high trestlework.

Really flat, Emery to Mitchell. Great cement US Highway 16, across sparse plains.....Windbreaks--7 rows.

Cumulus clouds <u>blur</u> together as rain threatens.

Look up JEDEDIAH STRONG SMITH, 1798-1831, first man to lead expedition across the Sierra Nevadas, overland Calif-Oregon, etc. B.

Bainbridge, NY. See H. C. Dale, "The Ashley-Smith Expeditions." A real pioneer hero--and pious--and a gd biography.

So often see tiny pond by road, with many blackbirds about it.

Many less trees about farmhouses in Dakota than in Minnesota, and less groves seen across country. Some farmhouses with no trees whatever.....In the mellow light of late afternoon, the flatlands become softer, sweeter.

The Sherman Hotel, Aberdeen, South Dakota--no dining room at all, but almost luxurious Blue Room--bar and lounge-like tables, with silver-paneled blue walls....In lobby, soft landscape paper, quite good.

The young men out here, even in the towns, a little heavy, earthy, inflexible and unreferential in speech. They could use some eastern Jewish-Italian influence.....Y men wear sweaters and windbreakers as girls wear slacks.

Minn and the Dakotas, more scientific feed stores than when I was a boy; proper mixes, grain & vitamins, for poultry, cattle.

MAY TWELVE, Tuesday. Cool and gray at 7 AM. Temperature Tuesday in Fargo, acc to Fargo Forum: 9 AM, 56; noon, 62. Aberdeen to Bismarck, NDak, through rain almost all day.

Beer at the Elks.

In flatlands, an eight-foot rise in the road seems an immense height and gives a View.

fol. 27

MAY TWELVE, CONT.

Always in the wheat land, some slews, a few lakes--which once in a while actually makes the road curve!

Though much winter wheat out now, also much harrowing, west of Aberdeen, and some plowing--a little. Aberdeen to Linton, no or few trees about farmhouses.

For hours today through a mist, which often congeals to rain. In the mist, plains kindly and mysterious.

Gullies in moraine range of low hills: here there is, on rocky soil, still virgin prairie. A house tucked in these green folds.

A note nothing to do with Dakotas: Affection for small objects, regret, almost personal sorrow, at giving them up: Marcella and her brass-buttoned school coat; I with a map of Minnesota which has served me well and now, wearing thru at creases, seems more important than new sister map......And a note later typed at Minnetonka, more in anger than in sorrow: how, in this quiet, machine gun of a woodpecker, power lawn mower, voices, will awaken one from nap.

No one has, so far I know, ever tried to make a prairie village which would be secure, beautiful, convenient. It would not have all straight streets, but curved; it would be walled, almost like a mediaeval village, with trees and shrubs--evergreens that would protect it in winter. It would not be ridiculous to think of tunnels, carrying communal heating pipes, connecting houses to schools and arcaded charming shops. No house, probably, to cost more than $7500; most not more than $3000.

At ten-thirty, the mist becomes definite rain. At eleven-thirty, we cross the border into: KIDDER COUNTY, NORTH DAKOTA. From Aberdeen we go 130 miles without a gear change--we might go 500. At noon, a chilly wind, and wet gravel road, chewed up, Jim has to keep "fighting the steering wheel," and the wet puddles, shining against brown gravel, makes it look even worse than it is.

At Linton, N. Dak., stopping for lunch, I naively order rare roast beef. That beef has been in the oven for days, and it's like chips. Plus radio, doors that crashes shut every time some one comes in, bawling radio, waitress girl, probably daughter of the woman proprietor, has tinted fingernails and tries to give me gravy-covered fork, used vainly on the roast beef, for the decayed raisin pie. Later today I take up the matter of this roast beef with the governor of the state, a supreme court justice in Bismarck, and the B correspondent of the Associated Press, but don't seem to get anything done about it.

Old grass, golden; some weeds russet.

Most of the day, flatlands, but after pass N.D. border, rolling rounded bluffs, where only agriculture is grazing, with a few sharp higher bluffs--good painting.....Much land thru here unfenced.

fol. 28

MAY TWELVE, CONT--2

At Sterling, junction with US Route 10 for Bismarck, country store which is also a museum: skulls of small plains animals, stuffed birds, old rifles. Here's a natural scientist. Here stuffed I found and can describe as I cdn't dashing by in car, a:

COCK PHEASANT: top of head, green and iridescent, with tufts like little horns; red wattles under the eyes; blue-green neck; white collar, back of neck; breast, gold spotted with purple; Paisley shawl back, many colors blended, w gray stipple. Green-gray long tail; dark green feet and legs.

Here I join the course I took with Gracie in 1916, when I motored, in a Model T Ford, from Sauk Centre to Seattle, then California, via Fergus Falls, Bismarck, Miles City. The most obvious change is in highways. The main roads, even, were then just dirt, but now are all cement or macadam; the side roads were mere prairie trails, worn through the sod; now they are blacktop or gravel. Top speed then was 15 miles an hour, now it is perhaps 100.....though just now, war rationing of gasoline and stoppage of all sale of tires may drop us way below 1916 standards.

Out here, everywhere shirt sleeves--e.g. clerks in quite good big-town store. And everywhere GUM, half the people at a movie chewing it. Everywhere "OK" and "You bet," for cheerful yes.

BISMARCK: Governor John Moses; 6' 4"; eyebrows like John L. Lewis. Supreme Court Justice A. M. Christianson, one with Art Hoffman, an older and plainer Agar--the eagle type. His brow wrinkles turn at ear & go up. The state capitol an 18 story skyscraper, right in the prairies--you look thru windows of atty genl's office to see grassland. Magnificent corridor of black marble columns with long brass chandeliers, in lower, 2-story wing of legislative halls.

Newspapermen: John Hjelle, Bismarck Tribune; Fred Compton, A.P.

Story of the Marquis de Mores, who married Medora von Hoffman of New York, a soldier of fortune--and rich--who came to N. Dakota and lived there about 1879-1883, trying to found an empire; vast ranches, own chain of packing houses. Tried for murder--just casually bumped off a cattle thief; acquitted. Built a castle at Medora, now property of state. His son, the Duc de Vallombrosa, still living.

MAY THIRTEEN, Wednesday. At Bismarck at 9:15, 38 degrees, and a cold wind so strong that it shakes car parked in capitol grounds as vainly try to find WPA N Dak Guidebook. Later, from Tribune, temperature in Mpls this day: (much warmer than in NDak): 8 AM, 59; 9, 62; noon, 74; 6, 71.

Bismarck to Fargo to Fergus Falls.

Calves being branded now. Lambing. Sheep shearing, June.

fol. 29

MAY THIRTEEN, CONT--

An angry day. Wind so strong it shakes the car, parked at the Capitol...Capitol, part just two stories, for legislative chambers; office part, 18 stories, with observation floor the 18th...Prairie comes right up to it.

Tumbleweed galloping across road, agitatedly. How many hundreds of mile a tumblewd might run if not stopped by fence.

From 11 on, a thin grudging sunshine. Wind on prairie like a wall when try to walk against it, and eyes assaulted by dust. Passing big fast truck, vacuum between.

Along the road, phone poles seem to come together in the distance. Seen over a rise, they are like a fan.

Silvery dry grass in an old pasture....Heat on in car today. The Dakotas have few silos, and almost none of the large rich farmhouses of Minnesota.....Swale....

Another BURMA sign--a chapter out of Babbitt:
When Junior takes
Your ties and car
It's time to buy
Another jar.

Town in NDak:
Cackle

Bleak lone weather-stained farmhouses. Some abandoned. Small low barns with such houses; some thatched with grass.

<u>Bismarck to Jamestown:</u> Spits of light rain, very strong north wind. About 40 degrees. With this, 15 miles of unfinished gravel road--building interrupted by war?--with crisscross ruts so that Jim again has to fite the wheel. And, the whole time, blown DUST, sometimes like smokecloud from a freight locomotive. Miserable! the whole time! Otherwise, would have liked the broad platters of almost houseless land. After Jamestown, the sun out, and some hard-surfaced road which, to a car, is like relief from rheumatism.....Sun again, 3:30.

Prairie lake edged with moraines, scattered stones.

Co-operative Shelterbelt. Department of Agriculture. Forest Service.

Flatness of prairie as come to Fargo then, back in MINNESOTA, Wilkin County, across the Red River, just as flat. Fargo-Moorhead and Whapeton-Breckenridge are each like one town, tho river and state line divide them....

MINNESOTA again.

Town of Finkle.

Breckenridge to Fergus Falls, over 20 miles, billiard flat & not many trees, then suddenly hills begin to swell toward Fergus, which is among hills, and a most pleasant town--good River Inn, and houses about Lake Alice. Inspiration Peak, a little over 30 miles E of Fergus.

fol. 30

MAY THIRTEEN CONT--2

Fergus Falls Daily Journal:
Elmer E. Adams, Prest, 2/6
RJUnderwood, secy-mgr, 1/2
WLRobertson, editor, 1/6
Carl Snowberg, reporter.

MAY FOURTEEN, Thursday. Fergus Falls back to Minnetonka.

Another perfect day, though cool, after 4 days mostly gray with fair amount rain. Temperature: Fergus Falls, 9 AM, 40; 2 PM at restaurant at Delano, on #12, 58. Mpls Trib temps, 14th: 8, 37; noon, 41; 6, 50. Midnite, at Minnetonka, 49.

Met at Fergus, Judge Himsl (Himsel?) of St. Cloud.

This is the tornado season. Three small ones yesterday in Minnesota; at Morton, Renville County, ten homes demolished. Wise man puts children in automobile and heads for country.

Radio in hotel lobby, beats on nerves. Clerk hates it but customers turn it on again.

The point keeps recurring of education of eye to see this land. After the flat W of Fergus, how important seem low hills.

Main Street, Elbow Lake (south of Fergus Falls), 900 population (Hasty notes driving slowly thru--not meant to be exact) Court House at end (brown, 3-story, like a high school) Grant Co.)

<u>Business section</u>

MDs' Clinic
Crossing
Gas & Chevrolet
Beauty Shop
Electric wares
Hotel
Herald print shop
Cleaners
Masonic Temple
Bakery
Korner Cafe
(crossing?)
1st Natl Bank, dentist over
Drug store
Cafe
Movie
Radio shop
Lumber, coal, hardware
Feed
Insurance
Market
Ford agency
Cafe
Red Owl grocery (rem RO's
big trucks on road)

Library
Park
Garage
Gamble store
barber
grocery
hardware
motor supply
beer
grocery
meat
beer
5 and 10 (Ben Franklin)
Red and White store
IGA dept store
Furniture
Barber
Optometrist
Drug store
Post office
town hall
Buick
Dress shop

Other end: Elevator & mill & hatchery; gasoline, depot

fol. 31

MAY FOURTEEN, CONT

Bright morning, lone white country church in a grove, with 1 cemetery, funeral. Cars parked abt church look too shiny, too mechanical, for the occasion.

In Brooten, pop. 676, are Lou & Al's City Club--just a saloon--and Elva's Gift and Beauty Shoppe, upon which some wholesaler must have unloaded--greeting cards, place cards, figurines, imitation cardboard pie, etc. Woman there "At the drug store you can get souvenir post cards of the school and the church." Such are the worst features of the constant urbanization of these prairie villages--along with the good features of increased tolerance and interest in world....In the Brooten cafe: sulky young waitress slapping down catsup bottles; travelling man trimming his nails....."Moderne" grocer's ad by road..All striving toward the urban. Chainstore city clothes--but shoes pierced

Here in the provinces: Vienna Jew who here is Fine Old Viennese family--Aryan implied; and Cockney who is English Gent.

And so back to Minnetonka, after 5 noble days--despite rain.

MAY FIFTEEN, Friday.

Tribune temperatures for the day: 8 AM, 43; noon, 51; 3, 59; 6, 62. Midnight, 46....Here at Lake, thermometer showed same 59 for 3 PM.

MAY SIXTEEN, Saturday.

Into Mpls for haircut at Hotel Nicollet--watch 'em or you'll have a round-neck cut & neck shaved. Day warmish, no rain.

MAY SEVENTEEN, Sunday. Another trip, all in Minnesota, to: 101 to Wayzata; 12 to Delano, Howard Lake, Cokato, (Finns) Litchfield, Willmar, New London, Belgrade, Sauk Centre. 18th: to Osakis, Alexandria, Brandon, Melby, Lake Christina, Inspiration Peak, Parkers Prairie, Wadena, Staples, Brainerd. 19th: to Mille Lacs lake; Milaca, Mora, Hinckley, Pine City, Rush City, Wyoming, Chisago City, Lindstrom, Center City, Taylor's Falls, Scandia, Marine on St. Croix, White Bear Lake, and home.

fol. 32

MAY SEVENTEEN, CONT., Sunday.

Tribune Mpls temperatures for Sunday: 8 AM, 53; noon, 64; 6, 62.

Start, at 8:45, cool, rain threats (which lasted all day, but only a little actual rain).....Children walking the tracks.

Roadside sign--the type was different in the two lines, but there was no punctuation

Only Jesus saves
THE GIDEONS

75th Anniversary of the First Congregational Church of Sauk Centre--and of the S. C. Herald (Ed and Chuck Rathe)

Church supper and my speech: Present: Present pastor, F. Thorley Johnson; ex pastors, Cecil Sparks of Forest Heights Cong. Ch, Minnepolis; Peter J. Jansen, Morningside Cong Ch, Edina, Mpls. In choir: Nellie Robertson. Dave and Hattie Caughren, my hosts, and Harry C. Laurel and Laura (Thompson) Kells. Ben and Julian DuBois and wives. Lynn Whitson, Doc and Mrs. Monahan. Mrs. APBrooks, (Anna Norris). Fred and Winnie; Carl and his wife; Bobbie. Pat Costello. Rydholm, the photographer. Billy Parker. Nelly Hanson.

MAY EIGHTEEN, MONDAY. Mpls Tribune temperature: 8, 49; noon, 49; 6, 52. Gray almost all day, and some rain.

The construction of cement highways where there were dirt roads, sometimes, for stretches, no road at all, completely bewilders one coming back, trying to identify old haunts. e.g. 52 to Osakis, up past 2nd and 3d slew. But about the arch, still grass and oaks, and Fairy Lake and picnic ground unchanged, because held by an estate--a blessing of absentee ownership and agin Single Tax.....Hoboken Hill, which once seemed so tall--because from it one really could see whole town below, and low hills beyond and to N, can't be over 80 ft altitude above town....Toward West Union--where I don't think there used to be any sheep--on grassy slopes by small pond seem Biblical....Is there increased wool-growing in Minn? Large wool warehouse at Wadena.

Ducks, singles and twos and threes, frequent during day, and once, a wild goose. Often, pheasants. Once--only--a prairie chicken.

fol. 33

MAY EIGHTEEN, CONT

Alexandria: Noonan maybe 50 small cottage development, public garden with cut-iron sign "Noonan's Little Bit of Heaven," and park, swans, kobold house.

Staples, Minn.: The Powder Puff Beauty Parlor.....Busses, 70 m.p.h.....Query everywhere: will gasoline be rationed, as is being in East, re war? What become of Northern Lake summer tourism?

Staples to Brainerd: for first time really seem to be in The North. Much more pine, birch, tamarack. Long strait roads through woods without a clearing or just clear in wds. Gray cleared soil...Brainerd very much in the woods.

In these small industrial cities, y couples who are liberal, literate, charming hosts yet simple, live in fine houses but speak ofselves as just provincials across the tracks--yet vicious re unions or Farmer Labor Party.

The Hotel Ransford, Brainerd--known to drummers as Hotel Rancid--provided the most depressing room I've been in in a couple of years. There was a landscape paper faded to an evil dirty brown; upholstered straight chair with the front edge of seat worn thru; pine desk and bureau painted to imitate rosewood but shrieking of cheapness and flimsiness. a hard rocker, a shaky old iron bed, a stained gray ceiling. The only lights, a clumsy attachment at head of bed, and a naked ceiling light which ingeniously managed to be both glaring and insufficient for reading. The view was on a narrow alley of brick walls and tarpaper roofs, like the courtyard of a factory. There was a bathroom but no closet. And very noisy--you could hear every faintest sound through ceiling--later that night I did actually wait for man to drop other shoe--and cars from alley......Later, new proprietor introduced himself, and when I told him what I thought, he was no nice, so explanatory about how he was recedorating all rooms as fast as possible--put back into them every cent he has made in his one year of ownership, and re lights, tourists steal almost every one of nice small ceiling lights--that I was moved to believe it was or soon would be a Ritz-Savoy, after all, and then next morning the coffee was undrinkable lye, yet thin--like the ceiling light, miraculously combined harshness and feebleness.....Bell boys here and in other small town hotels bored and re sentful, with Yuh as their cheeriest answers....But this the one really bad hotel I've found on these Minnesota tours, and two, the Prince in Bismarck and River Inn in Fergus, really admirable.

Evening with LIEUTENANT GOVERNOR ELMER ANDERSON, aged 30, 1st elected 4 yrs ago, newsdealer at Brainerd, Lutheran, no cge, looks like a kindly young Laval, his young wife, LILLIAN, and E. THOMAS O'BRIEN, Brainerd florist but classmate of Freeman in Harvard, candidate for Democratic nomination for 6th District against Knutson, St. Cloud, Republican. O'Brien's flat over parental grocery, retail & wholesale; father dead, mother and married sister there, unmarried, friend of the two bachelors of the Eveless Eden island, with tame fish and wishing well. And likes "Little Bit of Heaven."

See VALLEYS section for Inspiration Peak (in Leaf Mts., Otter Tail County) & Lake Christina, Douglas Co.

Kensington Rune Stone kept in vault, Alex Chamber of Commerce. Inscription seems too shallow to last. Where did they get chisel?

fol. 34

MAY NINETEEN, Tuesday.

Morning, again chilly, misty. Mpls Tribune temp for day: 8, 43; noon, 50; 5, 51.

In these towns, "cocktail bar" means any kind of a saloon.

Mille Lacs really like the ocean. Can't see all of farther shore, from Garrison, Many fishing boats out, some motor, and in fleets. Might be on Cape Cod.

By and near Mille Lacs a few Indians: one squaw in blanket with pappoose; one a young sport with cigarette. Chippewas? And here to sell things to tourists?

Vge of <u>Onamia</u>: Wooden teepee, office for gas sta., and taxi-service; Crosier Fathers, crowstep Flemish...On a garage, amateur mural that has everything: snowcapped mounts, human figures, lake, trees...."Moderne" stucco building, with chromium-strip decoration for door, black glass panel, hexagon windows--it's onlt one story but might be 1st story of a bldg in New York, and the sign is "Filipino Tavern: Chow mein, hamburgers, Grain Belt Beer." All this 5 miles from Mille Lacs, 25 from Elmer and O'Brien in a bright new village. Now figure out Minnesota for me....O'Brien himself is as impossible a combination as a recipe directing you to mix cornmeal, aluminum, and Mozart. A Harvard graduate wouldn't return to the lumbering town of Brainerd; if he did, he wouldn't be a florist--and there wouldn't be a florist in Brainerd, anyway, even though there happen to be four; and the last thing he could be would be an Irish Catholic Democratic politician; and in none of these roles could he be a loyal friend of the innocent little Elmer Anderson; and certainly he couldn't think that "Noonan's Little Bit of Heaven" was an endurable sign....in fancy ironwork!

Bradbury Brook, then Rum River--perfect New England combination, but followed by Burnt Lake Brook. Then Mike Drew Brook....Note brook, not creek. Town name, Bock.....Bogus Brook (real).....Remember as boy, perilous passage through The Arch, on stepping stones, with Hoboken Creek at least four inches deep.

In these North woods, flat round pasture, hidden, quiet.

<u>Some</u> sheep are already sheared, look very naked....Lambs <u>bounce</u>.

Jim's tongue-twister: The Leith police dismisseth us.

Sign by road:

After death the Judgment
Accept Christ
Accept　　　Refuse
↓　　　↓
Heaven　　　Hell.

M. Lacs south, rain and mist till 10:30, then fleeting sun. All afternoon, menace of black lowering heaps of clouds ahead, but never rained.

Millaca Town Hall: WPA murals by Boratko, showing lumbering, sawmill, bears, dear.....All thru Minnesota they say "murial."

fol. 35

MAY NINETEEN, CONT.

Vge of Quamba. Population maybe 65. Vge of Bock....A night club in the country called "The Streamliner." "Koffee Kup Inn." At Mora (once lumbertown), pop. 1014, large creamery. In Harry's Cafe: microphone for use in bingo games. Pinball that pays in money. Pirex coffee pots on monelmetal base. Fruits of Schnectady in the wilderness. More Dept of Utter Confusion.

Hinckley Fire: 3-5 PM, Sept 1, 1894; 400 square miles, four villages, burnt; 418 people killed. Jim Root, the hero engineer, who backed train clear back to Duluth, over burning bridge, saved 350 lives....and stuck to it though his hands burned to the throttle....What became of him?

In rather barren villages, big tapestry-brick schoolhouses with excellent modern lighting.

All this burnt 400 sq miles now plowed or in flourishing second growth woods, largely birch and poplar. But among them, you see lots of still burnt stumps, corpses of murdered trees.

A preacher's "relentless dullness." He knows the congregation is bored, but hell, so is he, and they've heard this sermon only once--well, maybe twice--but he's heard it 20 times.

Taylor's Falls: Chisago Hotel, still restaurant in cement-floored 1st floor. Built in 1852; Stephen A. Douglas spoke from balcony (still there) in 1854....T. F. pop 550.

Across from Taylors Falls, in Wisconsin, on way to St. Croix Falls, by the road is a structure in the shape of a river steamer, sternwheeler. The sign, to make this confusion Utterest, is:

Pleasure Cruise
Relax in the Beautiful
Hawaiian Room
STEAMBOAT ROUND THE BEND
St. Croix Falls, Wis
Fine Foods Prepared by
Mrs. Schnable

Lowell Inn, Stillwater. Perfect inn--but why no view, in this valley of views? Tucked in opp a small shoe factory!

And so back to Minnetonka.

fol. 36

MAY TWENTY, Wednesday

8:30 AM, gray again, at lake, and 52 degrees. Sun and warming up in afternoon. Mpls Trib: 8, 48; noon, 52; 6, 59.

At 8:30 the sun goes down, red, and its last trail on the lake is a knife of flame across copper water with silver and then blue-silver water, all calm, beyond. Looking out at 9:20, exclamation over incredible beauty. The lake is still light, but a burnt umber shaded to rose. The woods of the now mysterious islands reflected in perfect dark doubles. The lights on shore poignant. The dark clouds in sky, apricot to silver, are solid seeming and unmoving/ There is a new moon in sky that behind it still seems blue, and bats flit against clear spaces of sky seen behind silhouetted trees on the shore. There is a peace like a dream.

MAY TWENTY-ONE, Thursday. Mpls Trib: 8 AM, 46; noon, 63; 6, 68; midnite, 55. At lake, sun on and off all day. At 2:30 PM, 66. John and Betty Cowles, niece Virginia, Harts for dinner. Talk of Paul de Kruif and his advocacy of doubtful vitamin bread; of Henry Wallace's speech.

MAY TWENTY-TWO, Friday. First "perfect day" in a long time. At nine AM, cool, clear, bright, cloudless except for low wash of clouds at horizon. Trib: 8, 49; noon, 63; 6, 67. Noon at lake, 68, with softly cool breeze--a day to be out--birches so brilliant against bluest water, and a thrush gurgling....Evening, reading with Brenda Ueland, to see if she cd play Hedda Gabler in Bob Aden-Dorothy Tighe's Log Cabin Theater, at Excelsior. I think so. Her bewilderment at first trying to read a serious role as a real person's, to make it emotion, not words....Bob, Brenda, B's friend Elaine Norden, Bert Jeter, Molly George, Evelyn Snapp, Carl Nagell here from company.

MAY TWENTY-THREE, Saturday. 8:30 AM, clear, beautiful, rather chilly. PM, warm--in '70's. (Mpls Tribune: noon, 70; 6 PM, 73).....Now, already, despite chilly weather we've had, the fields, the yards that are uncut, have that deepness of grass, that thickness of leaves, that make the richness and luxuriance of summer. Soon, vines will be sprawling wanton over everything. All the birds long since in residence; and one crop of dandelions has already gone to seed....To Addison Lewis's; he just back from farm, contentedly dusty, breeches...His and Dorothy's daughters are: Dana (Mrs, Atkinson), Virginia, Charlotte (Chy), Gretchen, Carol (12)....Starke Hathaway, the psychiatrist, fishing with Hart; here in the evening; talk of psychopathic personalities.

MAY 24, Sunday. 7:30 AM, cool with a half milky sky; 9:30, 62; PM, languid. Trib: 8, 52; Noon, 73; 6, 77....McNallys and John and Bernice Dalrymple call in PM.

This note doesn't belong anywhere, but note that Margaret Prescott Montague of White Sulphur Springs, West Va., is the author of a book, 1916, called "Home to Hims Muvver," and Who's Who proves it.

fol. 40

MAY 25, Monday. Trib: 8, 61; noon, 68; 6, 59. At lake at 7 AM: warm, lowering, still. Heavy rain at one, with lightning. In the downpour, the farther shore of the lake disappears in the gray, and our mild lake seems to be the ocean....Camilla Wing, Mrs. Bessenen, in for coffee; strong, shining pale hair, Norwegian; so interested in own problems, only, and repeats stories; always a hint of "brave self-pity."

MAY 26, Tuesday. Trib: 8, 62; noon, 64; 6, 67. At lake, 9 AM, 66, but <u>seems</u> chilly, so coldly gray is the lake now, then alternate rain and mist, in which again the lake stretches out without farther shore--a sea...It is one of these damp, warm, suicidal mornings when nobody loves you, when everybody has done you wrong, when you want to go--away....Evening, in Coffman Memorial Union, at University of Minnesota campus, "banquet" of Delta Phi Lambda, literary fraternity. Some mild men and a lot of faculty members, including Joe Beach, but mostly young and middleaged women, plump, skinny, only a few pretty; all being coy about the attitude of being Writers and one reading a coy story about raid by punctuation marks, with Rotarian songs--q.v.p. (One sign of professional writers, p.c., their matter-of-fact way.)....Afterwards, at Marie and Eddie Ford's with Beaches, McNally (going to California) and Luther Weaver.

MAY 27, Wednesday: (Trib: 8, 59; noon, 66; 6, 71) At 8, rain is again threatening, but this morning it is not still and sulky but the world is nervous, quick, gray; the trees and waves stirring nervously....But no rain, and at 10 AM the sun. It turned into a fine, boisterous, rowdy, windy, sunny, lakeside afternoon; low cirrus clouds fast flying with never a halt, murmurmus steely waves fast flying, leafy branches seeming ti start to fly away, and high in air a bird trying desperately to balance itself against the wind. And boats on the lake flying too, and small boys, at baseball, shouting. Everything ALIVE.

Small green catepillars are devouring the maple and basswood leaves, for second year in cycle. Harris says a new crop of leaves will come this year...First dragon flies I've noticed this season....A rose-breasted grosbeak--black and white wings.

Nearly midnight: thuderstorm. Alone in the big house, except for servants at the back, lightning in the thick dark, the light windows and doors rattling as if by sinister hands--mildly terrifying.

MAY 28, Thursday. To Sauk Centre, for dope about Main Street at War for a treasury-department radio script. Tribune: 8, 65; noon, 77; 4, 85; 6, 83. Another perfect day--clear after last nite's thundershower.

X is born to be a secretary--but to resent it always.

Minnesota villages: Cosmos. Greenleaf.

Village of Silver Lake: Czech (with Catholic and Ch Presbyterian) and Polish (with Catholic Ch). PWA auditorium. Some vines on stores gave a gt difference to a prairie town....Saw a farm with a rock garden--there, seemed sensational! Flowers at Johannes Kirche betw. Dayton & Hamel on 101

fol. 41

with MAY 28

MAIN STREET WAR ACTIVITIES	USO—local—movies, Rotary Club meals—service men leaving, going thru Insert

Sts more quiet Sat even, with 80 boys in service. Mothers work faster to get to Armory for Red Cross work....Boy Scout troup SC collect 6 tons waste paper...Photographer, air raid warden. 3000 books Victory Book Campaign....Defense bond committee: Banker, lawyer, postmaster (secy of committee), school supt (chairman), publisher of weekly, 2 others. Special aim: get industries, such as creameries, to get employees to buy.

Creamery board meet to discuss patron allotment on defense bonds....Bankerm nayor, walk to work to save rubber.

Postmaster notes letters from boy in camp....Farmers discuss raise more soy beans, hogs, and milk more cows; combine on services and machinery and transportation; wives raise more chicks.

Creamery mostly dried milk to be shipped in barrels across the ocean. Experienced hands not available, men work 10-16 hrs a day. Coach and industrial teachers out of school; supt does their work.

Filling stations and car agencies closed. Banks encourage war bond sales to replace CAccts. "A funny war. No rage, no hate, no fervor, no passion, no speeches, no parades. Theh remember that like MacArthur, you can't dig in & shout at same time."

Red Cross first aid training--150 people--high school gym. 7 weeks—3 hours once a week—total 21 hrs. Eighteen members of volunteer fire department, take extra training; incl first aid and rescue....Carrying rescued down ladder.

500 troops from vicinity.

*****

RED CROSS SEWING PROJECT, abt 150 worked every day; now await new patterns--will have to buy own materials--did but own thread, buttons. Made socks, sweaters, scarfs; even layettes for refugees. and dresses. Mrs. Sartell, wife of NP, leader.

HOME DEFENSE UNIT, now called STATE GUARD. Dewey O'Gara, garage man, captain. Now about 50. 100 who have been in it (not in Natl Guard) now in army or on defense jobs. Dewey persuading high school students who will get college military training to join and get preliminary. (80 sent from former Natl Guard)

Billy Parker, CHAIRMAN OF RATIONING BOARD, sugar, tires. No pay but allowed one $1800 woman asst. Also has store inventories.

HOME DEFENSE COUNCIL: Mayor Steve Schwartzbauer chairman. Under it: Air Raid Wardens. Committee on Health and Safety, Moynihan.

Agricultural chairman, Borgmann, lines up farmers to grow more vegetables...Auxiliary police (3) and firemen (3). Moynihan in charge emergency, flood disposal, drinking water.....Publicity....Industry....Victory Aid w Boy & Girl Scouts collect waste iron, rubber, paper; books. Woman in charge of this but actual hefting done by volunteer men.

Rubber collectn

fol. 42

MAY 28 CONT:

Trick of beauty in villages seems to be more trees and gardens than architecture or arrangement, and that to depend on vision of first settlers--did they allow room for trees on streets. Thus one idea of some long-since-forgotten pioneer settler might entirely affect village, which becomes town, for a hundred years.

Hutchinson, the town of the abolitionist singers Asa, John and Judson Hutchinson, pre-civil war abolitionist touring singers--the cop says no Hutchinsons left now, nor even the Andersons, their in-laws....Adventist Academy on hill facing town.

A town policeman as hero of a novel. The one in Hutchinson lean, strong, lean-cheeked, affable. Blue shirt, uniform cap, badge, gun in holster. They see so much--who stays up late, who plays poker, who calls on what lady--but wisely do nothing about it....Remember By Carr, the woods ranger, rustic-seeming but cd handle the toughest fighter...He wd belong with the Whites and railroad man in The Happy Man.

These Main Streets have improved so much in solidity of architecture....Did the complaining Carol Kennicott help?

Prairie villages seem to divide about 50-50 on having Main Street at right angles running away from all important (once) railroad tracks, and running along parallel to and facing the tracks. That probably seemed natural before automobiles came to break the railroads' domination.

Hutchinson on Crow River, with falls--probably reason for original settlement here in 1855....How the rivers more than lakes dominate southern Minnesota: the Mississippi, Root, Cannon, Crow, Minnesota.

Little pond by fence: dandelions bright in pasture grass abt it.....New to me: (chicken) hatcheries in many villages....Lamb lying contentedly by its mother--neither yet shorn--a sheep madonna and child, future misery unknown, sanctified by calm happiness.

Willmar: WPA auditorium, hold 2000, dances and concerts. Stage 60 x 25. Sound-deadened roof.

At Green Lake, n of Willmar, and elsewhere, lilacs (in one place, a hedge) still blooming fully.....Willmar State Hospital for Insane looks the best I've seen as final refuge for self & friends.

Sign with a really horrible picture, on Nest Lake above Green Lake, Kandiyohi County:

Mink and Fox Ranch
Wanted: Disabled Old Horses.

Familiar old Dobbin as well as the mink slaughtered and bloody to provide Sadie the Cluck with a wrap.

New London and Sibley Park--see Valleys.

fol. 43

MAY 28 CONT--2

New grain elevators are likely to be covered with shining galvanized iron, instead of being painted red.

Hot in the car, all afternoon, but glorious and clear all day. No clouds. Evening <u>starts</u> well, toward dusk: water <u>exactly</u> mimicks yellow & smoke sky, so that the wooded shoreline, now black, seems a bar of dark cloud across a continued sky Sunset 8:45. Dark 9:20 CWT. then:

Evening: Jim Hart comes in to complain of not being used, hints that Gladys is irrepressibly raging. Finis.

NIGHT OF 28th: Awakened at 1:30 AM by heavy thunder which <u>shakes the house</u>--sic. It passes over; as I go to sleep, its distant grumbling, like an old dog's, is really comforting in that it isn't nearer. Reawakened at two by a hell of a lightning spasm: lightning incessant, furious, like insanely dancing flame, as seen beyond trees which spring into sudden lighted windows, and the thunder is now artillery. Then a mysterious slap on the roof of my sleeping porch, amd another--and realize that it is heavy hail. Can't sleep; put on dressing gown, have coffee from thermos bottle, contemplate: what would I save if lightning hit the house? MS, M's letters, a few suits! And am enough of a farmer to think of what this hail will do to the crops--on which so counting, these war days. Awake an hour, then in dark nightlike morning, slept till 10, unerhört.

On such a day as this has been, bright and not too hot, now that the wheat is a few inches up, the prairies are beautiful, luxuriant--provided too they have a little roll.

MAY 29, Friday: Tribune: 8, 64; n, 63; 6, 73. Cloudy all day, then in evening a good deal of thunder and lightning--not so much as previous night--but rain heavier, driving right through light summertime windows, soaking floor so that much dramatics with bath towels
Niece Virginia and Dorothy Bennett of U of Minn press here for night: playing Rachmaninoff Concerto 2, Beethoven VIII, and Afternoon of Faun on phonograph; showing off by listing names of states and capitols.

In this rain, one thinks again of the farmers and what it will do to their crops. Unlike NY, in and about a city like Minneapolis one is never far from farming and thought of it.

fol. 45

MAY 30, Saturday. Fitful sunshine all day--no rain till midnight, then not heavy. Tribune: noon, 71; 6, 76.

Re-reading my Main Street, for first time since it was published--because I'm to do a radio script for Treasury Dept. on "Main Street Goes to War." It is probably only just to the tight older people but doesn't take enough acct of the younger ones, who will carry out all of Carol's aspirations with none of her artiness or ego, and who will build the fine school building of today, nor enoygh of outside forces--the state wh will build the armory, the chain-store companies which, however brazen, will do competent merchandizing, the movies, which will become real drama....One thing is most unfair: the statement that the Midwestern spring is just one moment between harsh cold and blasting heat. Spring here, this year, has been as disconcertingly coy, as advancing and retreating, as it cd be anywhere in the world.

Virginia and Dorothy Bennett canoeing. Evening, to F. Peavey Heffelfinger's "farm"--a low luxurious house, retired--then to Woodhill Club, modest, golf and riding on plump slopes overlooking Minnetonka--for the opening of the club. Too many people drinking too many cocktails and talking nothing but golf and heavy kidding. This Minnepolis IS a provincial camp still. The men are heavily amiable, full of golf, hunting, fishing; surprising number--Heffelfingers, Pillsburys--with inherited money, muxh given to Yale and directorships and still rustic proconsuls; the women intrusive and important.

Three women in succession feeled called upon to show their activity, world-knowledge and superiority by insulting the cowering Celebrity: one insists that I have lied about being at Dahlberg's, Gott soll behüten, on Rainy Lake five years ago as well as fifteen, because her 17 yr old son saw me there; one volunteers that she has read in numerous reviews that I am a most lousy actor; the third, a pretty female of 30, married to a large fortune, very drunk after drinking cocktails all evening, comes up, introduces herself as the daughter of H.B., announces that I am lying when I say that I remember her father very well....Of course the American woman generally likes to do that. Because she's bored by husband? And women like Mrs. John Cowles, Mrs. A. M. Wilson, and the surprising Kay Perry, C.I.O. organizer amid the wolves invited only by the freakish independence of Brad Heffelfinger, are extremely nice and casual.....Of the other three, one has since then become a good friend! The damndest thing for a frightened Celebrity who likes peace!

(Robert McClure, Santa Monica, California; F. Peavey Heffelfingers; Mr. and Dorothy Bauman; Mrs. Philip Pillsbury; John and Bernice Dalrymple; Mr. Tierce(?)

MAY 31, Sunday. Trib: 8, 63; noon, 65; 6, 63. AM, cool, all gray, still. May be able to get a little rain! Agreeably at Al and Fefe Wilson's...In for drinks, Elizabeth Heffelfinger, Lt. Commander Truman Penny, USN., Bob McClure. Robt. J. FLANAGAN (lawyet: Holyoke, Mass, and University of Padua) Midnite, cold. No rain all day.

fol. 46

JUNE 1942

JUNE 1, Monday. Trib: 8, 55; noon, 61; 6, 67

A gray, misty seashore morning; 58 at 9 AM. At noon, fitful sun. At 4:30, a light drizzle starts--but no lightning.

Floods now in Wisconsin and Southern Minnesota, after unprecedented rains. On the Mississippi tributaries, bridges washed out. Root River, beyond Houston, above flood level. Meadows about here are flooded from Lake Minnetonka, and excited boys catch carp in them with their hands. (They won't eat carp out here; regard it as worthless; shipped alive in tank cars to Jews in New York.) Lake itself highest in years. Edges of some roads washed out.

The lake remains visibly light till 10 PM, CWT; pale streaks of rose in the dark gray.

JUNE 2, Tuesday. Marcella starting west from New York this afternoon. Looking out at Hudson? Her shorthand course is finished.

Trib:

7:30 AM, 64 degrees; another seashore morning; fog so thick that beyond the trees on the bluff above the shore there is nothing but a gray wall. Sun out in the afternoon. No rain.

The Old Log Cabin Theater, Excelsior, opens tomorrow evening, but it's sloping dirt floor, below level of sur. land, is a deep puddle, so that at least the 1st 5 rows will be useless, and the aisles are slimy. They will use gravel but----Rehearsal: girl who can't be heard anyway trying to use Irish accent.

8:20, the sun still up; lake all misty gold foil. Then turns to plum and silver, as sun lower. Then rose and bronze. I read on the roofed porch till 8:40....At ten, though on land quite dark, trees on shore still seen in lovely silhouette against the pale silver of the lake....I wonder what the lights are, peeping through trees: my God, stars! They had apparently resigned.

fol. 47

JUNE 3, Wednesday. 3:30 Marcella and her mother arrive, Burlington Zephyr, and we studiously view Minnehaha Falls, which is now actually falling--and people canoeing on Minnehaha Creek--and we consider Lakes Harriet and Calhoun and Marcella insists that Central Park is much more irrigated. And we stop by the Log Cabin theater and, against all probability, they have dried up the front rows with loads of gravel and planks across it.

Early morning, gray but sun working thru. Trib for day: 8,68; noon, 81; 6, 83.

This afternoon, the first real heat since April--felt a bit dizzy when I got out of car in Mpls street. Evening, we loaf on the porch. A background of ineffectual lightning.

JUNE 4, Thursday. Trib: 8, 70; noon, 76; 5, 84; 6, 82. Misty at 7, sun breaks thru at 8. The curse of summer life on a lake is the speed boat, on and on like an aimlessly malignant mosquito. All we need is a few more aeroplanes, also, to make Innisfree as gentle as a boiler factory.

Hot in late afternoon at lake. Fitful sun all day, thunder in evening, but no rain till late night, then heavy.

Evening: The Lewises, Addison, Dorothy, Charlotte, Dana and husband Atkinson; the Uelands, Brenda, Gabby, Sandra. Buffet supper with the Brats at supper on porch.....Talk of Swedes--out here, where all so pro-Norwegian, Swede neutrality a more important topic than the Japs.

Driving to lunch at the Lafayette Club, via St. Bonafacius--"Bonny," where we sneaked in the stage door and back stage at the white frame Catholic church: small storms of cottonwood fluff blow across road....Turtles, big and small, not hitherto seen at all this season (disturbed by high floor water, or just seasonal?) lumbering across roads everywhere, as in migration. Some get horribly crushed by car....Many less cars since rubber rationing; and now for a week speed been cut to 40 m.p.h.--which, after couple of days of feeling like crawling, again seems high

JUNE 5, Friday. 7 AM, hot, damp, clear--tropical. 2 PM, 87. Very cool at midnight. Trib: 8, 72; noon, 83; 5,90; 10, 77; midnight, 73.

In town, crushingly hot; sudden cloud burst for 5 min. as we pass lovely Lake of the Isles....WPA Writers' Project, 28 2nd St. NE, huge room over Public Baths; files. Gentle Roscoe Macy....Rem. island in Mississippi on Hennepin Ave.

Evening, at last see Peg o' My Heart; not violently bad, just dull; should have taken 2, not just one, cushion for bench.

Newspaper says this is, along of floods and tornados, worst spring season in 60 years.

fol. 48

JUNE 6, Saturday. AM, gray, cool, autumnal. 9:30, AM, 62, twenty-five degrees less than Fri. PM. 5 PM, 68 and still gray. Tribune: noon, 61; 6, 68; midnight, 60. Walk with Marcella....Trailer from Georgia. Wild roses. Some lilacs still in bloom, though fading. With Al and Fefe Wilson to Bob Flanagan's, at Stubbs Bay. Mrs. Nickerson to me, "Oh, I read that book of yours abt young people. An outrageous book!" Elmer Peterson, ex-reporter, radio commentator, "I've only read 1 bk of yours - Dr. Arrowhead."

JUNE 7, Sunday. Marcella to St. Croix River, canoeing with Virginia. 8 AM, cool, gray--62; 2 PM, 66. Gray all day, till sun out bright at 5:30, but no rain. Tribune: 8, 60; noon, 63; 2 PM, 63; 5, 71; 8, 74. When does a mound become a hill, a hill a mountain? At what size does a pond become a lake, an island a continent, a gay lady a bad woman, a Prominent Citizen a Celebrity? In such queries there is atheism and peril. Starke Hathaway in the evening.

JUNE 8, Monday. Another perf day. Cool and clear all day. 9:30, 66.....Tribune: 8, 60; 10, 66; n, 70; 6, 77. Drive west on #5 to Waconia.....Village name: Young America. Corn now up 6 inches, and being cultivated, and the washed-out patches re-seeded. Potatoes (there's a lot in Carver County) up a foot....Some cement roads now have cultivated and mowed grass edges. Dark at 9:50, C.W.T.

JUNE 9, Tuesday. AM, gray, quiet, not very warm. PM hottish, fitful sun....Trib: 8, 62; noon, 72; 6, 78. Evening: Wilsons, Russell Plimpton, Alan Priest of Metropolitan Museum, NY.

JUNE 10, Weds. 7 AM, gray, warm--70--but with delightful cool gusts of breeze. Sun out at 9:15; sun fitful all day, with sharp half hour rain 7 PM. Trib: 8, 71; n, 78; 6, 82. With Marcella, Mrs. Powers, to St. Paul--gaunt onyx Indian statue in artificial light, City Hall; State Capitol--the usual aimless marble miles.

JUNE 11, Thursday. Damp, warm, irritating morning. PM, clear, gt cumulus clouds, hot as hell--84 at 5 PM. In evening, while at Brad Heffelfingers, at 9 a 15-minute cloud burst, then the sky ½ late daylight, ¼ dark, ¼ sudden glow from just-setting sun, ¼ lightning, incessant--the whole a fast-spreading murky and menacing rose, as tho whole city afire to the west. Trib: 8, 71 12, 80 (noon) 6, 84 9, 81 10, 64 (note drop after rain)

JUNE 12, Friday; Marcella and Mrs. Powers return to NY--train leaving at 8 AM from Gt. Northern Station--which meant rising here at 6 AM, CWT--which means 5, God's Time, and damn early, but a cool washed morning, and all afternoon, (4 PM, 67) gusty with fleeting sun and booming clouds....Virginia and Dot Bennett coming in evening, to stay while I motor for a week. Evening: 8, 61; 9:30, 56. 12, midnite, 54 (at lake). Trib: 8, 61; noon, 70; 4, 65; 8, 62; 10, 53; midnite 50. (Trib thermometer on tower?

fol. 49

Sat, June 13 thru Wedn, June 17, trip to Duluth, North Shore of Lake Superior, Hibbing, Bemidji, Itasca, Detroit, Leaf Mts., back to Minnetonka; Joseph & myself in Buick. Mileage, Buick speedometer, 38307 to 39650--total, 1343 miles

JUNE 13, Saturday. Cool & bright all day--perfect day, all day Start at 9 AM, sirrus clouds; 51 degrees.

A wood pasture, grassy and secret, cupped in small hills, oaks or maples, if possible with moss and mossy stones, seems to be my particular Favorite Scenery. Let us call it in reference wood-pasture.....How people vary in what they consider good scenery--preferring Berkshires to Himalayas or vice versa, or hidden peaceful lake to ocean off Maine & v.v. But almost all really see only the conspicuous much-advertised Points of Interest to which their attention is definitely called.

For most of the data on this trip see section Minnesota Hills and Valleys.

Near Rush City, lupine on railroad embankment. In swamps, wild iris. Near Hinckley, burnt stumps.

Phenomenon of road ahead, perfectly dry cement or blacktop, looking as though it were wet, in shiny patches, which flee and vanish as rapidly approach them in car. These come particularly in places where road surface is rubbed a little smooth, and seems to happen only under particularly hot sun.

Junk in souvenir shop at Moose Lake: framed quotations, with flowers and drawings of children; a porcelain Buddha; Marquise figurines.

Cloquet: same Co-operative has two stores here in town and two outside, one in very Finnish village of Esko. Their own labeled condensed milk, breakfast food (corn flakes), paint, varnish, canned vegetables....In Cloquet, big Romanesque Catholic church. From bluff, good view up St. Louis River, with long island, to sunlit uplands....Around here, log cabins very much in use as farmhouses.

On tree in front of house hang, astonishingly, an old oxbow and a double-bitted axe. A private arboreal museum.

DULUTH as invididual and beautiful as ever--more magic than when I last saw it, now that Skyline Parkway completed. Enger Memorial tower--a merchant who liked to wander the hills. Remember: Superior Street, then London Road along lake.

On NORTH SHORE OF SUPERIOR, remember: Silver Creek Cliff--the road cut into it--Split Rock, fairly mountainous, with lighthouse. Two Harbors a lout of a town--the N. Shore not really start till after it. Night at Lutsen's. Robert & Ruth Pack from Minneapolis; Oscar Cwyser (?), old Charley Nelson, the white mustached pioneer who, 50 years ago here, used to row boat with 2 tons of fish down to Duluth in 24 hrs and row back supplies; now owns Lutsen's and the damndest double-arched fountain warted with Florida shells he

fol. 50

JUNE 13 CONT

picked up on Fla beaches. His son, hotel clerk, picks up by the tail a porcupine that comes wandering down the road, and sticks it up on the fountain arch, where it crouches with poor little paws up, shedding quills into the fountain.

That night, so cold heat on in hotel is welcome. Probably 40.

Baptism River. Temperance River (no bar at its mouth.)

JUNE 14, Sunday. Clear and cool on North Shore. In Mpls, by Tribune: 8, 50; noon, 65; 6, 73.

The whole North Shore is really sensationally beautiful--really is as beautiful as Maine Shore--probably more so. The hills seem mountains; the headlands are gorgeous.

Grand Portage, with its few shacks, is sensational in the way the mountains come down to a great curving beach, a crescent with points out at both ends. Not so much less beautiful than the original Carmel, Calif....Grand Marais, nearly as well situated in shore and descending hills, part wooded, part cleared and shining uplands, is hideous in its lumps of buildings, like a not very compact typical Minnesota prairie village: e.g., one block, two yellow brick cubes stuck together, a bank and a barber shop; then a vacant lot, then, alone on the corner, a white frame cube; "cafe and ice cream" with rooms upstairs. Across the street, a Federated Store with a cement slab of a movie theater across.

First the stores, then scattered small houses, then piles of pulp wood, shut off the beautiful bay, and no houses climb the hills. Brooten, Minnesota, on Monte Carlo bay!

Cool and delicious air at Grand Marais--57 degrees at 1:20 PM.

Here is transition from pioneer to modern settlement. Is all transition, spiritual and political as well as architectural, always harsh, usually hideous?

What a chance here for an architect--and he should use, but simply, the natural original architecture--log houses, in a crescent. It would be a village for the whole world.

Breakwater, fishing boats,.....See Valleys in general re north shore.

Everywhere in small restaurants in Minn: "What beverage do you wish." Nice Nellie.

In Grand Portage, replica of log stockade, with blockhouses; notable points; fine wooded island under shelter of which the Indians fish--for this end of North Shore is a Chippewa reservation

fol. 51

JUNE 14, CONT.

Farm cabin covered with green "granite paper," another with composition paper with pattern initating blocks of stone.....Lots of buttercups....Grand Portage Trail thru the birches.

At the US Border: "Sextus City--60 Cabins." Shocking.

Approach to the Canadian border at Pigeon River Falls: the typical straight road through the pines, the opening a triangle on its base, with trees on and near road blurring together into an apparent gate, is here filled with a mountain. Beautiful border; the Pigeon River runs thru a deep gorge with, on American side, mountains between here and the shore. Sensational.

All morning, cumulusclouds, some threatening, disappear toward noon; clear and cool.

You see no Canadian cars crossing the border--none at all, the whole way to Duluth (190 miles) because there are monetary restrictions in Canada, re war.

Lutsen charges $40 a week for one in a room (corner room) with bath, including all meals.

Fancy mail boxes at private villas along this road--an iron team of horses and walking driver, with the mail box as covered wagon; others painted red, white & blue. That ought to do something to somebody.

Lots of bluelets, buttercups.

Night at Hotel Duluth, Duluth; kept awake an hour by ore steaners thrice tooting for aerial lift bridge and bridge answering--been a block at the Soo canal and steamers come in a bunch.

Lake Superior beautiful as the ocean and as blue--depends on whether you like the irrepressible athletics of surf which, as Cabell noted, is on the repititious side. It has a certain aspect of YMCA gymnasia.

Interviewed by Buck of the News-Tribune (now, with Herald, owned by Ritters of St. Paul) formerly of Hibbing. Next morning, met Nathan--Nate--Cohen, culture reporter of same and clever; and Stewart, editor, Fitzgerald, mg ed.

JUNE 15, Monday. Cool, gray, cloudy, possible rain ahead.

Eveleth, first town in the Mesabi (or Messabe, etc.) Range a neat town, on a hilltop; only between it and Virginia does the range have tall hills with vistas.....Deep Missabe Mountain Mine, not being worked, war or no, till gets another lease.

HIBBING....Hotel Androy--part of town rebuilt by Oliver Mining Co when old part moved for mining--you still see remains of foundations, walks, where some day will be just a great hole. Androy: Crystal Bar, with great glass

fol. 52

JUNE 15, CONT.

screen; coffee shop, chairs upholstered in blue leather, fluorescent lamps on ceiling, composition table tops, wood panelling, balcony, composition non-echo ceiling. Picked up by H. L. Nides, insurance man, and Morris Stevens, highschool English teacher; joined by Mary Ryan, on her first day or newspaperwork, pretty Irish gal with firm jaw, grad U of Wisconsin.

The vast pit of the Hull-Rust-Mahoning mine, with trains struggling up its sides and multicolored heaps way down there--maybe 350 feet down. The highschool-junior college, with great auditorium, large library, electrical and woodworking and forge etc. shops preparing students for war defense work. Vast auditorium with, int al, little theater--no dressing-rooms!.....S. S. Patchin, sturdy and intelligent supt of highschool; Dean Dreacher (?) of the cge dept.

NAMES OF VILLAGES & Hamlets IN NORTHERN MINNESOTA

Amor	Shooks	Puposky	Kankel
Twig	Jelle	Lynx	Fram
Cotton	Jed	Moonlight	Jane
Zim		Bejou (sic)	Lambs
Local		Blix	Oye
and, with about six houses:			
Luce			

Remember as a boy: eagerness for anything out of Sauk Centre usual, or special in town: the derrick, a stranger in town, house with small tower, odd-shaped window in neighboring town.

11:15: Diffused blank clouds over whole sky get tucked up into cumulus with blue between, though no sun yet.

At Grand Rapids:

Club Alamo--Bowl and dance

Always today at trangular "end" of long straight road thru woods hang cumulus seeming unmoving.

Bena, supposedly on Lake Winnibigoshish--you cannot see the lake at all from highway. Fine sand roads thru woods down to it.....A store, with piled logs in the yard, backs up to deep wild pines....A bear, a moose, a deer, a porcupine, in winter a wolf, might come up--they're all still here.

BEMIDJI

Henry--"Heinie"--Z. Mitchell, prop and ed, Daily Pioneer, from St. Cloud as is his wife Grace. Judge Bailey. Alec and Myrtle (Johnson) Doran. On the lake front, statue of Paul Bunyan and Babe, his blue ox; of Indian looking to East; Information Bureau with, oh God, fireplace with stone from every state in Union and every prov in Canada. Hotel

Markham--Lycan--and Birchmont Lodge. The Oasis, mild roadhouse.

fol. 53

Duluth Little Theater -
director last winter,
Gregory Foley.

JUNE 15 CONT--2

Number of places in Bemidji to buy beer, but wine and spirits--"hard liquor"--can be bought only in the two municipal saloons; two not for financial undemocracy, but social; prices are the same but one too Elegant for lumberjacks, and a little too much of the painfully innocent atmosphere of an Ice Cream Parlor: wallboard in stripes, double bar down center of large rm once movie theater, Cocktail Rm with low tables, compo walls, stepped fancy wall-bracket lights--one could not tell a dirty story in this feminized place as one could in #2, which is a plain saloon. Owned by city, both of them, at good profit.

Paddy the Pig, old lumberjack with long hair and long dirty beard, was made king of a Bemidji carnival but spoilt it by cutting his hair. He highhatted the mayor of St. Paul with "And who may this be?" His life was ruined; he often goes into #1 now, and remains pretty clean, tho he still has the comfortable Elliot Paul belly.

Oil station men meet to discuss purchase salvaged rubber--they pay a cent a pound--natl 2-week drive which <u>may</u> obviate nationwide restriction on gasoline (which they now have in the East) to save rubber. Jim Preston (?) (Peyton?) Northern States Power head. There met James Sayers, property clerk at Red Lake Indian Reservation--¼ Indian, and as "white" as Vermont; buying drinks, explains no ¼ breed supposed to buy drinks.

JUNE 16, Tuesday. Cold, clear, perfect-day morning. Rain (1st rain on trip) begins in mid-afternoon, rain heavy that evening and probably all night. Tribune for Mpls: 8, 55; noon, 69; 6, 67.

RED LAKE CHIPPEWA RESERVATION. (Incidentally, Red Lake--270,000 acres--largest lake entirely included within one state in U.S. Shores all wild; mostly belong to the Reservation.).....Mess Club.

Mr. Bitney, supt of reservation. (Dr. Deutsch and anthrop wife not there.) Towns: Red Lake, Redby, Ponemah--last, pagan, no missioaries ever made good.

Fishing done with nets--stretched between stakes, or betw two boats. Gill nets--dragged in with fish, pulled out by hand by squaws and children, stuck in spaces; net must be washed with salt and dried, or decay. Nets dry on reels or racks by shore....Boats, a sort of dory with square stern; very seaworthy--particularly if just lie down....Fish boxes with handles furnished by Govt, which maintains fish warehouses (ship by trucks to Twin Cities, Chicago)--as well as sawmill making boards. Fish caught: whitefish, pike, pickerel, muskies, carp, particularly good perch.

Over each grave, near Ponemah, a little dog house, with a hole in front for spirit to exit, and tiny platforms in front on wbich for 3 days after death is placed food. In groups right in front of house.

fol. 55

JUNE 16--CONT.

Well built houses abandoned when several have died in it--TB the favorite disease here--and after a time, begin to be pulled down and boards used elsewhere.

You see good-looking young men, different only in being dark. The young and old men still show colors in violent colored and striped and crisscrossed flannel shirts.

Birchbark wickiups in most yards, at Ponemah, for storage--also larger one for pow-wow after y Indian recently murdered another, with gun on payday drunk.

Magic. Red or red and white rags hung on porch, or bush stuck into wall, to keep off evil spirits--all thru Ponemah district--superstition in contrast to plain scientific spiritual antisepsis of saints' images in more Catholic Red Lake.

Bitney on lady anthropologist who asked the squaws on their Sex Habits--the gals supplied what they thought wanted, and giggled abt it afterward. Bitney of New Deal idealist from Washn: I didn't know whether that was a practical plan or just a sparkle in his eye.

Back to Bemidji; evening, steak at Oasis--politicians from Clearwater County, incl County Atty Lewis; and the Bailey cottage on the lake--stone, porch, guest rm with private door.

JUNE 17--Wednesday. 8, cool, gray. Rain off and on for a few minutes from 8:15 to noon. Found had been heavy rain down in Ottertail County; and around Minnetonka, very heavy and sudden late in afternoon. Road Park Rapids to Detroit Lakes had fifteen miles of mush with crisscross ruts that threatened to let car slide off the road and of deep soft ruts where car threatened to sink--this a gap in hard road.

Trib: 8, 59; noon, 63; 6, 72.

Loud radio in hotel lobby a new terror to traveller.

Just south of Bemidji, meadows and then crops; but wd say the definite line between South and North in the state ran from Detroit Lakes to Park Rapids....The section roughly bounded--correct later--by Fergus Falls, Detroit, Park Rapids, Wadena, Alexandria, is the PARK REGION OF MINNESOTA and though not so spectacular as THE ARROWHEAD REGION, incl North Shore, full of beautiful hills and lakes, and better to live in year-round.

In the North, you see very few of the stretches of bare burnt stumps, with meager tarpaper shacks in prickly clearings, that were common even 10 years ago. Grown over and shacks better. Still sticks of dead trees, but 2nd growth a miracle.

fol. 56

JUNE 17--CONT.

Bitney on catastrophe of drainage of northern Minnesota--Willard's Folly did he call it--with result dry woods inevitably burned.

Great virgin Norway pines in Itasca Park. I learn here that they are also called red pines.

Inscription on monument at mouth of Lake Itasca:

> Here, 1475 feet above the ocean, the mighty Mississippi begins to wind its twisting (?--some participle) way 2552 miles to the Gulf of Mexico.

The river starts north, goes to Lake Bemidji. The beginning is a cheerful stream about four feet wide. Almost immediately it has a small bridge and a tiny waterfall.

No pheasants seen in the north. Belong to prairies? And despite the many waterways, no migrating turtles.

The layman's phrase--as he calls Rehearsing "practising," and asks actor how he can learn all those lines and Does he do his own makeup: a novelist *writes up* a theme.

Lakes, Park Rapids to Detroit:
Height of Land Lake
Big Twin Lake
Big Toad Lake.

A literal *sigh* of contentment at Otter Tail hills.

New business buildings in quite small Minnesota villages now are likely to use the modern materials of glass brick translucent windows, cement walls, curved corners.

A magnificent afternoon; rainy, drizzly morning quite forgot. Blue sky with giant cumulus.

Add Bemidji; in talk about having Fritz Kreisler--if not so spelled, at least sounds that way--and the honor thereof, it was some time before I discovered they meant a Univ of Michigam football coach.

Otter Tail City, which in 1888 had 5 hotels, is now just a grove of low oaks with long grass.

Remember as boy: poison ivy on Sunday School picnics.

Much yellow mustard now--sulphurous waves of it in rolling wheatfield.

Streets of Alexandria--called "Alec": Mother in slacks, 16 yr old daughter in overalls....Girls in these small-town "cafes," with booths and counters, meet many more Passing Strangers, out-of-the-tribe people than their "boy friends"--and have just as little interest in them....Head of a shop, coatless with fancy colored shirt, blue trousers, sports shoes with thick rubber soles....Old Scandinavian farmwives so happy chatting in Swedish and laughing, stopping together on street ¼ hour--probly rarely in town.

fol. 57

JUNE 17--CONT 2

Great caravel clouds--frigate clouds...."A great wide broad gleeful afternoon."

Clover being mowed.....Are clouds on the prairie not more beautiful even than those at sea? One cumulus a study in black (or at least soot) and silver, a hawk against it. One feels that if he were up there, he could climb through those snow-filled abysses in a mere week or two to its top--a snowy enormous mount.

First a hen peacock, almost the color of the speckled macadam road, tries to commit suicide in front of the car; then we see something like a pigeon dragging a train of sausages ahead--it proves to be a small duck mother followed by hurrying ducklings (She probably had told them, "Now you trust me--I'll take care of you," before leading them almost to death); then a dog feloniously following one car and trying to bite tires runs in front of us and again almost a sudden death.

At five PM, two meadow larks. Are they on the prairie only?

The village of REGAL, near Paynesville, has about 75 pop. Lake Koronis, Paynesville.

7:10 PM, almost back at Excelsior; been raining heavily here; clouds still threatening, but with a rainbow which lasts till 7:40 or later. Wet blacktop pavement, silver w dark blue shadows

Corn near here in some places 10 inches high; some places in north--where not much anyway--only 4-6 inch.

Virginia here for night, with Dottie Bennett & Mea Mann.

END NORTHERN TRIP@@@@@@@@@@

JUNE 18, Thursday. Trib: 8, 59; noon, 75; 6, 78. Radiant blue and green and golden perfect-day; lake a blue sparkle. 78 degrees at 2:30, but breeze makes it seem 70....As sun about to go down, just before 9 PM, CWT, its flat rays make the grass on the lawn a gold-green. As it does set, it seems to pour liquid gold over the dark wall of trees behind which it sets....Not quite dark outside at 10.

JUNE 19, Friday. Dim foggy AM turns into another radiant PM, not hot. 4 PM, sun gone, sky & lake turn a sad soft gray. Mary down from St. Cloud...Dinner, Wilsons, Harold & Mrs. Swett, Woods. Tribune: 8, 58; noon, 72; 6, 75.

fol. 58

JUNE 20, Saturday. Cool, gray, some dtizzle in AM. Beautiful clear PM. Do I imagine it, or is there really tendency in New England for clear early morning and cloudy or wet PM, and just the opposite here? Start actual writing of novel "Planish." Till now, planning. Trib: noon, 69; 6, 75. Evening: Log Cabin Theater: Biography. Not bad.

JUNE 21, Sunday. Cool, bright day. Trib: 8, 59; noon, 72; 6, 74; midnite, 58.

Swedish picnic at Svithiod Home, next door: choir of young men from Rockford singing. Little girls, costume of red pointed caps, embroidered aprons, dance in circle to accordeon. The Swedish banner, well placed yellow cross on blue, is handsome.

In lake here, tiny ducklings swim in wave-stirred isle-sheltered water at my dock, menaced by muskrat like a flexible submarine.

SHORTEST DAY OF THE YEAR; a clear evening, and the sun down behind trees across the lake at about 9:01 (remember this is CWT--Central Wartime Time--an hour later than normal, making it really 8:01). Sun drags down with it a tapestry of hot gold. It is dark at 9:55 CWT--till then can read watch outdoors--though there is also a half moon to extend the light....It is magic at ten: a half moon, bats in the clear sky, afterglow across the lake, and the waves silver and dark blue in the breeze.

A lake is always so alive, compared with hills; yet not contemptuous and menacing, like the ocean.

Evening, midges stroll right in through the mosquito screens; and cover a (closed) glass window right near a light in study....They will be gone in a few days....Gone where?

JUNE 22, Monday. AM clear, then gray. 56 at 7:30, at one, only 59; at 3, 61 and gray, with gray waves--a real autumnal day. 6 PM, 64; 9, 60; 11, 57, with a cold wind that makes it seem colder. Trib: 8, 52; noon, 56; 6, 60; midnite, 53.

JUNE 23, Tuesday 8:30 AM, gray, cool, hint of rain; 58. Trib: 8, 53 (5 degrees colder than by thermometer at lake), noon, 59; 6, 63; midnite, 54.

In Minneapolis, house-hunting for fall--after deciding to, not to, to, not to, and to stay in Minnesota till Xmas and teach at University.....Confer, Bert Blase....Edmund Burke house, Mt. Curve Ave.; Geist & Miller on River Road; Harold Swett, and Moorish house with balconies..Tooth at Dr. Everett MacGibbon's--Bunny of my boyhood...Lunch, AF of L business agents, in basement of Mpls brewery, much beer and sausage: Mrs. Brad Heffelfinger, Elmer Peterson, Myrtle Harris, Reuben Latz, Finkelstein, Bob Kraemer of Labor Review; Councilman Norman E. Carle. Re Brad, "How do we know any of yr bks are good?"--"I seem to hear non-union voice."

fol. 59

GENERAL—Minn

The town of Blue Earth is not in Blue Earth County but in Faribault Co.

The town of Faribault is not in Faribault Co. but in Rice.

Lake Itasca is not in Itasca County but in Clearwater & Hubbard Co's.

Red Lake does not even touch Red Lake County--it is in Beltrami and Clearwater Co's.

Carl<u>e</u>ton College has nothing to do with the town or county of Carlton.

Cottonwood not in Cottonwood County, but Lyon

Marshall not in Marshall County but county seat of Lyon

fol. 60

JUNE 24--Wednesday. Trib: 8, 52; noon, 69; 6, 77--25 degrees in 10 hrs. AM fresh, clear, cool, beautiful--bright and windless, though cool, and the lake in gentle colors, so that now the lakeside is clad in perfect peace, "a cool ecstasy."

PM, drive about Lake Minnewashta, a couple of miles south of Minnetonka--hills andthick woods; New England hill hollows, even with two old maids in a white NEng cottage with delphinium, golden glow, and (if I remember) hollyhocks....Ten youngsters stooping over a strawberry patch--lots of berries about Tonka....Oats ready to cut.

Evening, drizzle at 11, but very cheerful with Al and Fefe Wilson here.

JUNE 25, Thursday. Trib: 8, 59; noon, 62; 6, 60; midnite, 61. 9 AM, 60; chilly, gray, promise rain--which comes and lasts all through afternoon, heavy at four, quitting at seven--when it is 62.

In heavy rain, the distant wooded shores become a charcoal smudge.

Evening: Mea Mann, George Leonard, John Leonard (Wash'n Bureau, Wall Street Journal) & wife; Tom Clarke of the London News-Chronicle and daughter Pat....Drunken sailor, name never quite clearly got, comes with Northwestern Univ instructor to call on the Celebrity, is quite drunk and becomes offensive, and invited to get out, whick he does with a grave reluctant feeling that injury has been done not only to himself but to his favorite, Ibsen.

JUNE 26, Friday. 9 AM, gray--60. Trib: 8, 59; 9,59; noon, 64; 6, 73. In Minneapolis, saw houses of P. Wheeler, 1800 Dupont, and that of my admirable at-present, at the lake landlord, Chas Lane Harris, 2112 Pillsbury Avenue--colonial of gt charm...McNally's back from California...Dinner, John & Mary Baxter: Ben Woodward, Helen Baxter, Brenda at al.

JUNE 27, Saturday. Trib: 7 AM, cool, gray, threat of rain. Noon, sun out and for first time in many days, hot as hell--80 at 8 PM. Saw CLHarris again--$3000 for 8 months, Sept to May 1st. Pillsbury Avenue, arching elms--a fine New Eng street.

Farmer-Labor Party convention: Elmer Benson, Bob Kraemer, ballroom at Nicollet; curving ceiling corner indirect lites. Susie Stagelberg old-timer... Most of the delegates dirt farmers with cigar brown hands and cheeks--brow whiter where shielded by hat....F. H. Shoemaker, No. Redwood, ex-cogressman, did time in Leavenworth in 1917 as conchy.... Howard Y. Williams of Union for DemocraticAxtion. Farmers' best suits; soft shirts, mostly blue. Many, coats off. Benson, keynoter: "these differences vanished like dew beneath the rising sun of Japan"--maybe an unfortunate metaphor! Benson & some union agts. like young mpls bus. men

fol. 61

JUNE 27, CONT.

Suddenly, at midnight, rainstorm breaks the heat, with lightning not loud but quivering without a pause.

Do I again imagine it, or do thunderstorms come in Vermont mostly in late afternoon, but here just after midnight?

JUNE 28, Sunday. Three-day trip, Sun-Mon-Tue, to Otter Tail County, including Henning-Vining-Clitherall-Battle Lake, to Leaf Mountains, Elbow Lake to Evansville to Lake Christina, and Maplewood Township Hills east of Pelican Rapids...Trip: 726 miles.

Tribune, heat in Mpls for Sunday: 8, 66; noon, 75; 6, 70.

Storm must have stopped during the night and begun again at 6:45; anyway I was awakened by thunder, and thought "No trip." Heavy rain. Had cooled off to 66, by 7:30. Grass and trees a menacing yellow-green in unnatural darkness.

Rain down to a drizzle; sun out at 9:30 and start for Otter Tail County.

Through trip: a lot of corn, re recent excessive rain, which has been 50 % more than normal, is only up to abt 4 inches, especially north of Sauk Centre, and will probably not ear out. But a lot in the south, e.g. Benson to Willmar to Minnetonka, up two feet or a little more.....Lots of flax near Fergus Falls--no more beautiful blue than the electric blue of flax, which is now in flower.....Wheat tall, mostly headed out but very green.....Haying begun....In one mile, corn will vary from 4 inches to 2 feet.

A pasture flayed for sod.....Horses necks together in pasture. The earth, just the earth itself, in Southern Minn so black, is very beautiful, striped in long curving lines with young corn across low knolls--like the bubbles in boiling water suddenly fixed.....Rolling hill, a <u>swelling</u> on the prairie.....Many fields ruined by mustard.....In long grass by railway, blue bells, lilac-colored wild phlox, wild roses.....One old haystack has a door covering its eaten-out den.

A moody day. 11:30, remains cool, with tender blue between dark clouds..Yesterday's heat spell was for only one day....2 PM, bright hot sun. At 6, hastening into Fergus Falls, a heavy rain, which lasted only an hour--and permitted me to go out and see movie, "Blondie's Happy

Event," impossibly bad in sentimentality and improbability, yet had the nerve to make fun of parent trying to explain birth via bees and pollen--5-year-old knows more than father. Audience applauded spirited movie of Offenbach's Gay Parisienne ballet done by Monte Carlo ballet.

Sign at Collegeville and elsewhere thru state: Caution. Deer Crossing.

fol. 62

JUNE 28, CONT.

> At ease, she said,
> Maneuvers begin
> When you get those
> Whiskers
> Off your chin.
> Burma Shave.

New architecture, cement with glass brick, curving corners, at a lumber warehouse in Elk River, a surprising high school in hamlet of Albany.

Villages like Albany, Freeport, each dominated by a towering Catholic Church, usually brick, often new, a parsonage, parochial school.....But they try to be up-to-date: saloon in a store building in Freeport: "The Yellow Canary Cafe."

Just north of Melrose, historic site sign that a farm there was homesteaded in 1860 by August Lindbergh, grandfather of the flyer, who served 2 terms in the Swedish parliament before coming to America....This near the Sauk River road-crossing.....Grownup, returning, may care much more to learn all about a district than did as child. Often he also has a much more affectionate attitude. Is this more normal--or more beaten?

Some of the differences in Sauk Centre....Two years ago, noted chain stores, stores have new fronts with tapestry brick; black and translucent glass; neon and fluorescent lights....Even second-rate country roads hard-surfaced. Saloons imitate city cafes....Beauty shops in small places;

women using many cosmetics, have hair dressed, nails colored.....Add to these now; great cement roads connecting not only with The Cities but other points. Main roads enter and leave the town at pts different from the old roads--whose course now hard tp remember. Many gas stations, including on hill, at entrance to town, which was of old just pasture; and near it, cabins for tourists....Signs advertising all towns with any pretentions to being "resorts" along the highway.

In some places along the G.N., snow fences up permanently.

Eating, when motoring, especially if one is alone, is just a Vile Necessity--at least, is indifferent--and to be postpned to two, even three.

OSAKIS: Did find my semi-circular window, remembered with interest from youth: it's on the Red (   ) store.

Good resort hotels: Osakis: Idlewilde Inn. Alexandria, Geneva Beach. Dunn's, Lake Lizzie. Blake, Lake Homme Dieu.

Town nicknames: Alec, Fergus, Tonka (lake),

OLD CLITHERALL. A mile West of Clitherall, on a pleasant bluff overlooking Lake Clitherall (named after a major who was in charge of land office). A few modern tourist cabins on one side of an old brown house, sinking into the earth,

fol. 63

JUNE 28, CONT--2

<u>Old Clitherall cont:</u>

built before 1870, belonging to Chancy (sic on tombstone) Whiting; a white school; a still, white, severe, sharp angled roof building with sign "The True Church of Jesus Christ." On monument near shore: "Site of the first permanent settlement in Otter Tail County, Minnesota. Members of the Church of Jesus Christ came here from Iowa, May 5, 1865."

Talk with Lester Whiting, farmer-legislator, sharp brown jaw, one glass eye, clean blue shirt, standing in his potato patch in Clitherall--farmer for many years, now lives in town....When Joseph Smith murdered at Nauvoo, Brigham Young took as many as he could of the Mormorns to Utah. Others maintained that Jos Smith, Jr. son of the prophet, the true leader. Others refused--among them, the people who came by ox cart from Manti, Iowa, in 1865, and founded Old Clitherall. Their few descendants still there; they have no missionaries--fault of the world if damned.

Old Lester was brought up there, but he and his six brothers made a further secession and joined the Reorganized Church of Latter-Day Saints, who prophet is Frederick Smith, son of original Jos Smith Jr., who has headquarters in Independence, Mo. They have about 1000 adherents in Minnesota; churches in the new Clitherall (a sweet modest little gray shingled building, with no label, well-kept lawn), in Mpls, St. Paul, Duluth, Bemidji). Lester is Elder of this new church; like the missionaries, no salary--tho missionaries may have their families supported. There are also the priest, teacher, and one other. At Independence, 3 bishops, with Smith and asst.

Half Mile from Old Clitheral, on Route 3, on an oak-shaded hilltop, very peaceful, very pretty, with vistas of both Lake Clitherall and West Battle Lake, and off to the S.E., the Leaf Mountains, is MT. PLEASANT CEMETERY--not exclusively but mostly populated from the old Mormon colony.

Stone in it:

CHANCEY (sic) WHITING
1819-1902
Father, lonely is thy bed,
And the turf is overhead,
Cold earth is thy cover;
But thy heart hath found release,
And it slumbers full of peace.
The calm spot where thy body lies
Gladens (sic) thy soul in Paradise,
It is so still and holy.

<u>Other names in the cemetery</u>:

Editha Whiting	Effie Sherman	Nelson Wendell
Mary Burdick	Seth Fletcher	Emma Trowbridge
J. J. Tucker	Joseph "	Winfield M. Gould
Orison E. Tucker	Jasperson	

Graves as late as 1940--Father Barnhard C. Nohe--surely not a Mormon.

fol. 64

JUNE 28 CONT--3

<u>Old Clitherall cont--2</u>

Very curious gravestone--only it's a carved grave<u>wood</u>, the inscription badly blurred. Part of it seems to say: Willie (   ) Lewis and (AND with the N turned around) Elba Albertson d. Dec. 27th 1881, aged three months and (N turned around) four days. Born on same day, died same day in epidemic? Lester says they had epidemics of black diphtheria.

From Mt. Pleasant Cemetery, the colored counties indeed--together yellow mustard, brown hay, green wheat.

The urbanization tendency of America. A cross-roads hamlet tends to become not a true village but a small city; shirt-sleeves and guffaw to cheap "sports outfit"--green blouse and trousers--and talk of golf and Rotary (only into shirt-sleeves, even in restaurant and movie and the guffaw pretty easily!) O'Meara's in Fergus, with its black glass, and the movie theater and River Inn, are small-city....One of the few Minn towns that at all uses its river or lake front is Fergus, with rock garden below River Inn and sloping lawns at Courthouse and Federal Building, down to Otter Tail River. (Also Bemiji, with park, homes, information bldg).

On Sunday, all farmers here go fishing--catch or not--cars parked by bridges, on which farmwives also fish.

JUNE 29, MONDAY. Morning, cool, very gray. Trib: 8, 68; noon, 74, 6, 76; midnite, 66.

"Atmosphere" under the gray sky, a melancholy prairie slew among low hills--dull water, gray muskrat houses, long drooping grasses. But under sun it would be lively with blackbirds.

A state like this needs more eccentrics and more Jews.

The writer, loving or thinking he loves, the hills busy taking notes about them instead of looking at them.

Climbed Inspiration Peak again--just in time to get caught by sudden rain. I could see it coming and, being so high, abt on a level with raincloud, could look down and see its filmy tails drooping as it came....Instantly the path up became a slippery earth gutter.

See VALLEYS section re most of today.

Going north of Route 3 to see Maplewood hills....When you go, especially motoring, wondering whether roads are wet, into a new country even on a bright day, it seems to the imagination all in darkness, with the roads confused--likely get lost.

fol. 65

JUNE 29 CONT.

All day long--sprinkle, pour, sun out, gray again.

On Route 108, just east of Lake Lida, a small old log cabin without windows, abandoned in a field. Like a Roman Remain in England.

Pelican Rapids to Dunvilla: passed the shallow, commonplace road cut where the Minnesota Man was found in 1932. Not a mile away, marker of the 1825 line, SE to NW, supposed to divide territories of Sioux and Chippewas......Dunvilla, Dunn Lodge, plaster; maybe 30 cottages with main dining hall; graceful small bridge arching over inlet to sandy beach; power house at tiny falls of Pelican River, here entering LAKE LIZZIE--a pretty lake, with some bluffs.

Evening: William Robertson, editor of the Fergus Falls Daily Journal--born in Canada, been on the Journal for 51 years, now abt 65; and CARL SNOWBERG, reporter on Journal but also Chairman of the County Commissioners; both thin, tall, quiet, don't drink--and Carl's mother-in-law keeps trying to make him stop smoking cigarettes!......

Their stories: when great Tornado (1919, summer I almost went to live in Fergus came; tornado smashed all hotels, one frame one to matchwood; killed 60 in all) Robertson was home; thought there was quite a wind, busy holding down swing windows--and looked out to see garage gone with car standing there.....Train robbers, about 1890; not caught--probably sheriff in with them; gang that was caught were nothing but poor honest bank cracksmen who registered at a hotel (in Moorhead, I think) at 4AM, clerk suspicious at their looks, found to be loaded down with guns and nitroglycerine, and sentenced for the train robbery, tho they provided an honest alibi that they had spent early part of that night in a whorehouse!.....Colored settlement in Fergus, migrated from Kentucky; oldest one, preacher, married 4 times, was born in slavery.

At the State Hospital at Fergus is Dr. Lindley, brother of Ernest.

Chief diff a hotel like River Inn to train the indifferent temporary bellboys (one sits day dreaming while I wait at door of elevator) and waitresses....So good a hotel pay?....It's only deep wickednesses: "coffee shop" (universal name in America now for a hotel restaurant) not open Sunday evening; no closet in my room nor yet hooks on bathroom door--that a very bad wickedness--andthe damn courthouse bell rings the hours and halves.

fol. 66

JUNE 30, Tuesday. Trib: 8, 64; noon, 70; 6, 76. 7 AM, at Fergus, very cool and apparently foggy. This "fog" continued, as a haze, all day, from Fergus almost 200 miles to Minnetonka. I wondered if it could possibly be smoke from a forest fire and on Wednesday found it really was--from fire in Northern Saskatchewan or Alberta, nobody knows quite where. The day before, it was seen in Montana. By night, Tuesday, it was gone from Minneapolis.....Jean Piccard, professor in University here, claims he saw smoke from a Minnesota fire in China. Not impossible. Note how smoke from one cigarette will fill a huge room. But anyway, the damn haze kept me from climbing Inspiration Peak--where rain drove me down on Monday.

East to Battle Lake: a grassy hollow, ringed with oaks, cattle reclining--a Landseer pastoral in Minnesota.

In this haze, all hills become mysteriously higher and Battle Lake becomes a hilltop mediaeval village--and that, for B.L., is some becoming!

Remember from boyhood: streets lighted by arc lights. The tender, John MacGibbon, threw away the used carbon--picked up by boys. In June, bowl of arc light half filled with burned insects....Light associated with pum-pum-pullaway on st corner.

New Yorkers--a <u>distressful</u> and neurotic people....He wrote with vigor and valor......Crows piratical in the mist.

Lake George, nr Inspiration Pk, been dried up for several years, till this wet year. Hills, unlike lakes, do not dry up.

Much of Otter Tail County Scandinavian, but NYMills Finn, Perham is German.

Ever-normal Granary govt tanks seen, so far as I remember, only in Southern part of state.....Litchfield has a village green......I've seen migrating turtles only near Minnetonka, tho been by so many lakes--returning Tuesday, saw one turtle crossing road.

On these long straight roads, any curve, even a right-angle one, seems a joy and very beautiful.....Re this mirroring of cement roads--you can see nickle of approaching car reflected in it....Mirror smoothness comparative--I suppose an actual glass mirror is rough under a microscope.

Everywhere at filling stations, gt piles of the rubber now being salvaged for war--tired, inner tubes, overshoes, garden hose.....Will this war finally end the notorious American waste of resources--and end it too late?

Return to Lake Minnetonka. The house so spacious, yet private; so much cooler than prairies in car; shining, belonging to <u>me</u>.

Warm in PM, sun through misted gray sky. 74 at 4, when ret. Evening, at 7:40, sudden wind and heavy rain--thermometer drops to 70. Storm lasts only 20 minutes--a spit of bad

fol. 67

JUNE 30 CONT.

temper. Then the wind gone, the late sun genial and unashamed, on flat silver water.....At 9:45, when already dark on shore, the stilly lake half silver, half rosy, and against it the trees silhouetted, every twig, every shrub, clear. So beautiful--and a sound of distant singing--Edelkitsch.

One cause for a man getting married--a foolish notion that he will save the trouble of going on making engagements for evenings--the week after this always so empty.....A frivolous manner can be a defense just as much as rudeness is.

<u>JULY</u>

JULY 1--Wednesday. At 9, 62; clear, cool, radiant, perf. day. Cool all day--at 1:30 PM, only 69. Excellent! Can't get the Harris house--he has an offer to rent it 2 years unfurnished. May take the Wheeler house, 1800 Dupont--not like it so well but save about $1200 in 8 months. This can be put down as a typical example of forethought--not being <u>able</u> to get more expensive, I don't.

Most beautiful day in weeks. Should have had it like this at Inspiration Peak....A man seeking a harbor might miss it because of the fortuitous look of it on a stormy day, and so change, or rather fail to change, his whole life.

Tribune, Wednesday: 8, 57; noon, 62; 6, 68; midnite, 58.

Lscking Harris house, drive into Minneapolis again, again look at Wheeler house, 1800 Dupont--too grim, and no silver-linen-blankets. Look again at Burke House, 1500 Mount Curve Ave.--"bijou"--200 a month, vs 1800 for 8 mos at Wheeler's, 3000 for 8 mos at Harris's. Only Joseph wd have to have a bedroom made of the handsome basement "game room," as they call it here (and sometimes, oh God, romp room) Joseph likes it....Evening, took Joseph to "White Cargo," at Log Cabin; pretty good, especially Robt Aden. Nobody (esp the author) has seen the real moral--that the vaunted White Man has no damn business in the tropics, in Africa, expropriating and hating the hatives--of Kipling, also. The world cd not realize that till now, with the semi-revolt of India and China--really more in revolt in Japan..This is a three-cornered war, a Battle Royal, of democracies vs dictatorships vs enslaved "colored" countries. I felt like apologizing to Joesph for taking him.

At theater: God how these Midwestern girls make their mugs ugly by chewing gum!

fol. 68

JULY 2, Thursday 7 AM, gray, chilly--59. Sun out suddenly, 10:05 AM. Trib: 7, 53; 8, 55; noon, 68; 6, 75.

Between living right on lake, with no town near, driving, and keeping this diary, very conscious of weather all this summer. To real urbanite, weather doesn't exist. To the rustic, all important, chief topic of talk, exasperatingly human in its moods. More of Lewis Browne's eternal feud of urban vs country....The urbanite misses an excitement, a collector's triumphs, in ignoring the daily rare specimens of the thermometer, the time of sunset, the amt of rain which are unknown to the warmed and lighted city.

To Mpls. Signed for Burke House, 1500 Mt. Curve Ave. ?Will I occupy it after Xmas?....Buick, with which started out in Beverly Hills 2½ yrs ago, passes 40,000 miles. Like the weather, it has become one of my most interesting friends.

Dinner with Chas Bolles Rogers, old family house, LaSalle Ave. Portrait by Diego Rivera. The flour aristocracy here, all of which hates even the New Deal, shocked by his having Rivera paint it. All the guests complain of recent "cold." McNallys, Alfred and Mrs. Pillsbury--she, eyes gone almost, still the grand lady of Mpls; born Boston, knows the stage, knows such authors as Evelyn Waugh, Saki; Bruce Douglas, long sculptor in Paris, now lives mostly in Carmel, Calif., his pretty French wife, and his mother; Newells; Madame Black Bey--is it Black?--sister Oscar Kalman, married Frenchman who was Turkish ambassador to Vienna.

Home in blinding downfall of rain which started at 10:30, lasted an hour; cars edging in terror along Excelsior Bvd.

Note, Lake Calhoun, in Mpls. Young people bathing, bicycling, older ones, with dog and stick, walking around it; many-colored canoes, red, green, blue, on beach. Sailboats, anchored, all head up same way into wind. This is a lake that is <u>used</u>, yet not littered like Central Park.....As far as water and woods go, young people out here do live.

JULY 3, Friday. Clear, chilly--62 at 9 AM. Trib: 8, 57; n, 62; 6, 69. Phrase: "That pleasant section of Minnesota called So. Calif"

Drive to Shakopee, Savage, where, re war, tankers being built on Minnesota River...Best corn seen yet--well over 2 ft; real farms, so near to Minnetonka. Nr Chaska, sugar beets (refinery in Chaska) 4 inches high...Toward 9 PM, descending sun naked in slight haze, and sun path on lake narrow copper.

A note: man mutely turning away eyes, one compact of misery, no protest, when severely scolded.

fol. 69

JULY 4, Saturday. AM, cool, gray; 9:30, 65. Gray, cool, all day; occas sun. Trib: noon, 66; 6 PM, 67. (These important data re Saturdays always scant--complete table not given in Sunday paper)

Perhaps first eve of July 4th, and 4th itself, in life, while in America, that didn't hear one firecracker explode, one toy pistol. Forbidden, re war. Many people on roads in another putative last fling before threatenied gas rationing. Egypt now menaced by Rommel--we talk mostly of that, if mention the war at all.

Evening, to Wilson's; Fefe's charming mother and handsome, slim, international father; Addison Lewises, Brenda Ueland, John MacMillan--building tankers at Savage but app prefers Hitler to FDR, Harold Sweats, Porter of War Dept., and Sumner MacKnight--of Christ, a classmate, with whom I probably never exch nine words in 4 years at Yale but who now drips with "Harry." A weedy little man, who has been in the State Senate and owns millions--thousands--of acres and banks. An American aristocracy, mostly jumping from chewing tobacco to spit--"the first chews tobacco and the 2nd does nothing but dribble."

Somebody claims to have seen fireflies evening. (Later: very few here as cf. w. Conn.)

JULY 5, Sunday. AM, cool, gray; 9 AM, 63. Trib: 8, 56; n, 66; 6, 61; midnite, 57 Gray all morning except for a few leers of sunshine and one embarrassing belch of thunder, not fol by rain. PM, 70 at 2; dark, with mist-storied shores across tranquil lake. CBS concert on radio, premiere of "Music for Elizabeth" (for Betty Furness) a fantasia by Johnny Green, gt charm.

Sun sinks a red disc, gigantic; the water all rose. Down on the dock, at lake front, the lake so fresh, the channels & shore beyond islands musterious.

JULY 6, Monday. Trib: 8, 53; noon, 65; 6, 72. Clear, cool, perf-day; 9 AM, 62. For weeks now, been only one very hot day; not till today taken meals again out on porch; needed extra quilt every night on bed.........PM, drove St. Bonifacius, Fefe & mother. Evening: rehearsal of Amphytrion at Log Cabin. They want me to direct Dodsworth--cut, with unit set for all the scenes.

JULY 7, Tuesday. 9 AM, bright, clear, cool--9 AM, 62.

fol. 70

JULY 7, CONT.

<u>Trib</u>: 8, 56; noon, 73; 6, 81; midnite, 71.

Tea with Mrs. Mac Washburn--Rube--Penny--in small new house in Tyrol Hills, off Wayzata Bvd.--a new world of small white houses that actually do have a little ground.

Dinner with Addison Lewises, and Mr. Atkinson, and finally met the beautiful daughter Virginia. Chy so charming--and smokes too much. The whole family combine the modern habit of complete freedom between the generations on any subject with Addison's old-fashioned "wish t' God they would do a little work." Atkinson highly anti-Semitic--he's in "mercantile business"--i.e., as "Harold's" sells women's clothes on several well-carpeted floors; "anybody that ever did business with the Jews knows they won't keep their word." Yet he is a kind man, not aggressive, not money-grasping. The merchants agree to close at 5:30--the Jews sign the agreement--and keep open till six.

JULY 8, Wednesday. AM, very gray, pretty warm. Summer really begun? 9 AM, 68. Used no quilt on bed last night, plus regulation light blanket; the first time in weeks....Queer gray <u>listening</u> sort of still day. All afternoon, warm, dim sun, a sulky feeling in the air.

<u>Trib</u>: 8, 62; noon, 79; 4, 87; 6, 87; midnite, 72.

Mosquitos now active in the evening; they replace the Extra Blanket as a Minnesota diversion. An enevvating day, so that sleep badly Wednesday night--despite Gideon been going well, and have and have played a new record of the Beethoven Vth.

JULY 9, Thursday. Morning not so much hot--74 at 9--as soaked with humidity. Very hard to sit and work. At 2:30 PM, only 80, but with gray sky, day so damp and breathless that it feels like 95; requires resolution to sit at typewriter--though Gid just meeting Peony....But one gets interested in the writing just from going on with it. Till now, I have really just been planning Planish and experimenting--with more interest in exploring Minnesota.

<u>Trib</u>: 8, 67; noon, 80; 2 PM, 84; 6, 73; midnite, 69.

"The only reason why Man has any chance at all in the eternal war with Woman is that so many women ate traitors to their own side and always singing fondly the battle-hymns of the enemy."

fol. 71

JULY 10, Friday. Morning, clear, fairly cool; PM very hot. <u>Trib</u>: 8, 66; noon, 80; 4, 87; 6, 86; midnite, 74. Summer <u>has</u> begod begun.

With Penny Washburn to tea at Clarence (?) Williams house on West Lake of the Isles Bvd; dinner Minneapolis Club. Driving in, explore charming hill country south of Hopkins--about Glen and Shady Oak lakes.....Bought new radio; an RCA Victor; at Schmidt's.

JULY 11, Saturday. Morning, fairly cool, sun off and on; 75 at 10 AM. <u>Trib</u>: noon, 83; 6 PM, 88.

Evening, as typical when alone here: Summer Symphony from New York on new radio, from CCNY Stadium, brings a touch of homesickness, remembering being there with Tony Minor & Frances. German lesson on Linguaphone. Reading Folwell's Hiatory of Minnesota. 10:30, phone Marcella, who has just finished her two weeks as the gay lady in "Ah, Wilderness" at Peterborough.

JULY 12, Sunday <u>Trib</u>: 8, 74; noon, 86; 6, 92; 9, 76; 2 AM, 73. Much the hottest day so far; what they call a scorcher. With a cool breeze, day starts well at lake; 74 at 7:30 and 84 at 10:30 but cool breeze. The breeze keeps up with the heat--out here; a hot, voluptuous, hoydenish day--the heart of midsummer. 90 here at 3, but on the porch by the lake, the cheerful breeze keeps it pleasant. But, at 6 PM, when the breeze goes down and it's still 90--then the thoughts have to pass to the typewriter through hot thick gravy, and are probably not undamaged.

After half an hour of menacing, mocking thunder, a rain comes, at 7--a very little rain. That over, there is a wild green light among the agitated trees for a while, the sun coming and going. The thermometer drops from 86 at 7:30 PM to 76 at midnight; but the upstairs cottony with heat, and it will be the first night this year when heat will affect sleep.

JULY 13, Monday: Trib: 8, 66; noon, 64; 6, 77; midnite, 67.

But I did sleep; indeed, before morning, needed to pull the light blanket up over me; and when I woke, at 7, the thermometer had dropped to 68, but, gray, with cold and stormy though rainless wind driving in off lake, from the north, it seemed more like 50 degrees....A nervous, exciting morning: thunder, then no rain but just gray with a steely wind; then sun out a minute, brilliant on hydrangea bush, just outside the porch, in the foreground, against fretful gray background of wide lake.

At noon, still only 68, but grayness dissolving. Midafternoon, 3:30, 74; a bright, cool, perf-day with light breeze. Many birds combative on lawn.....Dinner: McNallys, Dot Bennett. A cool evening

fol. 72

JULY 14, Tuesday Trib: 8, 63; noon, 78; 6, 82; midnight, 70.

9:30 AM, 68 and bright, p.d. (abbreviation for the inexact term "perfect day," to be used hereafter). Cool evening.

Bob Hanscom here wanting me to direct "Dodsworth" for Log Cabin Theater.....Evening, Brenda Ueland's; her brother, Arnulf; Helen Rand, Wilsons, Chas Schoerer(?), McKinnon-Woods. Driving back after, first time this year seen Northern Lights--faint, though they were faint lightning....Fefe says that Al has no perceptive friends here save me. She finds it hard to have an easy circle to whom really talk.

JULY 15, Wednesday. Cool gray AM--69 at 9:30. Trib: 8, 67; noon, 72; 6, 73. Whole Log Cabin bunch here; refuse to direct Dodsworth--hard work for little possible reward; trust--as actors--only 3 in company....Evening, Wilsons; Douglases--Mahala, Bruce and his wife.

THURSDAY-SATURDAY, trip to Hudson (Wis), Afton, Pt. Douglas-Prescott, Nininger, Rollingstone, Whitewater Park, Rochester, Troy, Chatfield, Houston, Caledonia, Yucatan, Brownsville & Reno, Waukon and Decorah, Stewartville, Owatonna. 769 miles. All in a real HEAT WAVE.

JULY 16, Thursday. Trib: 7, 70; 8, 71; 10, 82; noon, 86; 4, 94; 6, 95; midn, 85.

Broiling all day; exploration really hard work. Afton and Rollingstone charming new villages--see Valley notes for practically all of this trip.

By road: Michaelmas daisies--very tall; mustard; Queen Anne's lace; lupin; red and white clover. Much tall white wild clover--is that right?--by road. Black eyed Susans....By driveways of farmhouses: hollyhocks, nasturtiums, tiger lilies

Oats everywhere ripe, and in many places being harvested--by horses as often as by tractor.....Ripe oats seen afar on blufftop seems flame-colored and flame-breathing, on such a day....A lot of corn now 3 ft high; many fields of soy beans, maybe 1½ ft high...Some wheat, not much, about ripe.

Bridges out after "flash floods" in small streams now almost dry....One tilted but could cross it, queasily.

Not as hot down in valleys as up on unsheltered prairie, in sunglare.

Can't from absolute, map altitude tell what the hills are. Here in S. E. Minn, wide ranges of them <u>below the level</u> of the flat-looking prairie, worn by streams.

fol. 73

JULY 16, Thursday, Cont.

So very high bluffs along a river and actually lower than the prairies beyond....Not so with moraines, as in Otter Tail County.

Girl cashier in a movie theater--a small-town career--she meets so many Gents.

IGNATIUS DONNELLY HOUSE, at NININGER--just it and 2 or 3 other houses to show where gt city was to have been. Big square elaborate; loophole-atticwindows 3d stort to watch for Indians. Porch rotted away, whole house will go unless cared for. In hallway, pictures of I. D., BOFlower, Pingree, Richard Ely and other early Radicals as editors of NEW TIME....Study, portrait of Napoleon is significant....Books, eceonomics, physics, literary history....In drawing room--two niches instead of fireplaces--old square piano....Just rim of trees between it and Mississippi. Three miles W of Hastings, with magnificent bluffs of the Missip all the way.

WEATHER: Broiling all day. In the car, baking, uncomfortable. Dust from the many gravel roads we travelled covered hat, shoes--cigarette case felt gritty. This is a real heat-wave....It did not let up in the evening--went to a movie, very bad, because it was "air-conditioned" and cool....No electric fan in room, even in the renowned (and excellent) 9-story Hotel Kahler, with its rate of $6.00 for a good corner single room; its wood-paneled dining-rm with portrait of Will Mayo...So sleep all nite with just sheet over me...A weariness to crawl thru the streets, even at 11 P.M.....Sticky juicy Jewish city women in the lobby....talking of the heat and how bored by their Diets.

(Next night, also stayed at Kahler--had a fan--25 cents. Mayo Park, with huge outdoor music park and band stand; zoo with monkeys, and bears who seemed cruelly ill-used in their narrow prison-cell cages, in this heat. Fine modern auditorium--ice skating!

Villa Maria Academy, with its red roofs, at Frontenac is, they claim, on site of old Fort Beauharnais, built 1727. But site also claimed for Sand Point, nearby.

At Lake City, "souvenirs" in window: book ends, vases, lip sticks.

Along the Mississip and Lake Pepin you now see, on both sides of the river, the amber of ripe grain atop the gt bluffsm in contrast to the heavy green of bluffsides, trees & grass.

My beloved deep meadows not so good now--because they've just been cut. And in them you see already dry bales of hay, already baled.

Whitewater State Park in glorious ravine country, along the Whitewater River, but it's only 60 acres and, oh God, has a golf course.....Roads here for the time have surface taken off by recent flood, in low places by river, leaving a prickly surface of broken stone.

fol. 74

JULY 16, Thursday--CONT 2.

Corn strips in contrast to grain is startlingly darker--from a distance you wonder what crop that may be.

You can see the tower of the Mayo Clinic from the East 9 miles away across prairie. I don't know how many stories it is--the coupola is tricky.

Late afternoon, the soft light on sides of grazing sheep--a Landseer, and quite romantic and unreal.

JULY 17, Friday. Rising at 7 AM, seems much cooler, but from 11 AM to midnight, more broiling than Thursday. That evening in park in Rochester, oldish men with bandaged heads, arms, evidently outpatients living at the innumerable boarding houses ("$1.00 & up"), sit drawling, always in shirt sleeves. Such men now wear quite narrow suspenders or belts. Too hot for them to stroll--or for me!

TRIB: a complete schedule of a Minnesota July-heat-wave day: Friday, July 17: 2 AM, 85; 8, 81; noon, 89; 3, 94; 6, 88; 10, 85; midnight, 81. In the Rochester paper for the same day: Maximum, 94; minimum, 74. Year ago today: Max, 85; min, 53.

Same day:	Max	min
Chicago	96	77
Duluth	68	56
N. Orleans	88	75
N. York	84	70
Miami	87	75

In Fremont, a hamlet near Chatfield with one store, one school, one hall, a creamery, four or five houses, an old-fashioned quite New England country store--white bldg, old, with worn steps; amiably suspicious wrinkle-faced Yankee storekeeper; straight chairs so worn they're strapped with iron; litter on shelves and boxes--patent medicines, wrenches, straw hats, thread (but, as usual in such stores now, an elab modern enamel ice box with bottles of Coke, Whistle, Seven Up, on ice). I ask directions and he, "What business you in, Mister?"

NORWEGIAN NAMES, from a country cemetery (on #30, E of Chatfield

Olson	Brakke	Lilvestad	The spruce-shaded
Amdahl	Reishus	Wraalstad	cemetery remarkable
Pederson	Tollefson	Sandvig	cool in baking prairie.
Sandli	Fossum		

Previous question of these notes, while Joseph drives, interfering with seeing the very country of which make notes. But they do keep one awake and attantive--& easy to fall asleep on hot day if not responsible for driving.

fol. 75

JULY 17, Friday, Cont.

For me, the hills have personalities, and strong and cheerful ones. Even just to motor among them cures me of depression.

Round and octagonal barns.

JULY 18, Saturday. Return to Minnetonka; in at 4:10 The heat wave ends. Agreeably cool in morning, hot in PM, very; heat ends with thunder disturbance without--at the Lake at least--much rain.

TRIB for day--for once complete in Sunday paper: 8 AM, 77; 11, 90; noon, 89; 4, 93; 6, 90; 7, 90; 8, 84; 9, 76; 10, 71.

So far, I could conceive of living, permanently, in Minneapolis, St. Paul, Duluth, Winona, Rochester, Preston, Chatfield, Fergus Falls, Marine, Afton, and possibly Detroit Lakes, but in no other towns in the state.

An article on the vast difficulty of knowing all of even one county, to say nothing of one whole state or country or continent--as a Johnny Gunther nimbly pretends to. And Pearl Buck in her contemporary "East & West Association" wants us all to know all about Burma, Celebes, China.

Animals seen crossing the road, roughly in order:
gopher--quick and seeming gay
pheasant--sparrow, crow, woodpecker, dove
snake
woodchuck
skunk (but always dead!)
turtle (rarely in late July)

Meadow lark seems to be on prairie only.....Metal top of silo like a small observatory at distance....

Southern Minnesota town names:

Moscow	Elba
Albert Lea	Etna

Religious signs: "Repent Ye and Be Converted." "Prepare to Meet Thy God."......God can't touch the Hotel Kahler in his outdoor advertising.

Should see Hollandale, south of Owatonna. WPA guide says it has Dutch houses. Sign about it: "Paul Jones, Inc. 15,000 acres of onions, potatoes, cabbage, carrots."

Owatonna: Neither hotel prop, Fred Johnson, once of Palmer House, Sauk Centre, nor prest Security Bank, has read Edgar Wesley's book Owatonna, tho he does town almost too much credit--the Owatonna Hotel dining rm isn't that good. If they had had to pay him $75,000 they'd all read it, give it to strangers. Probly cant be bought anywhere in town....Metropolitan Opera House--Albrecht Stock Co still plays there--canvas in summer

fol. 76

JULY 18, Sat., Cont.

Sign in Faribault (tent): "Val Cloud, the dynamic evangelist from California."

When arrive here at lake at 4:10, it's 91, though seems much cooler than on road. Certainly a lot more quiet and comfortable! At 4:35, starts to thunder, but no rain by 5:30, and still 88. A sprinkle at 6. At 9, 78 and raining a little. A wild haggard green light after sunset.

As startling to see 93 on a thermometer as on a speedometer.

JULY 19, Sunday. p.d. cool, clear. 70 at 8 AM, 74 at ten. Does get up to 84 in PM, but enough breeze to be p.d.--here. PM, heard premiere in Western Hemisphere--in all parts of the world save Russia, and England, where it was played on June 29th--of Shostakovich's "Seventh Symphony," given by NBC orchestra on radio, Toscanini conducting. Predict it will be permanent part of world's really great music--power and melody.

Trib: 8, 67; noon, 75; 6, 73.

JULY 20, Monday. AM, p.d., clear and cool. Trib: 8, 64; noon, 75; 5, 78; 6, 75; midnite, 67. Evening: reading Clinchy's "The Mask of Sanity."

JULY 21, Tuesday. Morning, gray, very cool, 64 at 9 AM--autumnal. <u>Trib</u>: 8, 62; noon, 68; 6, 70; midnite, 60. Tea with John Crosbys: Mr. and Mrs. John, Mr. and Mrs. Albert Crosby, Mrs. Bovey, Mrs. Willard (?--Mrs. C's sister), Bernice Dalrymple....Dinner, Addison & Dorothy & Charlotte Lewis, and the Wilsons. Met Bob Piper, to marry Ginny (the Addisons' Ginny). Stopped a few minutes with Wilsons as the Buckthorn, Long Lake--walls covered with arms.

JULY 22, Wednesday. <u>Trib</u>: 8, 53; 10, 64; noon, 70; 6, 81. A delicious early-fall day; slightly veiled sun, with tender light. Cool--67 at 10 AM, 76 at 6:30 P.M. Afternoon, drove to Victoria to Chaska to Carver to East Union to few miles from Belle Plaine. St. Nicholas Catholic Church, on hill on n side of Carver, in glorious site, with wide Minn Riv Valley view; red brick with cement-covered butresses and white pilasters in front--they happen to be only white-painted tin, but never mind. An ancient-seeming abrupt-sided stone house, seeming very old, probably once the rectory but now occ by a family. Roman remains again?

On this mild day in midsummer, with none of the itchy irritation of such flayingly hot days as last Saturday, the countryside--especially with even a little roll, and even small valleys, like that S of East Union--seems so secure, protective, home: amber oat stubble, deep corn, farm houses with thick groves, small shaded streams.

fol. 77

JULY 23, Thursday. Cool, bright, p.d. 10 AM, 70. Evening, a little sprinkle. <u>Trib</u>: 8, 61; noon, 79; 6, 82. Even: With Wilsons, Addison Lewises, Virginia L and Bob Piper, and Katherine Overstreet, pianist, to Excelsior Amusement Park. The whip, bump-the-bumps. Sailors with girls in slacks. Heavy discussion of Al and Addison: The War and "Mpls business men shd discuss it more."

JULY 24, Friday. AM, damp, a little warm, but cools as, at 9:30, begins to rain, as gently and persistently as a money-borrower, Quits at 11, and a mild sun.

<u>Trib</u>: 8, 67; n, 71; 6, 79; midnite, 69.

Evening, to recitative at Lyman Lodge, YWCA camp on Minnetonka. Most of the girls only 12 to 18; counsellors, U of Minn undergraduates. Manager, Mrs. Raft--nice. The entertainment a recitative song of the Mississippi flowing from woods down to city--sound like birds of fresh young girl voices, lovely. Then a radioo-like script of Mpls street sounds, by Ruth Cole., The camp amiable, non-pietistic; they have their own services down by dock on Sunday morning, finding most visitng preachers too show-off, but Catholic girls taken to church in town. Some Jewish girls in camp--no distinction...RC church opposes their girls going--some priests obey bishop, some not. Sweet little children in infirmary who missed the show.

They have some homesick kids whom they cure by keeping them busy....The swimming dock a quadrilateral, making safe pool in center....Much canoeing.....22 acre tract (rite on lake) of virgin timber, part of the Great Woods tract; was Indian camping ground--found arrow....Counsellors in swimming, canoeing, photography.

...Is it only as one grows older that he loves "scenery"--an escape from human involvments.

JULY 25, Saturday. Trib: noon, 75; 6, 82; midnight, 66. Morning, gray and feels a little warm, but only 68 at 9. Clears by 10, and though 74 at 10:45, feels cooler. p.d. 3:30, 82 and feels like rain--apprehensive--but clears. That apprehensiveness of a coming storm, when you try to attach the feeling to some definite object of worry--and find a dozen.

"The trouble with always doing exactly what you want to is that you so rarely find anybody to do it with you, and pretty soon there is nothing that you very much want to do.""

Mrs. Rath, Ruth Coles, the hard keen Alice Rose, come over in evening to listen to Beethoven on phonograph.

fol. 78

JULY 26, Sunday. 7:15 AM, 68; 9:30, 70; 76, 6 PM: cool, bright, p.d. really "p" Trib: 8, 64; noon, 75; 6, 75; midnight, 66.

Already, in this northern land, you begin to feel autumn coming. The brilliant hydrangeas have mostly faded; you hear crows calling more often.

Harvest, acc. to paper: Some southern Minn counties already past peak of harvesting. North Dakota: harvest begun in early oats, barley, winter rye; wheat not for 2 weeks yet.

JULY 27, Monday. AM, gray, cool, misty, may rain. A seashore morning; a listening day. Pale sun at noon--it becomes a p.d.....TRIB: 8, 63; noon, 75; 6, 80; midnite, 70. PM: haircut. Tea at house of Mrs. Williams, the pretentious Englishwoman who, to use the phrase she would use for others, isn't quite "out of the top drawer." She volunteers that she knew Walpole, Galsworthy, Drinkwater. But two decent men there: Paul Harris of the Art Institute, and Wilhemus (sic) Bryan of the Blake School. Evening: C. L. Harris, dinner. Dr. and Mrs. Zierold, Casey Kant, Clarke Fletcher, Weaver Dobsons, Addison L's.

JULY 28, Tuesday. Trib: 8, 64; noon, 67; 6, 75; midnite, 70.

Awake to coolness and a steady gray rain, which is over by ten, with a mild sun coming and going. The afternoon is cool, bright--p.d. Again an example of how, in what seems a contrast to New England, the day starts bad, becomes lovely. A real *** p.d. all afternoon, tho clouds promise rain which never comes....The lawn thick today with robins and squirrels. Rabbits come out of the woods.

Evening, a full moon battling with fast troops of dark clouds--celestial cavalry. Dinner, Dalrymples' on Crystal Bay: Wilsons, Carl Jones once of Journal, McNallys, Gideon Seymour editorial writer, Dana Macmillan.

JULY 29, Wednesday. Trib: 8, 66; noon, 78; 6, 80. The morning fairly cool--68 at 8--somewhat gray, becomes by 9:30 a p.d. of the veiled sort, with a thin sun. Last night's promised rain did not come. It is now dark by 9:40, CWT, with the lake still light. Evening, reading "The Long Boats Passing," by Havighurst--a saga of the Great Lakes. Mrs. Rath, Alice Rose and Ruth Cole come in, listen to Beethoven II; Ruth plans verse history of Minneapolis--the 90 yrs of Miss Godfrey.

JULY 30, Thursday. Trib: 8, 68; noon, 74; 6, 84; 9, 80; 10, 77; 11, 71; midn, 72. Note16 degrees rise 8 AM to 6 PM and 13 degrees drop, 6 to 11.

Morning, slightly foggy, slightly warm, 70 at 8. Sun out at 10. Afternoon, bright, cool--p.d. Hanscoms and Bert Jeter again over from Log Cabin Theater to ask me to direct something--anything.

In the dim thick woods west of the house, a scattered stipple of light on the bushes, as sun shines thru trees.

fol. 79

JULY 30 CONT.

Evening: the sun low, its path is a flaming copper; the water to east of it, tender-colored and various: luminous pale blue, a duller blue-green, and a pale copper, Sunset about 8:40. At 9:25, looking out from porch on tranquil citron-colored water, attention attracted up, to East, by lightning, and there a vast cumulus cloud, snowy with black edges, is rolling in fast with lightning in its heart; then thunder, but very low. Later, the lightning seems to between layers of the cloud, a dark layer low, above it a snowy layer which is lighted rosily by the lightning. A celestial Vesuvius. And nothing happens--the cloud rolls by and no rain.

JULY 31, Friday. The dirtily tricky sort of day you don't expect here: at 9 AM, the true *** p.d., only 70....Drive to Hutchinson, Stewart, Glencoe, Chaska, back. The day turns into a gray one, with diffused glare; then rain, from 2:30 to 3; then sunny but humid and rather hot--no day for brisk work or anything else.

Notes en route: Lots of corn over 4 ft high; some must be 5; quite a little, though, has been permanently dwarfed by the early rains. Most of the oats have been cut and shocked. Corn and oats seem to be the gt crops in the region traversed; don't believe there's <u>any</u> wheat.

CARVER-MC LEOD COUNTY HAMLET NAMES:

Hollywood	Corvuso
New Germany	Cosmos
Sumter	
Lester Prairie	

Most of the country, west of Cologne on 212 and a few miles w of St. Bonifacius on 7, is pretty flat, not much roll, and on a gray listless day like this, it's a pretty DUll view, pretty boresome.

On an almost imperceptible rise W of Hutchinson, the "Hilltop Inn." Is there a craving in the flatlands for hills and "views"?....Near Silver Lake, a former store-building out in the country: "Bohemian Reading and Educational Society.".....Near Hutchinson, several brick farmhouses....Everywhere in Minnesota, towns now marked not only by church steeples but by tower-supported water tank with name of town lettered on it......Southern Minnesota villages much more than those in central and northern parts of state are likely, as you approach, to seem pleasantly buried in thick trees.

Friday TRIB: 8, 65; noon, 74; 6, 81. Evening: Brenda's: Rolf, Baxters.

fol. 80

A U G U S T--1942

AUGUST 1, Saturday. Trib: noon, 77; 6, 81.

Rain which started about 2 AM seems to have gone on all night; it was still raining at 8:30 AM, when it was only 68. The sun came out by 9:15 and was in and out all day, with no more rain. Sunset now, 8:40.

Evening: Martha Ostenso, once a good writer, with three female friends, one Kay Taggart who works for Thorpe Bros, real estate, came out, all drunk, loquacious, flattering, rowing, and highly unpleasant.

Hopkins, suburb of Minneapolis, "the raspberry queen." Many fine large raspberries for sale by road--taken from luggage compartments back of cars.

AUGUST 2, Sunday. Trib: 8, 66; noon, 70; 6, 74; 2 AM Monday, 59.

A real p.d.; brilliant, only 69 at 10 AM. Clear and fairly cool all day. At sundown, lake in small waves a steel blue. Drove to Robbinsdale, Stillwater, Somerset (Wis), hoping to call on Joe Beach at his cottage, nr East Farmington--not there. Route 35 from Somerset of Hudson, fine views across the St. Croix River into Minnesota.

Eager among Micky's coming from the East--arr. Wednesday.

AUGUST 3, Monday. Trib: 8, 56; 9, 62; noon, 73; 6, 79; midnight, 66.

Another p.d., all jade and sapphire. No place can have more beautiful days than Minnesota when it behaves. But some summers it goes up to 100, remains over 85 for weeks.

Squirrel on stone bench here in yard sits up primly behind an imaginary little desk......Evening, to Wilsons'. Sunset spills all over the water in lavish burnished bronze.

AUGUST 4, Tuesday. p.d. tho partly slightly misty. 9 AM, 69. Trib: 8, 60; 10, 71; noon, 80; 6, 83; midnite, 70.

fol. 81

AUGUST 5, Wednesday.

Trib: 8, 65; noon, 74; 6, 81.

9 AM, 68; sun comes and goes, rather gray, may rain...Thunder at 12....Michael arrives on train Hiawatha from Chicago 7:45. Take him right to Wilsons' to meet David. Sudden savage rain, lightning, at 9, lasts till 10; just as we arrive at Tall Trees, the lights go out, so that is Mick's welcome to what must have seemed to him a dark, gloomy, haunted, big old house. Lights come on after quarter hour and Micky much relieved to bed. Rain goes on till late.

AUGUST 6, Thursday. Trib: 8, 65; noon, 77; 6, 82. Gray, lowering, cool morning; rest of day warmish. 10 AM, clear, p.d. Micky seems happy here. Spends much of day with David Shiras, at Wilsons'. Family life as one doesn't see it in NY: Fefa's day: (1) David (a) has infected finger, (b), going to ride in Woodside Club horseshow on Saturday, (c) he's getting acquainted with Mick, to see if they want to go to North Shore together. (2): Their dog having pups. (3): Peter home from farm with gt splotches after anti-tetanus injection, after having stepped on rusty nail. (4) Question of Is Win overworking this vacation at Honeywell plant.

With Mick to call on Addison Lewises--Virginia to be married Saturday.

TRIP WITH MICHAEL, DAVIS SHIRAS, and JOSEPH TO DULUTH, GRAND MARAIS, HUNGRY JACK LAKE Hibbing Gull Lake. Total 996 mi. (Davis remaining in Excelsior to ride in horseshow; joining us Saturday evening by train.)

AUGUST 7, Friday. (Trib: 8, 66; noon, 73; 6, 76) At 7, dark rain threat--can we get away. Wait for mail and pack and do. But rain on and off all afternoon, on way to Duluth--some sudden and heavy showers when hard to go on.

Go via St. Cloud; Mick meets Mary and Virginia--a little uninterested in them, I thought; more impressed by Claude, whom met at office, because Claude knows the Big Woods, of which, just this moment, Mick feels that he is master--in anticipation. He uses and misuses terms like "back track trail" in some confusion of Back and Pack.

Golden rod everywhere now. Oats stacked. So little wheat even toward Duluth.

AUGUST 8, Saturday. Gray, cool, quiet all day....Shopping for Mick's camping supplies: scout axe, knapsack, maps, note book, which he will never use, laces for boots--hard to find, sun lotion etc. To movie "Mrs. Minniver." David arrives at 8, and I send the kids to bed. To Flame restaurant with Nathan and Mrs. Cohen, another newspaperman - name like Sydenham--Sigurd Arne of World Wide eatures, and meet there Bart Heffelfinger, en route from C.I.O. convention at Ely....Sigurd finds Duluth ugly and "unpainted," I, charming and impressive and neat!

fol. 82

AUGUST 9, Sunday. Trib: 8, 60: noon, 73; 6, 80. Off from Duluth for North Shore. Rain on and off all day. Lunch, Lutsen's--now jammed with the Old Ladies....In grayness, hard to tell where sky ends, sea of Lake Superior begins--glancing once, fishing boat seems to be an aeroplane in sky. The boys think well of the falls of Gooseberry River--once Groseinnliers River.....From Grand Marais, new terrain--GUNFLINT TRAIL, north. In real wilderness--birch, pine, spruce; probably don't actually see Misquah Hills, highest in Minnesota, but do see Pine Mt. Sometimes road, mostly washboard gravel, up and down like roller coaster.

At 5:30 to Gateway Lodge on Hungry Jack Lake, abt 3 miles from Canadian border. Cottage for 2 boys and Joseph, who seem friendly; small one for me, of which I become fond--so simple, concentrated.

Next page--see description of Lodge.

I am badly trained as a parent; conversation of both Micky and David wears me out. It is incessant, as we drive or eat. David asks unanswerable questions--when will we get to Gateway, will we like it, will there be fish, if we have a guide, will be be white or Indian, what time will supper be, what will we have to eat, where will we go next.

No questions for Mick: he is too exhibitionist, proud, show-off--and also intelligent and dominant. He lectures without stop on How Indians blaze trails, How much Chinese coolies are paid, how tiresome it is to see Coco-Cola signs along the road (this with a Lucius Beebe sneer), How Merlene Dietrich gets her effects....He is 12, just a year older than David, and twice as big....Joseph and I in front seat of ststion wagon bent mutely to the verbal storm....Mick talks as much as either his father or mother, which Christ knows is twice too much.

Evening, heavy rain, after seeing kids off to bed, sit cozy and warm in my small cottage (perhaps the selfishness of its being entirely mine is what I like) and read Blegen's schoolbookish but interesting "Building Minnesota," and to bed at 11 and sleep 8¼ hours.

AUGUST 10, Monday. Trib: 8, 63; noon, 70; 6, 74.

Send Mick and David off for all day in canoe with Ed, pleasant workman-type guide, fishing; I plan short story, "All Wives Are Angels," written to pay the rent, now that I have novel with Gid just fired from Heskett Foundation--a place where I can halt for a while.....Pleasant, writing here in woods, alone. David loses his perilous hunting knife. We'll keep it lost.

The boys come back at 5:30--not a fish, but happy, and ready to repeat, with new lakes, tomorrow.

Last night, cold enough to want extra blanket; this morning, wearing sweater along with coat, and gray morning. But sun out at 10, and all afternoon pleasant, fairly bright, warm in woods, not out on lake--where rowed with Joseph.

fol. 83

AUGUST 10, Monday, CONT.
Extract from letter written today.
GATEWAY LODGE, HUNGRY JACK LAKE.

beginning of carbon copy of part of a letter to Marcella Powers

The camp here is a mixture of wilderness and almost too ingenious woodsy decoration. The boys have a cabin, and I have one to myself nearby--all in thick woods with the lake below the slope. There are no bathrooms; my mind goes back to Sauk Centre and that questionable period known as youth as I wash with a tin pitcher and bowl, and attend the country backhouse. But the bed is astonishingly comfortable; I have a little stove of my own; there is room (between a Rustic Table and a Rustic Bureau, apparently made here, of split pine rods ornamenting pine bodies) for the card table which I have with a fussing of merit made into a literary desk; and I have a tiny porch of my own where I sit in a deep canvas chair, looking owlish and vacationed.

The main lodge--where you dine and where the food is pretty good boarding-house--has gone a little mad on Rustic Decoration....It is built of varnished logs. The chandeliers have strings of pine cones; on the table are hand-carved lumpy candlesticks ornamented with pine cones; the chairs are handmade of pine, with fringed deerskin cushions. The buffet is an immense effort of handcarved pine, the drawers ornamented with little dark pine trees made of pine cones against backgrounds of birchbark pasted on the pine end of the drawer. There are stuffed ducks, wolf skins, a moose head, a deer head.

In the lounge, an immense room which repeats the same idea, are enormous chandeliers with very small bulbs, a vast stone fireplace and, among other vivid but now unperilous animals, a tiny stuffed bear cub....There are even homemade pine picture frames with photographs of local scenery.

It's interesting, all this earnest effort for no very particular purpose. I suppose all vigorous people do it, in innocence worthy of a wise two-year-old child; you busily perfect a line which you are sure is going to raise the entire standard of the theater, and me--like these home-made-pine-coners--I set up my little table and write like hell in the innocent (and quite home-made) belief that I shall impress you!

The people, Mr. and Mrs. George Babbitt, mostly, or their 24-year-old young on honeymoon, not only do go fishing, and every day, all day, but they actually seriously talk about it in the evening, at dinner table, and recall the time when "Well, I thought I'd just make one more cast--I was using a Silver Widgeon, and I just gave it a nice easy toss-----"

But the reason why GOD really led me here is this: last evening (Sunday), after dinner, the wife of the hostess, a not-young woman, who was wearing a flowery blouse, blue overall sneakers, a maid's hair-band and a maid's tiny fluffy apron--which against the blue overalls looked somehow extremely unmodest, like Venus with a monogram on her fig-leaf--after having helped serve dinner sat quietly down at the piano and played, first, "Yankee Doodle" and then part of Beethoven's "Moonlight Sonata."

end of letter carbon

fol. 84

AUGUST 10--Monday--CONT 2

Sunset; festoons of crimson cloud--just brilliant wisps; the water silver and, in shadow of high trees, black....What one notes about these trees of the wilderness is the white streaks of birch trees in the dark body of the pines.....A rocky, not too hospitable country; and I don't know that I get any especial kick out of backhouses and no baths. Query: do the beefy Babbitts enjoy it so much here as an escape from realms where they can't, because slower and heavier witted, feel dominant?...The little inn-keeper enjoys a serene feeling of hospitality. His story of the woman who complained of no bathrooms and proud of his ansqer "Madam, there are people who come here who could bathe in gold bath tubs." She was supposed to be crushed.

AUGUST 11, Tuesday. Trib: 8, 56; noon, 72; 6, 78. At 7 AM, misty, dark in the cabin, and when open the doors for light, very cold; me with trousers, dressing gown, sweater, and winter scarf over pajamas before courage to strip and dress. Couldn't have been over 45 degrees. Warms rapidly with sun up. When sun still low in East, looking away from the lake, the impressive tall dark columns of the pink trunks stand out theatrically against golden mist of the birch foliage behind them. I drink coffee from the thermos bottle Joseph has left and contemplate.

Bright and warm by nine. Mick and David off for a two-day canoe trip, with Ed the guide, with tent for sleeping out overnight. As they go off, scene very pretty in a hardware-store-Xmas-calendar way: the graceful canoe, curving up fore and aft and moving so easily to the paddle strokes, the red and green of Ed's and Mick's mackinaw shirts, all against smooth water and then the solemn woods on sharply rising hills across the lake.

I stay home and write story "All Wives Are Angels." In the evening, instead of reading Minnesota history, read detective story, "Murder by Latitude" by Rufus King; he writes excellently, and so inevitable result that when the tightwad management turns off the electric lights at 11, I can't go to sleep, and hear all about the solitary cabin in the pines--not murderers and fog-horns, from the story, but merely creeping wolves, blundering bears bound on breaking in to gobble my toothpaste.

AUGUST 12, Wednesday. <u>Trib</u>: 8, 62; n, 75; 6, 81. Early morning, the lake, being narrow and hemmed in by wooded hills, is so much more hidden, shy, secret, even magic in th morning, before sun has risen high enough to expose it, than a fine broad lake like Minnetonka.

fol. 85

AUGUST 12, Wednesday--CONT

Important new use for young birch tree--sharpening pencils against it; just right texture.

Boys back from 2-day canoe trip; slept well in tent but caught only two fish. Gapon, proprietor, says there have been too many May flies lately. Ed the guide instituted "periods of silence," to get a little rest from the boys' chatter, and kept Micky from cussing by telling him that such language was regarded as Sis among the hardy men of the North.....Amateur movies of the region in hotel lounge at night. All amateur movies <u>must</u> show water-falls--and each for an extensive period.

First evening warm enough not to be rather uncomfortably chilly in cabin.

Mrs. Gapon--with the apron over slacks--is appropriately named Sue. She says (after, naturally, that they're "not ready for freedom yet and of course England will give it to 'em when they are") that Hindus are heathen, so <u>must</u>, for religion's sake, be held by Xian nation like Britain....And she actually told the story "For God's sake" (only she made it "For pity's sake") "drop the other shoe" which I remember having first heard told by Allan Updegraff (to me and 2 pick-up phone girls) in 1904.

Pa Gapon, a small man, proud of retort to woman who complain ed of lack of bath tubs, showers, and indoor toilets, "Madame," I said to her, "there are people who come up here who could bathe in gold bath tubs." I'm afraid she didn't say "So what?"

AUGUST 13, Thursday. Trib: 8, 63; n, 71; 6, 74.

Warm, bright, breezy at 7:30. Via Little Marais, Ely, Soudan & Tower (which shd explore) of Vermilion Iron Range (the boys fish an hour on Lake Vermilion) to Virginia and Hibbing, last hour in heavy rain. Evening, Hotel Androy. Met Lt. Commander McDonald--who volunteered to everybody, "I'm from Boston"--and Lieut. Rome of Navy Aviation recruiting, and heard them broadcast, station WMFG, basement of the Androy. Miss Coe, the business mgr of station, small, fine, quick, spinsterish, interested in Serbs-Croats-Slovenes, now proud inhabitants of Hibbing, and the bewildered Finns, who dont know whether US is for or vs their native land.

AUGUST 14, Friday Trib: 8, 65; n, 72; 6, 77 AM, pleasant; again with Dr. Morris Stevens of Hibbing h.s. to Hull-Rust-Mahoning mine, to show it to the boys. He pointed out high new Cyclone fence abt headquarters bldgs of Oliver Mining Company, and said the town murmured this indicated fear of coming labor war....Everybody in town wonders whether in 7 to 10 years, the high-grade iron ore will all be gone in Hibbing, then the low-grade, then the place a ghost-town....On road along Mesabi range,

fol. 86

AUGUST 14, Friday--CONT.

even the cement roads are ruddy from iron ore carried by tires....Looked over Coleraine of which the Oliver Mining Co makes so much as a "model town." Very commonplace development, distinguished only by Trout River, placed there by God, not Oliver......Hour's rain; through Brainerd to Gull Lake, and Ruttger's Sherwood Forest Lodge--again a cabin for me, and one for Jos and boys.

TOWN NAMES, NORTHERN MINNESOTA
Babbitt
Embarrass
Swatara
Finland

AUGUST 15, Saturday.

This Ruttger Lodge so much simpler than Hungry Jack--no coney chandeliers or bark pasted on furniture; but bathrooms, h&c, in every cabin, and lights (elec) not turned off at 11 every evening but on all night. Logs also, but simple and seems honest, and I think that helps to make the guests friendlier, as they certainly are.

Whole trip, doubt if thermometer ever over 75, even the warmest midafternoon back in the still pine woods, and nights probably down to 45-55, all of them--in mid-August.

Chilly and windy all day. Boys fish from dock of Lake Margaret, on one side of hotel pass, all morning--catching one pencil-sized perch--and out on Gull Lake with guide in PM. They seem to love fishing better even than movies--next to sleeping, eating, and screaming over recondite jokes.

Afternoon, great triumph: on Gull Lake, with the guide, the boys caught 20 fish, including one 4½ Northern Pike, which Micky caught--he had to rush right down to near-by taxidermist to have it mounted and sent to him in Vermont.....All the older people in the lodge discussed this catch and envied/,,,,,By the time he reaches Vt, Mick will have caught 60 that afternoon--<u>all</u> 4½ pounders...Much pleased as they caught only 2, whole time on Gunflint Trail. Saturday night--must have gone below 20; <u>two</u> extra blankets

"looking down on the contemplative plain."

AUGUST 16, Sunday. <u>Trib</u>: 8, 52; n, 68; 6, 73. Return to Excelsior, on p.d., except that whitish horizon made diffused glare hard on eyes. Lunch among the coy mottos and guns at the Buckhorn, Long Lake.

Saw wheat in shock. So much less wheat now in Minnesota.

A study of when children make a couple old; when, as the tradition has it, "keeps them young."

fol. 87

AUGUST 17 - Monday.

Trib: 8, 57; noon, 71; 6, 78. Damp, gray, airless in morning....6 PM, lake veiled and beautiful in mist; almost first time I've seen it so, though hear there's been lots of fog while I've been away...Micky, day at the Wilsons'.

AUGUST 18 - Tuesday. Trib: 8, 63; noon, 73; 6, 79. Gray, damp, fairly cool. Sun a red surprised eye, then vanishes. 3 PM, only 68. Mick goes in town with David. Evening, all the kids together at dinner: Mick, Winfield and Peter and David Shiras, Fefa and Me--Al in Detroit.

AUGUST 19--Wednesday. Trib: 8, 68; noon, 80; 4, 90; midnight, 74. At 8 AM, warmish, gray, promise of sun. Later, clear. A great sunset, the lake a flood of gold, from Lafayette Club, where dine with Mick after tea with Mahala Douglas - "the Duchess of Deephaven" - and Bolles Rogers. Evening rather hot. Heat wave coming?....Two weeks from today, shall be in Peterborough with Marcella.

AUGUST 20 - Thursday. Trib: 8, 64; noon, 83; 4, 91; 6, 89; midnight, 74. No heat wave yet out here at lake; cool bright day, p.d., tho horizon veiled. 70 at 9:30 AM. PM, islands seem floating on stilled lake. A perfect early fall day. The most beautiful thing about it, the hot light on birch trunks standing on edge of bluff, seen against pale blue water. Hot in town, but not here.

AUGUST 21, Friday. Trib: 6, 75; 8, 75; 10, 82; noon, 86; 3, 91; 6 PM, 91; 9, 85; midnight, 81; 2 AM, 78. Clear and cool in the morning, p.d., but heat wave does hit here in PM--88 at 6:15 PM. Micky off to Chicago, Albany, Vermont. In town, thermometer front of Hotel Nicollet 90 at 2 PM. Evening here, first real heat I've felt since July 16-17-18.

AUGUST 22, Saturday. Trib: n, 64; 6, 65; midnight, 59. The heat wave has lasted just 3 days in Mpls, only 1 here. AM, 7, it was 68, with high gray rushing wind. The sun out at 7:45, in and out all day. Midnight, 60 here. Evening: new people met, Hartwell, grain, be neighbor on Mt. Curve Ave.; Allison, X ray doctor, wife was on NYTimes; Luyten (?) University astronomer.

AUGUST 23, Sunday. (Start East week from today) Trib: 8, 49; 9, 50; noon, 55; 6, 61; midnite, 52. 56 at 9 and 10 AM; heat on in house.

fol. 87v

Lake colors at sunrise: pale rose, the shores & channels magic; sun up, a cloudy red ball; then water amethyst, then burnished gold; then rippling silver edged w. gold

fol. 88

AUGUST 23--CONT.

60 at 6 PM. Afternoon, however, comfortable in sun outdoors: at Wilsons, watching Al, Peter, Mrs. Potter, and son, and John and Marx Baxter place tennis--the woods thick beyond the court, phlox thick in borders behind. Sunset about 8:10; after it, watch on East, rose and pale gold, on west, cold blue-gray with woods feeling wild against it; and black trees on islands standing out against water so much more than when both in light....The obviously greater coziness here, when cold, with lamp lighted inside.....I shall miss this lake, its companionable incessant changes. Midnight, 52°.

AUGUST 24, Monday. 7:30 AM, 52; gray, then sun comes out for p.d. Addison Lewises, evening. Trib: 8, 44; 9, 51; noon, 63; 6, 70.

AUGUST 25, Tuesday. Trib: 8, 61; noon, 73; 6, 78. AM, clear, cool--not cold - p.d....Doing nothing but work on novel, to be able to lv it when go to NY...Addison in small while in evening re Aaron Burr and Long Lake MSS, (no--wrong - he came on Wedn.)*

AUGUST 26, Wedn. Trib: 8, 62; n, 64; 6, 70. AM, gray, 64 at 9:30. Rained last nite. Even: Dr. Arey & wfe, then Addison.*

AUGUST 27- Thur. Trib. 8, 68; n, 76; 6, 79. AM all gray; 7 to 10, 70. Sun out before noon and perfect PM with sweet slight tang of autumn...Late evening, 3/4 old moon, sharp tree shadows, lites across late. Mosquitos terrible...Strain from work, hard to go to sleep--hear burglars, dragons, characters!

AUGUST 28, Friday. Trib: 8, 63; n, 69; 6, 85 mid, 76. 9:30, light fog, 67. Sun out at 12. PM hot and very moist...Even: with Wilsons, Congressman Dick Gale & wife 'Pete' to Earle Brown for Sheriff rally in Mpls.

AUGUST 29, Saturday. A bright summer ends in rain--tho it's pleasant to sit out on porch, overlooking lake, in rain, and hear distant train-whistle.

This will be a furlough on this diary - August 30 to September 23--off tomorrow evening to Fort Sheridan, to see Wells, Peterborough, New York, and back.

fol. 89

AUGUST 30 - Sunday. Last night and night before last, much too hot for refreshing sleep, but this is a radiant, cool, perfect day with which to wind up Minnesota summer: the trees such deep, rich, joyous green aianst the blue water....The effect of moving leaves seen through the slats of the sleeping porch blinds is magic--like a living moving picture.

Phrase: "It's going to be a scorcher today."

Eleven PM, leave for the East.

AUGUST 31, at Fort Sheridan with Wells, now a 2nd lieutenant.

SEPTEMBER 2-3: Peterborough Players, New Hampshire; Marcella in "Quiet Wedding."

SEPTEMBER 2-21: at the Dorset, 30 W. 54th St., NYC.

On return, Joseph reports that during almost all of the 3½ weeks that I have been away, it has been chilly in Minnesota, with lots of rain.

fol. 90

SEPTEMBER 22, Tuesday. Evening, return from New York by the Burlington Zephyr. Joseph has moved my bks etc. from the lake to 1500 Mount Curve Avenue, Minneapolis, end of Humboldt Ave.--a pleasant stucco "English style" house with casement windows.

Sept. Equinox
WEATHER SEPT 22-26. Flurry snow 10 minutes, Thursday 24th. Night of 25th, snow all evening and night; morning, at 7, trees all carved of silver, but most of snow gone from street by 10, lawns come out green again - but lumps of snow on trees make them like gt hydrangea bushes. Snow all gone, mid-PM...Evening before, snow flies abt street lamp globe like swarms of silver bugs.

Duck hunting season opens Sat 26th, so Johnny Baxter, Addison Lewis, et al. went north day before and are caught there on snow.

Temperature: Wedn, 23: TRIB: 8, 46; n, 43; 6, 44; mid, 39. Thur: 8, 33; n, 39; 6, 39; midn, 31. Fri: 8, 33; n, 44; 6, 43; midn, 33.

Sept. 24, Thursday: office, 318½ Folwell Hall, seeing students for writing class; PM, tea at Huntington Brown, Eng. prof in U: Beaches and Dean Thomas there; met Robt Penn Warren, Tremaine McDowell, Clark.....Evening: housewarming, John-Mary-Helen Baxter, McNally's, Addison & Dorothy Lewis; Fefa Wilson and niece Ginny Lewis in.

Sept. 25, Friday; again office. Evening, home reading Maritta Wolf's "Night Shift."

Sat. 26th, home most of day, getting order at last out of mess of papers, ready to go back to novel. Ginny and Dorothy Bennett in for tea.

fol. 91

SEPT. 27, Sunday.

Trib: 8, 32; n, 36; 6, 40; midn, 31. Two churches: St. Luke's, dead respectable imitation of English country life, neat Gothic interior, congregation--"women in gloves"--lifelessly intoning service and singing, rector, Mr. Tyner, a Canadian with a hell of an English accent, a Manly Athlete, too, who writes golf notes for the paper, droning a sermon to the effect that We ought not to do things for us but for Him and Humanity.

Then the glorious, free, melodic crook church of the Christian Temple: pastor, the Rev. Isebelle Hall, a slim, active, almost tap-dancing young vaudeville gal, in white with, I think, bare legs, rasping voice but skill in leading congregation who sang the originals of Hallelujah I'm a Bum etc. as spiritedly as the IWW cd have; and the visiting evangelist, Mattie Howard, God's Miracle Woman, fat behind and bosom, calm, drab, thick-skinned, lizard face. The two women hate each other. THREE collections; one, you carry it down to pan on platform; two, they come after you; three, God's Miracle Woman having arrived late, takes her own. This is new to me in the glorious world of Gantryism.

SEPT. 28, Monday. Trib: 8, 26; n, 40; 6, 50; mid, 44. Warming. Sun through shrubs throws blotches of pure gold on white bathroom curtains, turning them into figured tapestries, in early morning; the l3af shapes just a lil blurred on the curtain, as tho drawn.

11 AM on, bright and sunny. Curious that after the recent snow, the trees here in the coty not turned yet--quite green.

To Grace Flandrau's--the old Flandrau House on Pleasant Avenue, St. Paul, down under Summit, with old farm still stretching up back of it; frame house of the '60's; small library, old Turkish Room, picture gallery--built by the old Judge to house portrait of his wife which son Charles took out in yard and burned. Small library, also, with high top book shelves--"to breed mice," said Grace. Walter Murray, of my class in Univ, and Harry Woodward, radio, there.

Fefa Wilson says that for a prosperous young married woman here, however capable or restless, to take a paid job wd be socially doubtful, if not disgrace. They must stick to committees, Red Cross work, etc.

SEPT 29, Tuesday. Trib: 8, 37; n, 54; 6, 65; midnite, 57. It is now light from about 6:30 AM to 7:30 PM (CWT equals 5:30 to 6:30) Afternoon clear and beautiful. Walk to end of Mt. Curve - overlook city....Would-be woman student for my class calls; mind a mess of criticisms already recd from teachers, husband & other relatives--so she wants some more! Hartwell, grain buying executive from Genl Mills, next-door neighbor, studying Spanish and Swedish in Univ, evenings. Has been in South America.

fol. 92

SEPT. 30, Wednesday. Trib: 7, 44; 11, 55; n, 60; 6, 74; m, 56 Summer again. My first class at the Univ. With weak good nature I have let in too many middle-aged woman "Special Adult" students, so I have 52 students instead of the 20 or less that I shd have. But some of the youngsters look gd.

Evening: "bachelor party": Al Wilson, Bill McNally, Russell Plimpton, Bob Flannagan.

Sunset in clear mirror of prairie pool, amid fields grown dark.

OCTOBER 1942

OCT. 1, Thur. Trib: 7, 55; n, 64; 6, 70; mid, 60. Evening, Beaches, met President Coffey of Univ--a broad round capable Methodist executive; Castell, philosophy dept; Morgan, lawyer, room mateof Joe Beach at Harvard, where met him with Arthur Upson. Mrs. Harding, U of M press.

OCTOBER 2, Friday) 502 mile trip to Otter Tail County, probably
OCTOBER 3, Sat) last of 1942; that, at new Federal speed of 35 miles an hour, re rubber saving, is equal to 700 mile trip last summer.

(Trib, Friday: 7, 51; noon, 62; 6, 77.

Leaves just turning on way to Benson; up in Otter Tail, well turned, but this year--frost too early? or contrast with Vermont?--don't seem very high color; and on Friday, leaves dusty--seem a little better in rain, which came Saturday noon and lasted most of the way back to Mpls Saturday even.

Corn is somewhat less than half cut. The stalks where standing are all gray. In general, the green almost gone from the country/ You now see stubble fields and straw stack; and couple times saw late grain threshing....Near there, wheat dust in the air adds to feeling of brown fall.

All day, Friday, smoky horizon, not see far. Saturday, in wetness, the brown low hills below Fergus like a moorland--feebly makes one think of Hardy's "Return of the Native" which now reading, but softer, more sympathetic, than Egdon Heath.....And less ancient human life! Blackbirds gathered for fall migration--excitedly discussing the journey south--they whirl in black clouds. ....Saw NO ducks or geese, tho now season.

Late PM light, Friday; the corn stalks a delicate russet shining against the black soil.....Part of the PM really hot; you felt uneasy, as if cyclone weather.

River Inn, Fergus: tho a good inn, rooms lack either bedside table or a closet; and the courthouse bells nearby a nuisance.

Saturday, rain washing off dust, colored leaves brighter.....How brave of the hunters to attack the tame pheasants with nothing but shot gun--ph season open, 10/15

fol. 93

OCTOBER 2-3, CONT.
(Copy of a letter)

beginning of carbon copy of part of a letter to Marcella Powers

At the entrance to the River Inn in Fergus Falls, Minnesota, a town of 10,000, there is a book-magazine-"souvenir" store, not bad for a town of that size; actually has some books--a feature not invariable in small-town book stores.....I go in for my evening Fergus Falls Journal, after the day's motoring, to see what movie I shall attend this Friday evening; hitherto, on visits to that quite competent little inn, I have been waited on by a slim, nervous, busy woman who has spoken of her husband and his (proper) admiration for the works of SL....Now the husband himself is there; thin, spectacled, school-masterish, a young fifty. He practically grabs me; gabbles "I was one of the first people to read your first novel--not that I care a damn what <u>you</u> think--I have just been out for twenty-six weeks with a circus as a mind reader--here!" He thrusts into my hands, now trembling with a fear of getting hypnotized, a blank sheet of his business stationery and a blank envelope. On these he appears as PAUL PERRAULT, but in private (if any) life he is not less admirably named HAROLD FEATHERSTONE.

He speeds on, "If I were to tell you about the inside of the phony medium game, I would give you a plot that would make you a best seller.....I'm in intimate touch with the FBI--they come to me for all their dope about fortune-tellers who blackmail poor gels living in apartments in Minneapolis--janitor sorts their love letters out of their waste-basket and sells 'em to fake mediums--the FBI are depending on me to show up the Ku Klux Klan, which is starting up again in Otter Tail County--oh, I come back here because I was born here, but I get around everywhere--Minneapolis, Rochester, Iowa, Missouri, travel with my own mind-reading show in winter--I meet everybody, Abbott Deutsch of the Benedictines at St. John's College--bankers, manufacturers, with great big houses, all brick, they come to me and say, 'Mr. Perrault, if I'd only come to you twenty years ago, my whole life would have been different, and I would know now which of my four children are legitimate. Lewis, I'll take you out this evening and introduce you to a lot of people you ought to meet here--fine girl, used to be with the Russian ballet, got sick of travel; she's opened a photographic studio here, she's also a fine painter; decorated the studio herself; you'll see. She's just as good as Steichen....Wait, wait, here, I want to show you--you see these mimeographed books--from the Nelson Enterprises Company of Columbus,

fol. 94

OCT 2-3 CONT.--2

Ohio--and then here's their printed catalogue--heft it--you don't think they'd get out a big catalogue like that if there weren't a lot of crooked fortune-tellers buying this magic junk--you bet--I could give you a plot for a story that would make people's hair stand up! The things I could tell you about this town--22 churches and 11 bootleggers--supposed to serve nothing but beer, but I know about 'em--I said to the county commissioner, 'Say, instead of a four-sided clock on the court house, you ought to have a two-faced one--that would be appropriate, eh?'

"Some time I'll take you out to Underwood and show you where Doc Cunningham lived--English remittance man, used to be a gun-runner, always carried a .44, murdered his wife's lover and somebody always trying to get him--died of the D.T.'s, his daughter was in a convent in Texas--the druggest there, Sam, he was a dope-fiend, one time the Doc laid down a bill somebody sent him on the counter, and damn' if Sam didn't pick it up and fill it--thought it was a prescription."

.....

But by and by I saw that Mr. Featherstone-Perrault wasn't so much a village boaster as a sort of small boy, inappreciated in this village and trying to show his new toys to the stranger/

end of letter carbon

Friday, Saturday; so many newts and frogs crossing road and killed by cars; Sunday, so many garter snakes.

SIGNS ALONG ROAD: Christ Died for Our Sins "And him that cometh unto Me I will in no wise cast out." Gospel Signs, Minneapolis.

Return for peaceful evening, Saturday.

****

OCTOBER 4, Sunday. Trib: 8,53; n,61; 6, 68; midnm 52. So beautuful in morning, drive with Joseph to Taylor's Falls, down by now under-repair #95 to Scandia, Copas, Marine, on to Stillwater. Glorious Indian summer weather till abt 3:30 when suddenly black rain which pursues us in.....See notes under Valleys.....Sunday Tribune states for 3d time, wrong, that I'll direct Bob Hanscombe and company in Dodsworth at--gymnasium of Wesley Methodist! Again I call John Sherman and Bill McNally at Trib to complain--tomorrow shall see Dr. Mecklenburg and Handsombe. (PS--do!)

Trees along St. Croix seem to me more nobly colored than up in Otter Tail--note dark green pines and white birches standing out more than ever among the scarlet-amber...Guilty of disloyalty to Otter Tail as look across St. Cr to those Wisconsin cliffs and uplands. Think I shall get a farm here--not too near to Marine and the intelligensia--or wives of brokers, who are the same thing.....The sumac a bright scarlet.

fol. 95

OCTOBER 4, Sunday--CONT.

The road--old 95--N from Copas (above Marine) being rebuilt--left, probably re war, a welter of mud. Just where this repair begins, I stood on hillock on edge of road looking toward the St. Croix, and realized that just then and there I had Indian Summer at its very best: sweet cool-warm air, the sky blue with touches of cirrus and vast cumulus; far off, in Wisconsin (and to see another state is always deceptively better!) the distant blue-gray hills to N without which no scenery; nearby, silver-brown corn-stalks and year-old hay stack; across the river, a pale sage-green pasture; just below, on slope going down to river on Minnesota side, the massed trees orange and a dozen shades of green (leaf, sage, silver, yellow); maroon, cherry-red, terra-cotta, with the deep green of unchanged pipes, and white birch trunks the more dazzling against this high color. Then across the river, red barns on uplands.

Perfect ripe beauty and peace--perfect but for the lack of a girl....And, motoring on, in less than half an hour it was raining like hell!

OCT. 5, Monday. Trib: 8, 48; n. 58; 6, 65. Re the false news about my directing, a slightly scared Hanscombe brought in by Dr. Mecklenburg, the town's large Methodist preacher. He is fat and amiable. Says he is gt friend of Bill Stidger; that his own radio program is the most popular in the Twin Cities; that he is Qdoing one of the greatest social works in the Northwest."

Radiant Indian Summer day. The leaves in the city now more than ½ turned; streets are golden avenues. And heaps have fallen last 3 days; few before. Seem to be few scarlet leaves in city—except sumac... Shd have noted in Otter Tail: crickets in drying grass, very antic.

OCT. 6. Tue. Trib: 8, 49; n, 64; 6, 67; mid, 50. Tho been only a very slight frost and no real storm, suddenly the leaves are all falling; nearly ½ gone in 2 or 3 days. They heap the walks, roadways, lawns up here on the hill in smooth mounds; thru suddenly bare trees, you see the valley below as formerly could not from this house (1500 Mt. Curve)

Sunday, above, cont: Tourists gather at stated "view" on road down to Taylor's Falls; and at bridge where loudspeaker ann a 3-mile trip thru dalles....What wd tourists do without camera, radio in car, gum, postcards, signs telling them where to look at the obvious?

Monday 5th Cont: Bob Hanscomb, Log Cabin Theater last summer, started amateur players in Wesley Methodist Gym; ann I wd direct Candida & Dodsworth; had to stop him, had him here with the large, plump, much travelled Dr. Mecklenburg (berg?) of the church; then pretty girl from Candida company--Timmy Sabor, who lives mostly in Hollywood.

fol. 96

OCTOBER 7, Wednesday. Trib: 8, 42; 11, 62; n, 66; 2, 77; 6, 77; midnite, 65. NOTE rise of 35 degrees in 6 hrs, 8 AM to 2. Indian summer continues, golden pd's. So warm in PM that what would have been glorious as a summer day was resentfully warm, with so rapid a rise in temp--such a lull now when one had been prepared for battle of winter.

Second class at Univ: rem. Love Cruickshank, Marion Lee, MarionEdwards, Ruth Cole, Adeline Berg.

Fefa's notion abt prosperous women who cdn't work here back by Lily MJ's apologetic explanation that she works extra hrs in a shop and is part-time companion to an old woman "just to pass the time."

OCTOBER 8, Thursday. Trib: 8, 51; n, 60; 3, 65; 6, 63. Another perfect Indian Summer day....Except for lawns, shrubs, a Lombardy poplar that I noted, all still green, the leaves left are now all yellow, and with the pale smoke from burning leaves, one looks out at a world not of green but of sun thru fretworks of gold and silver.

OCTOBER 9, Friday. Trib: 8, 41; n, 56; 6, 66; midn, 49. Finished first draft of novel GIDEON PLANISH today.

Another perfect Indian Summer day; cold in AM, hottish in PM. Drove to Minnehaha Parkway, very pretty along the creek, and attractive Lake Nokomis, where season less adv than here; more green and in turned leaves more scarlet; I never knew that fall coloration differs so much a few miles apart. The lake utterly placid, a little misty, trees and red roofs mirrored in it. Many planes from nearby Navy training gield...Back here, near dusk, the mingling of a low glow from sunset, smoke from leaves, gold leaves, and bare graceful elm boughs, a rather wild beauty in peacefulness.

OCTOBER 10, Saturday. Another perfect Indian Summer day. Drove to St. Croix Valley again, explored North of Taylor's Falls, far as Almelund. As beautiful as TF to Stillwater...Coppery oak leaves, rich and metallic, against blue sky....Trees a good bit faded since last Sunday....How river comes toward you, not side to, as you drop to Taylor's Falls, and Wis side, grassy upland mounds as well a dalles and woods...

Turkey farms, with outdoor roosts.....Stacy, Minn., pop, perhaps 40: Wally & Myrtle's Lunch....Lunch at North Branch, Minn.--horrible blotting paoer "Denven Sandwich," all quiet till 2 high-school senior boys in sweaters come in; the dull-faced barelegged waitress brightens, radio is turned on, vast shrieks and bawls from it giving weights and heights of members of U of Ill football team--the nadir in interest--the boys scrape their stools on cement floor and cackle....People do NOT like quiet.

Evening, to Helen Rand's big marble house, on Lake Harriet, for dinner; talk mostly to Sigurd Ueland...On way, Lake Calhoun--the smoky sunset-colored lake, with white sailboats at anchor. PM, tea: Ginny, Faubion Bowers, Tom Sakamoto & Mrs. Tsukahira from Army Intel. lang. school.

fol. 97

OCTOBER 11, Sunday. Another pd Indian summer. Trib: 8, 46; n. 66; 4, 76; mid 57 Range 30° Undergraduate part of my Univ writing class here for supper.

You find a sleek, urbane person like Billy Parker who has little travelled, who knows no known language; you find rustic, awkward, American-toned people like Norman Davis, Cordell Hull, Col. House, who have been in every strange land, dined with kings and professors, may also know no languages or may know a dozen. Travel does what?

Among writing class here: Ruth Cole, Love Cruickshank, Janet Nelson, Joan McQuary, Adelyne Bergm Pat Brueckner, Mr. Dodge the unwelcome who wanted to talk about phallic symbolology, Marian Lee, Marion Edwards.

OCT. 12, Monday. Trib: 8, 48; n, 63; 6, 71. Another Indian Summer p.d. Lunch with Governor Harold Stassen, tray on his desk in his office, with portraits ex-governors, incl Knute Nelson. Ice cream and blueberry pie--the noblest food. Stassen may be Republican candidate president in 1948 --if re-elected this fall, he will resign after legislature session & enter navy in wh a lieut commander in the reserve. He wore a double-breasted blue coat with a faint red stripe, no vest or belt; elbows shiny from desk. Pleasant, intelligent. Talk of India, of nations restoring resources to subject countries.

Evening, dull reception-supper for new faculty members. Talks on Washington information bureaus by Ralph Casey and Nifsinger (?) of U of M Sch of Journalism,

Some English words one may suddenly see as being more curious and improbable and ugly than any Russian word: FEW, ASK, O'CLOCK, POCKET HANDKERCHIEF BORDER,

OCTOBER 13, Tuesday. Trib: 8, 48; n, 61; 6, 72; midn, 54. Another Ind Sum p.d. Walk ih the placid suburb-like section here on Kenwood Hill--PM still and brooding Ind Summer.

OCTOBER 14, Wedn. Trib: 8, 44; noon, 59; 6, 71. Blackout, 9:30-10. Johnny Baxter a fire warden, with red-lens electric torch.

OCTOBER 15, Thur. Trib: 8, 43; n, 60; 3, 71; 6, 68. Another I S p.d., a little hazier, cool & sweet. If I go to New York in December, I shall miss this quiet, the trees and lawns and shrubs seen framed by net-curtained casement windows, and plenty of rooms & room. Dinner, Mr. and Mrs. Toffef Jacobson--Lily Mac Gibbon--Ginny, with Steve Harris in afterward.

fol. 98

OCTOBER 16, Friday. Trib: 8, 45; n, 62; 6, 66. With today, 13 days of unchanged I.S.p.d. Evening, Brenda Ueland's: Gabby there, engaged to Dick Brueckner--Pat's bro, son Univ prof, soon going into army--Brenda, and Meridel Le Sueur, ardent communist fictioneer, was 10 years an actress for Belasco et al, still darkly handsome.

OCTOBER 17, Sat. In this last of the autumn radiance, air so thinly sweet, every twig clear. PM, walk with Bill McNally along Mt. Curve to Kenwood Park and Lake of the Isles; pretty low hills.

OCTOBER 18, Sunday. Trib: 8, 40; n, 59; 6, 67. Walk with Ruth Cole to Kenwood Pk., then class here, with Alice Rose; Mrs. Eugene Horne, an "adult special."

Best writers in my class, as noted so far: Sheila Alexander, Janet Nelson, Mrs. Horne, Mrs. Irene Byrne, Mrs. Geo Rosenberg, Mrs. Louise Clayton, A. C. Regli.

OCTOBER 19, Mon. Trib: 8, 44; n, 62, 6, 72. Sixteenth day perfect Indian Summer. 4-6, tea for English Faculty at the "Institute for Continuation Studies." God how I hate desultory crowds. Miss Jackson, poetry teacher. Scotty of the Minn Bk Store. Robert Penn Warren, pal with Allen Tate and John Peale Bishop, who don't like me, as ever posed over his pipe, eyes down, listening and nodding as one who quietly knows better.

Only shrubs, pines, lawns in leaf now. 6:30 PM, look through bare enlaced elm boughs to a bright ½ moon, above it a pink cloud.

OCTOBER 20, Tue. Trib: 7, 49; 5, 56; n, 65; 6, 64. Late PM, walk with Janet Nelson. High wind, dark clouds, threaten that this, the 17th ISpd, is about the end of Indian Summer....Steve Harris in, talk of Ginny and her parents.

Evening, at huge house, formerly belonged Backus, of Stanley Hawks for dinner to Steve Benet, here for lecture: Gid and Mrs. Seymour, Fefa Wilson, Bolles Rogers being a h.a. Imperialist and actually telliny the story of "I was in London, storm (but Bolles made it Fog) and paper "Continent Isolated." Jesus but London must 've been crowded with Amers that day.

OCTOBER 21, Wedn. Trib: 8, 42; n, 41; 6, 40; midn, 34. First gray morning in over 2 weeks; at 9, down to 40 by thermometer here at house, with feel of snow coming. In early evening, it comes, a light snow melting as it falls. End of Indian Summer. Class....Joan McQuary here for dinner. Stories of Mitropoulos, conductor of Mpls Symph Orchestra; Bird or Bird of psychology dept; Dagmar Beach; man wanted Mitrop conducting 5th Symph to make V for victory with fingers end of --- --.

OCTOBER 22, Thur. Trib: 8, 35; n, 35; 6, 35; midn, 32. AM, gray, not snowing; sun out mild, 11:30. Snow 4:30, few minutes

fol. 99

OCTOBER 23, Fri. Trib: 8, 30; n, 33; 6, 38; midn, 34. Now light from 7:30 (CWT, 6:30 GT) to about 7.

OCTOBER 24, Sat. When awaken, drizzly snow, which lasts till mid-morning. Shrubs with snow-clusters like shining white flowers. All day at Minneapolis Indtitute of Art, judging exhibit of Mpls-St. Paul artists, with Gideon Seymour, chief editorial writer of Mpls Star-Journal, and Fred Sweet, hd dept painting, Chicago Art Institute, with Russell Plimpton and Mrs. Marjorie Sirich there; Mrs. Alfred Pillsbury, the local duchess--the wise, cultivated, Boston-born Gretchen--and Macmillan (which one?) at lunch at Institute--creamed oysters in front of fireplace...We "judged" oils, water-colors, drawings amd etchings, and even sculpture. Pathet rough stone sculp which a local negro sculptor submits year after year....Follrath, 1st oil (houses) and drawing--both excellent. Evening, late, McNally's: Forrest and Mrs. Spencer, whom I knew in American Legation in Vienna; Miles and Alice McNally; Dr. Strachauer, who operated on Gracie for appendicitis, over 20 yrs ago.

OCTOBER 25, Sunday. Trib: 8, 25; n, 27; 4, 26; 6, 26; mid, 21; 2 AM, 19. Snowed during night. Snow starts again 9 AM. Lawns that were bare and green yesterday covered all day, while I enjoy not going out to Japanese student dinner at Savage. Alternation, snows, quits, sun out a few minutes; world of elms, snow, uptilting Mt. Curve Ave, stone Rogers castle beyond, become at etching. Call M long distance. Eddie Ruben, theater owner, across street.

OCTOBER 26, Mon. Trib: 8, 19; n, 26; 6, 34; mid, 28. Snow sticks for a while; lawns white at 8 AM. But brite sun PM melting, lawns 2/3 green again.

OCTOBER 27, Tue. Trib: 8, 29; n, 31; 6, 34. John Baxter north to hunt teal. Doing nothing but revise and copy Planish.

OCT. 28, Wedn. Trib: 8, 27; n, 32; 6, 37. Noon, snow all gone except pockets. 2 PM, gray promises new snow, but it rains, 8 PM on. Fefa Wilson to my class; lecture on magazine taboos; with her & Joan McQuary to The Varsity for coffee.

To Grace Flandrau's, Pleasant Av. St. Paul; Franklin P. Adams and Dorothy--yes, D. Thompson, both in St. P, tho independently, to lecture, one in PM, one evening, for St. P Institute--for dinner. Amiable. To D's lecture in Auditorium--11,000 people! Ben Ritter of Pioneer Press in afterward, and D train at 10:55. Joseph and I lost in darkness & rain returning to Mpls.

OCT. 29, Thur. Trib: 8, 36; n, 38; 6, 44; mid, 50. All day, fog, drizzle; snow all gone. Even, speak to English section, Minn Educational Assn--teachers--"do you know enough?"

fol. 100

OCT. 30, Fri. Trib: 8, 38; n, 39; 6, 48; mid, 38. Bright, sunny, cool but not cold all day...Mrs. Margaret Bovey (sister of Anson Jackson) and son, an ensign, in for tea. Joan McQuary, dinner.

OCT. 31, Sat. Trib: n, 40, 6, 45; mid, 33. p.d., brilliant sun--early October again!...Nothing more beautiful than shadow of bough on plaster wall. Tea-supper, Eddie-Marie Ford: Thorp, swimming instructor; Starke, Ginny Hathaway, Mrs. Kenn (Eng husband a prisoner in Singapore).

Sky over river an etching of satisfying elm boughs against sky pale, then black-streaked green.....Virginia & Steve Harris.

NOVEMBER

NOV. 1, Sunday. Trib: 8, 30; n, 42; 6, 42; midn, 35. Fairly bright all day....Class here. Note: Love Cruickshank, Ruth Cole, Adelyne Berg, Joan McQuary, Eugenia Horne, Marion Lee, Janet Nelson.

NOV 2, Mon. Trib: 8, 33; n, 36; 4, 38; 6, 37; midn, 29. Gray AM, clear bright PM....Lunch, panelled and beamed Mpls Club; McNally and

Sumner McKnight....Dinner, Lilian MacGibbon Jaconson, Hildred Howe Smith, Kit McNiece (Mrs. Roy Hoople). Beethoven in Paris on wall.

NOV 3, Tue. Trib: 8, 22; 11, 32; 1 PM, 40; 6, 43; midn, 39. AM, softly bright, frost glitter on lawns. Day mostly clear, bright. Sunset: plates of gold in layers; dark sparkle about the trees in late sunlight.

NOV 4, Wedn. Trib: 8, 38; n, 42; 6, 48. Light abt 7:30 to 6:20 CWT (6:30-5:20 GT) AM, no colder, except penetrating wind.

NOV 5, Thur. Trib: 8, 37; n, 34; 6, 32. Dinner, Alfred (and Gretchen) Pillsbury's graystone castle on Stevens & 22nd--varnished woodwork, nooks and alcoves and panelling. Alfred, son of old Gov John Sargent P, founder of Univ. Dorothy Atkinson, Pierce Butlers, Bob & Ruth Pack, Mme Silvercruys sculptress.

NOV 6, Fri. Trib: 8, 23; n, 28; 6, 33. Fairly clear, some sun all day. Mpls Symphony in Northrop Auditorium Dimitri Mitropoulos conduct; Rudolph Serkin soloist--Brahms concerto in D minor. Carved proscenic arch, graystone, with cge symbols, looks Celtic. Mitropoulos like a Russian mummy; extra long dress tails, stride; hands flutter like snakes, hands arch. No baton or score. Serkin on bench before playing is erect, lifeless--a Charley McCarthy, ready for DM to talk into him....Applause is like beat of heavy rain...Lois and Bill McNally here after the show.

NOV 7, Sat. US INVADES NORTH AFRICA Snow starts, big soft flakes, melt as fall, 10:30 AM, and quits and sun out at 10:45. PM, sunny, fairly warm.

fol. 102

NOV 8, Sun. Trib: 8, 31; n, 38; 6, 46. Hazy but sunny day, fairly warm. Lunch, Mahala Douglas, Deephaven, Minnetonka. Road out, houses and higher hills that were unseen in summer re foliage now surprise you; from terrace at Waldon (sic), for first time see noble bays of lake, and islands. Bolles Rogers: “I don’t care much for Nature.” How that must hurt Nature! Evening: Baxters, Dr. Lewis & Hannah Daniel.

NOV 9, Mon. AM gray, raining, chilly. Temp all day: 20 to 30

NOV 10, Tue. Lewis Daniel's office for injection/ Evening: McNallys, Alfred Wilson: (he will rent this house when I leave at $150.00 - I lose $50.00) Faubion Bowers, now a lieut. Tom, Tsukahira and lovely wife Lily.

NOV 11 - Wedn. Ar,istice day, no class. Misty AM but pd PM; radiant blue sky--Columbia Heights seen from Mt. Curve. I've missed being out in such glorious weather - still revising and copying Planish ALL the time. Sunset: sheet of crimson at end of Mt. Curve, against it, the delicately etched elm twigs; at the point of this true Gothic arch, the line of st lamps as jewels; utter quiet, with lights coming on in homes. Evening, dinner at Steve Harris's house--he not there; in army. His mother sister of Sidonie Gruenberg. Nice polylingual Jewish bunch; Grauben, 1st cellist in Mpls Symph Orch.

NOV 12, Thur. Warm, hazily bright all day; 30 to 40. Evening: Bob and Ruth Pack (now living same luxurious 2-family house, Lincoln and Girard, as Chas Harris; he is abt 70, looks 55; retiring soon as prest Northern States Power Co.). Helen Rand, Bolles Rogers, John & Mrs. Pillsbury, "Mike" (Richard) Elliott, univ dept psych and a Boston Brahmin--his wife was in American Library in Paris; Swedish Consul Hellstrom, Betty Cowles....Reading popular theology aloud starts discussn.

NOV 13, Fri. Gray, 20 above all PM. Symphony: Brahms 1st; Carroll Glenn girl violinist soloist in MozarT Concerto 5

NOV 14, Sat. Indian summer back; pd, 40 at 4 PM, clear, brite

NOV 15, Sun. At last broke down, cursed the novel, and in warm weather, maybe 45, drove up to Rush City and E to the St. Croix, down to Sunrise, abandoned vge, to Almelund. Sure from soft dark woolly clouds would snow--didn't, and NOV 16, Mon. dark all day, snow-threat --warm, 45 at noon, up to 60 in PM--but actually, just a little rain in evening. Dinner, Hildred Howe Smith. (Sunday, no snow; ponds frozen only at edges)

NOV 17, Tue. Brightist, warm all day--30 and over. Dinner, Meg Bovey's --De Laittres etc.

NOV 18, Wedn Dark clouds but brite sun comes, goes. Joan, Love, Beth Singer make up a gang--abt 20--rave abt Mitropoulous.

NOV 19, Thur. Gray, some rain. 10:30 abt 25. Damp earth smells like spring.

fol. 103

NOV 20, Fri. Abt 25 all day. Gray. Snow been promising for a week but none come. Symphony: Rachmaninoff hilself, playing his Concerto #2--a noble, gaunt, channel-faced figure. Mpls really knows music. My students, Mary Baxter, John Pillsbury, equally interested. They all worship Mitropoulos, cf him to Stowkowski w scorn. But he seemed small and scrawny beside tall figure of Rachmaninoff, tho R (tho but 69) seemed to walk feebly.

NOV 21, Sat. Indian Summer p.d., air sparkled. Drove out to Little Switzerland, south og Hopkins.

NOV 22, Sun. Ind Sum p.d., about 30 to 35. Evening, Starke Hathaway's, modern house, like Lippincotts, designed by Mr. and Mrs. Close, who were there, with Fords, Daniels, Rolf and Mrs. Ueland.

fol. 104

NOV 22 CONT (from a letter)

beginning of carbon copy of part of a letter to Marcella Powers

Sunday November 22 and God what a day what a day--clear and sweet as a little silver bell, just cold enuff to be brisk--the grass not just dry and gray but sparkling. And so was yesterday. But except for a little run out to some lovely hills in "Little Switzerland," SE of Mpls, I have just stuck here and typed--typed--typed. I'll be finished by the end of this week and 3 weeks from day-before-yesterday, if you get me, I'll be HOME in NY.

NOV 22 <u>CONT</u> (from a letter)

Sunday November 22 and God what a day what a day --
clear and sweet as a little silver bell, just cold enuff
to be brisk -- the grass not just dry and gray but spark-
ling. And so was yesterday. But except for a little
run out to some lovely hills in "Little Switzerland,"
SE of Mpls, I have just stuck here and typed -- typed
-- typed. I'll be finished by the end of this week and
3 weeks from day-before-yesterday, if you get me, I'll
be HOME in NY.

Good, on Friday evening, was the Mpls Symphony Orchestra
(former conductor, the great Ormandy, now the great
Dimitri Mitropoules, who uses neither score nor baton,
and Makes with All the Members, like Dora Miller) with
RACHMANINOFF himself playing his Concerto #2. He's
the greatest musician I ever saw mit the eyes, and he's
thrilling -- looks as <u>should</u> this last of a world of
Tolstoy, Chekov, Gogol: tall, broad shouldered, gaunt,
his hair short like Carl Van Doren's, his face deeply
graven with lines of thought and emotion -- soldier cum
artist.....When he tottered out to the piano, he seemed
15 years older than his actual 69, but he played with
all the fire in the world.

Curious: Minneapolis, which has no little theater at all,
which sees few even of 2nd rate touring shows, is music-
mad and music-wise. Everybody from the flour-king
Pillsburys to the kids in the University talks and
amazingly seems to know music.....Mary Baxter and Al
Wilson learnedly (and I shd say without faking) com-
paring Mitropoulos, Toscanini, Stock, Koussevitzky --
dear God, just to remember their NAMES is a strain on
this poor outworn literary brain.

NOV 23, Mon. 9:30 AM, fm frost on roofs as sun comes thru
morning haze. 9 AM, 19 - 5 PM, 45. Clear, sweet, cool, ISpd.
PM to Stillwater and Marine.
Even: Addison and Dorothy Lewis and Brenda Ueland dinner,
then all to John Cowles, where Richd Wilson Mpls Trib Washn corr,
"Stuffy" Walters, exec ed Trib, Philip and the unlikable EMMMM
Eleanor Pillsbury.

NOV 24, Tue. Not <u>very</u> lite at ':15 CWT, and flamboyant sunrise,
crimson tapestry on pale blue rising to dark blue. Some sun
in PM....Even: dinner at Dr. Lewis Daniel's. David Shearers,
Daniel and John Baxter doing Christ-mas charade; John imper-
somating MMM Hitler.....The bunch to "The Happy Hour," Nicol-
let Ave, owned by Kit Cann of the booze interests....A soldier
was shot in the washroom here last nite....Carlo Molinari's
rhumba band,,MMMMMM booths on elevated platform.

NOVEMBER 25, WEDN. WINTER BEGINS, and I get ticketM for NY,
leave for home in 2 weeks and 1 day!
The AM cloudily dark. Snow starts at noon, heavy snow all

Fol. 104, showing shift from carbon-copy of letter for Marcella Powers (first three paragraph blocks) to directly typed diary entries (last three blocks). *Yale Collection of American Literature, Beinecke Rare Book and Manuscript Library.*

Good, on Friday evening, was the Mpls Symphony Orchestra (former conductor, the great Ormandy, now the great Dimitri Mitropoulos, who uses neither score nor baton, and Makes with All the Members, like Dora Miller) with RACHMANINOFF himself playing his Concerto #2. He's the greatest musician I ever saw mit the eyes, and he's thrilling--looks as should this last of a world of Tolstoy, Chekov, Gogol: tall, broad shouldered, gaunt, his hair short like Carl Van Doren's, his face deeply graven with lines of thought and emotion--soldier cum artist.....When he tottered out to the piano, he seemed 15 years older than his actual 69, but he played with all the fire in the world.

Curious: Minneapolis, which has no little theater at all, which sees few even of 2nd rate touring shows, is music-mad and music-wise. Everybody from the flour-king Pillsburys to the kids in the University talks and amazingly seems to know music.....Mary Baxter and Al Wilson learnedly (and I shd say without faking) comparing Mitropoulos, Toscanini, Stock, Koussevitzky--dear God, just to remember their NAMES is a strain on this poor outworn literary brain.

end of letter carbon

NOV 23, Mon. 9:30 AM, frost on roofs as sun comes thru morning haze. 9 AM, 19 - 5 PM, 45. Clear, sweet, cool, ISpd. PM to Stillwater and Marine. Even: Addison and Dorothy Lewis and Brenda Ueland dinner, then all to John Cowles, where Richd Wilson Mpls Trib Washn corr, "Stuffy" Walters, exec ed Trib, Philip and the unlikable Eleanor Pillsbury.

NOV 24, Tue. Not very lite at ':15 CWT, and flamboyant sunrise, crimson tapestry on pale blue rising to dark blue. Some sun in PM....Even: dinner at Dr. Lewis Daniel's. David Shearers, Daniel and John Baxter doing Christ-mas charade; John impersonating Hitler.....The bunch to "The Happy Hour," Nicollet Ave, owned by Kit Cann of the booze interests....A soldier was shot in the washroom here last nite....Carlo Molinari's rhumba band,, booths on elevated platform.

NOVEMBER 25, WEDN. WINTER BEGINS, and I get ticket for NY, leave for home in 2 weeks and 1 day! The AM cloudily dark. Snow starts at noon, heavy snow all

fol. 105

NOV 25 CONT

afternoon, and wind--a small blizzard. ,Have to go to class and return--windshield clouded, skid at every turn, dif crawl up ascents even on 1st, though never make Lowry Hill--and we were just in time; about 6, cars were stuck in a flock on Hennepin at foot of hill--uneasy crawling thru fog of snow with windshield coated. Glad staying home that evening, reading a Dorothy Sayers detective story. Down to 19 during nite. (At such times, they talk here of famous Armistice Day Blizzard of 2 years ago, when many duck hunters frozen.) Note on Dec. 7: this snow, above, still lasting--winter really had set in).

NOV 26, Thur. Trib: 8, 14; n, 14; 6, 19. AM, not snowing, but snow ridge on twigs and flat on lawns and roads. Sun out at 10. THANKSGIVING. Had been invited to both Wilsons and Lewises at the Lake, fortunately had refused--these Minnesota Vikings would expect me to plow out there. Addison Lewis goes home in evening even thru a blizzard--pt of pride. PM cloudless, snow-glare. Walk at 3--20 degrees. About the first really cold nippy walk I've had in years....Last rosy light on the housetops and chimneys up the hill at 5:30, and a blue darkness begins to seep up from the snowy dooryards.

NOV 27, Fri. Trib: 8, 10; n, 14; 6, 17. Finished copying last draft of Planish--now final revise. Vaguely light at 8 AM, bright all PM but the snow not melting. Din, Arthur Hartwell (grain executive--lives next door, just across a driveway). Gretchen Pillsbury and theater chronicles. New people--Phelps. NOV 28, Sat. Mild son all day.

NOV 29, Sun. Trib: 6 AM, 3; 8, 5; n, 14; 6, 22; midn, 10. Good sunrise slow abt 8:15; some sun in AM, then starts snowing at 1 PM, lasts one hour. Last class party

NOV 30, Mon. Trib: 6, 6; 8, 8; n, 18; 6 PM, 22. Gray, almost foggy in PM. Letter from Dorset, NY, have suite there. Even: yellow lights--snow--Xmas calendar vge scene, & delightful; colorless street lamp light on ridges of snow, magic shadows....Din at Mike Elliott's--trying to find in, over on St. Anthony Hill.

DECEMBER

DEC 1, Tue. Trib: 8, 12; n, 12; 6, 7; midn, zero, 2 AM, -1. First below zero....Today begins wartime gas-rationing for West as well as East; no more exploratory motoring for a year or two. A normal (non-war-worker) ration, 4 gals a week. Bright sun at 9:30--arch of trees over Mt. Curve Av to W a living brown....Big optical co 4th floor Medical Arts Bldg, fitters called "counter boys" Medic students? Small sprinkles of snow during day. No snow melting.

DEC 2, Wedn. Trib: 8, -4; n, zero; 6, 10; midn, 4. Early AM, frost painted on windows, 1st time noticed. 9:30, brite sun--when it hits frost on windows, the frost is full of diamond-point and green sparkles, and crimson.

fol. 106

DEC 3, Thur. Trib: 8, 6; n, 11; 4, 20; 6, 18. Bril sun all day. Joe & Dagmar Beach, Baxters, Gid and Petey Seymour and Helen Rand for dinner. They all say, "You <u>must</u> come back to Minnesota," which naurally pleases me.

DEC 4, Fri. Trib: 8, 16; n, 20; 6, 22; midn, 14 Week from today, New York! I shall be glad to go there, glad some day to return here. AM, slow snow. Good work day.

DEC 5, Sat. Finished last final revision of GIDEON PLANISH! Read radio scripts from Martin Jones who wants me for show. Phoned Marcella--so gay. AM, brilliant sun. I had almost fprgotten how beautiful are <u>all</u> effects of all lights on snow: sharp and delicate shadows of trees, twigs, wh would be lost on grass; shadows in hollows, warm sparkle and glow of sun on shadowless snow stretches, interest of human & animal tracks. Evening farewell party at Baxters': Addison Lewises, Al Wilsons, McNallys, Hannah Daniel (husband abed, bad heart), Russell Plimpton, Helen Baxter, Brenda.

DEC 6, Sun. Trib: 8, 16; n, 18; 6, 22; midn, 10. Packing. Light now 8-6 CWT--only fortnight to shortest day of year, then blessed turn of sun.

DECEMBER 7, 1942. Monday. AM, <u>not</u> dreary here in snowy yards; delicate variations in the gray mist of early AM, and house lights cheerful; dawn glow in skies goes on, gold to rosy, almost till 9.
Dec. 5, finished Planish MS
Dec. 7, Pearl Harbor anniversary
Dec. 9, next Wedn, last class at University.
Dec. 10, " Thur, leave
Dec. 11, " Fri, arrive NY, lunch with M, deliver MS.

So I close this Minnesota Diary, hoping to reopen it in a year or a year and a half.

#######

fol. 107

Feb <u>1943</u>

Minn. Weather—1943

<u>Feb.</u> Average mean temp. St. Paul is 17.9. Feb. 43 was 19.3. Highest, 45° on 19th, 21st, 27th. Coldest, -16° on 14<u>th</u>. Only .54 of an inch of precipitation   Feb 24 to 27 varied from -8° to 24+

<u>March 2</u> -11°, coldest March day in 30 yrs (-17° on Mar. 2, 1913) nite of Mar. 2, Internat Falls, -25°, Duluth -23° Bismarck -12°

Feb. 27. Sat. 7 AM (WST) old moon, river. dim silver, lights on bluffs across river in West St. Paul.

March 20, when Al Wilson left Mpls for NY, foot of snow w. such treacherous ice underneath that cdn't make driveway at 1500 Mt Curve—then, here in NY. Central Park getting green.

fol. 108

May 1943

<u>1943</u>

NY to Minneapolis et al. for two weeks; return to NY

MAY 12, Wednesday, at Minneapolis. Trib: 8, 36; n, 44; 6, 52. Trees almost out, but about 10 days behind New York.

THUR. MAY 13: 8, 36; n, 53; 6, 57.

FRI. MAY 14: 8, 42; n, 60; 6, 62.

SATURDAY, May 15: rain steady and chill all Saturday, and till 9 Sunday AM. Everybody: "Certainly was needed for the crops--1st big rain this spring."

Possibly the most tiresome people in a provincial city those who try to be metropolitan--to to keep proving to you that they smartly are so--and at least more knowing than you, when you don't care a damn whether you are knowing or not. The man who asked me to read his play and then, on not too severe criticism, "Well, I know at least as much about the drama as you do."

Young man's approbation in 1943, "WERE YOU EVER HOT!"

SUNDAY, May 16: 8, 42; n, 43; 6, 53. To the Lewises at Long Lake. Trees two weeks behind Mpls, just feathering. Wolffeld estate and private lake. Dana and Addy--Harold Atkinson, 2nd

MONDAY, MAY 17. Gray and chilly till PM, then warm and bright. 8, 42; n, 58; 6, 61.

TUESDAY, MAY 18. First real day of summer. Sun glare, and 8, 48; n, 63; 6, 69.

THUR, MAY 20/ Off to explore Southern Minn. Ed Thye as Governor. Lilacs not quite out in the cities, yet scent of them in the air....8, 56; n, 65; 5, 78; 6, 64.

Pretty low hills south of Invergrove to junction of 52-55-56 and SE of Mendota on 55, with wide view to the Mississippi as approach Hastings...."Sibley Tea House" that of his secy, Hypolite (spelling) De Puis who married Evangeline Renville. Built in 1850. Alex Ramsey's daughter, Mrs. Furness, still living? Sibley and Ramsey likely to be buried in Oakland Cemetery? Some day see Hector Dousman house at Prairie du Chien.

Late PM. rain threatened, the sky copper under dun clouds. When rain comes, the tiny moon-craters of wiped rain drops on windshield.

Unpainted farmhouse with colored-glass stop to large window.

Cannon River valley worth tracing--rem. crossing it betw Hastings and Red Wing

fol. 108a

FRIDAY, MAY 21, 1943. Spent night at Red Wing--no bath. Trib: 8, 50; n, 70; 4, 79; 6, 80; mid, 65 At Red Wing: Levee Park, from it seen the curving shining river, green shining isles, hills beyond. A cool, clean, delicious Minnesota morning.

Typical tourist error: just seeing Red Wing motoring thru, just front street with tile factory, shoe factory, though it altogether dingy. BUT: charming park with modern limestone-glass-bronze courthouse (Goodhue County--contains int al, ration office for war) and handsome Citizens' Fund Insurance Company; levee park; "yacht club" of many bayou-reminding boathouses on the river; abandoned Norwegian seminary on abrupt bluff behind the town; valleys at edge of town, with suburban houses overlooking a petty Switzerland with whiffs of fruit trees coming into blossom on the tilted fields.

Most peace in valleys.

Summer camps by Lake Pepin; Norway pines, violets in grass.

Mourning doves unafraid in the road.

Frontenac; white lilacs all open, purple ones partly. Utter peace up there, on just slightly misty but PD.....Spring foliage, along with tender green of leaves, has something of the russet of fall.

PEOPLE MET IN
WINONA

Ward and Frances (Prenny) Lucas, and Jack.
Mr. and Mrs. Tearse
Geo and Mrs. Little
Gretchen (Grata) Lamberton--(Mrs. H. M. Lamberton Jr.)
Archie and Trude (Weil) Bauman--Little Theater.
Mrs. Choate
HMLamberton brother of Mardy (Mrs. Chas) Swett.)

Watkins Medicine Co now run by a Mr. King.

SUNDAY, MAY 23. Trib: 8, 62; 6, 64. Rain on and off all afternoon, and all day Monday. Sunday nite at Albert Lea--Love Cruickshank.

Minneiska: gay cheap lunch with families at Sunday fete. Signs on walls: "We don't know where Mom is but we got Pop on ice." "Two pints, one quart; four quarters, one gallon; one gallon, one fight; one fight, two policemen; two policemen, one magistrate; one magistrate, ten days. Drink sensibly and go home." "If I don't cash your check, you get mad. If I cash it and it's no good, I get mad. I'd rather have you mad than me." Coco cola signs of semi-naked girls. War posters. Juke box. Punch ball."

Holy Ghost Baptist Church of Jesus Christ--small building.

fol. 109

1943

SUNDAY, MAY 23, cont.

Houston. Young man in Sunday girling garb: painfully neat sports coat in tweed, tan trousers, clean blue shirt.

Local bands named for the leader. They have printed posters, spave left blank below to write in name of village and hall where hold dance.

This year, all the girls bare legs--and not entirely due I think to war lack of stockings!

After the hot days of last week, trees in Southern Minn all out fully.

Strangest thing about this country, spiraling up and up not to a peak but to level prairie.

Village chicken hatcheries and fancy stock foods new since my boyhood.

PRESTON: good effect of stores on all four sides of the central courthouse square. The courthouse itself--Fillmore County--is spotty with cream colored bricks among the brown. The damndest cupola, with winged serpent windows, curving shutters, electric lights strung, decorated globe.

<u>The</u> hill south of Preston has a farm on top whence have 300 degree view--road as over moors to East, town below, hills to north.

MONDAY, May 24. Morning, chilly, steady light rain. Cows go through culvert tunnel under road. Gothic stone-fronted "mortuaries" on Main Streets.

CROSSING THE PRAIRIES, So. Minn.: same wood-lot, long grass and oaks and stumps; same Schmidt City Club beer sign; same house and grove with red barns and tile silo; same tousle of young green oats in very black soil; same grassy ditch or brooklet by road. Land and land and land. Solid, worthy, necessary, Swedish, dismaying. A relief when run by river, under bluffs, with no fields. One gets so tired of eating bread alone!

Rem: attack on Mpls school board and supt schools as crooked, grafting on contracts, teachers' salaries.

A recently rustic vge like Shakopee now all night clubs with names like La Parisienne. Slot machines, maybe heavier gambling.

fol. 110

<u>1944 Winter Notes</u> 300 C.P.W N Y C

With even snow, nite, satisfying golden glow of St. lamps in park, & gay green & red

Whirling snow-devils on N.E. terrace in semi-blizzard, & result. Sculptured drifts mit bare spots on floor of terrace

Feb. 19 1944—7:30 AM—quite light, umber clouds to faint pink, life & spring delight in air; waning moon a big bright fragment just risen

Feb. 21—7 AM—dawn drama in 6 layers from terrace: lake, dark lead; city dun w. lites, band of murk, dusty rose band, pale blue band glorified by frail old moon rising & one star, dark blue top almost-night sky & stars

fol. 111

Winter notes—NYC—1944

Feb 23—Great rolling nimbus snow-clouds, fast; thru them, lite shaft hits tenement on Jersey heights, & a moment it is a heavenly castle.

Mar. 29—winter all over, grass green in park, 2nd blanket off bed. 1st lightning storm Mar. 25. Then half hour snow flurry on 29th. But spring is here

Apr. 5—heavy snow all day. Trees still brown

Apr. 10—grass much greener. Trees, wh were all-brown, have (esp willows) burst into green

May 5—after 2 days of record-break 83° temperature, Park in full foliage—cherry & plum trees full bloom Penn Station—sur-real of elevators, dark passages, stairs, tracks overhang like cliffs

fol. 112

Remember

"Pie plant"—rhubarb—& stalk color. Mullein silk. Hayseed cigarettes w. newsp. wrapping

fol. 113

1944
Arrive Minneapolis May 6, 1944

Saturday, May 6, arrive. Average temperature about 40. Trees, seen from train, about three weeks behind New York City, after NY's 83° for two days with almost full summer. Grass on bluffs abt Winona still gray.

Sunday, May 7. 8 AM, 39, 4 PM, 62. Spring galloping on. Lake of the Isles (walk with Robt Penn Warren) lovely with lawns about it, trees, islands, children playing. Kenwood Park beyond. Mpls singularly anti-Semitic--Geo Leonard attributes it to strong Yankee influence of founders--Pillsburys etc....People here, like Dr. Roy Swanson, rougher, more ready to call pretenses and errors....Highly respectable women as hotel chambermaids, nice girls as waitresses.

May 8, Monday, 8, 48; 4 PM, 53.
May 9, Tue, 8, 44; 4, 63.
May 10, Wed, 8, 49; 4, 66. Evening, heavy rain, pools on streets. Mississippi river mildly flooded.
May 11, Thur. 8, 59; 4, 76. Gray.
May 12, Fri, 8, 65; 4, 72. Gray and humid, threat of rain all day.

May 13, Sat. Lowering early, then clears to the first bright but cool sweet day since arr. Temperature probably reaches 75. Suddenly full spring--abt two weeks late, this year. Immense change in the week since arrived. Willows along Calhoun (party at Brenda's) in pale green fire--leaves not full. Pleasant on porch at Brenda's, like bright beyond not-quite-full trees. Baxters, Rufus Rand, Addison, Mrs. Allison, Osborns, Ueland bros. et al.

May 14, Sun. 8, 64; 4, 84; 7, 85. Hot on River Drive. Luke Rader, evangelist, in bldg like warehouse with stagy choir loft up behind him--3 girls in red sweaters giggle while Rader prays. Among miles of 2-story houses, drug stores. Rader: "Prest Roosevelt guilty of high treason." "Negroes not fit to demand equality."

May 15, Monday. To Winona. Trees and grass now almost fully green. Flooded Mississippi up to tracks, islands disappear & shacks stand amid water. But not in sts of towns. Tuesday, lunch at Mrs. Earl Russell Thoemen's, top of bluffs above Homer, S of Winona. Walnut library, new bks; bar open on rm inside and terrace out; swimming pool, on slops, winter cover, window so see sunset when dive; MINK COVERED PILLOWS; butler and chauffeur--money from JBWatkins Medicine Co--W her grandfather, King her father. Temp in Minneapolis Tue, 8, 62; 4, 85.

Wed May 17, lv Mpls hot and raining; ARRIVE DULUTH clear and 20 degrees colder, with wind so strong cant open windows in hotel.

fol. 114

Minn diary—1944

Mon, May 15. 1st heat death in Mpls, Temps. there, 8, 60; 4, 81; Midn, 65. Winona hot & humid, like NY. Good show in Anvil Theater, but stifling—& fire trap....Train down, islands flooded over w cottages standing in water...Misty river, w phantom Eng. city across. Elms well out in Winona sts. Quince & plum flowering crab...Hotel, light well lobby, Blue Blazer coctail lounge. Glass brick Winona clinic *

Tue May 16: <u>Hot!</u> Mrs. E. R. Thoenen house on bluffs, mink pillows in walnut library. Window in swim pool. Blown up & illuminated fotos. Butler Chauf. <u>Now</u>, at Winona, trees all out, fruit trees in bloom... Fine barley for malting in brewing in Winona Co

* Mon cont: Ward Lucas circular drawing rm, low white, bedrooms down, on declivity. Wren houses. Orioles, cardinal wanted in at glass—& rattlesnakes.

fol. 115

Temp. Wedn
17, Duluth max
63, min., 39.

beginning of carbon copy of part of a letter to Marcella Powers

DULUTH AT
LAST!!!!!

Hotel Duluth
Thursday, May 18
1944

Looking for houses! I've seen a couple already, nothing yet satisfactory, see some more today.

It was a mild adventure to come up here yesterday from Southern Minnesota. I had heard how much colder it is here, except for hot spells in July-August, but hadn't quite believed it. Monday evening, at the Little Theater show in Winona, it was stiflingly hot; one fled downstairs between acts for a little tepid air. Wednesday morning, when I left Minneapolis, it was about 72°. I arrived here at one, 4½ hrs later, to find it 52, with a fine Nor'easter brewing across the vast gray lake; and last evening when I went to Margaret Banning's very handsome house for dinner--meeting president of the Oliver Mining Co and a pianist--all the integuments which had been drippily removed Way Down South in Mpls--undershirt, vest, topcoat--were frenziedly reassumed.

And this morning when I got up the Noreaster was rolling pretty large breakers up on the shore, especially over at the entrance to the Canal, where the long ore boats come in with coal and go out with iron, and the lake was almost black w. white-caps. It was raining and cold--yet I sort of liked it. Y' know--fresh. But the little buildings way down below the tall hotel, shops and warehouses, looked so bleak, with their big, flat, foolish-looking roofs.

I've looked at several houses; nothing quite possible yet--may even not be able to find one at all, of course, but think I shall. Most of them have been too horribly domestic--the photographs of Aunt Ipzabah's boys, the hand-knitted whoozit, the one bath for four bedrooms, the small itch of lawn.

But when, this afternoon, the real estate man drove me along the glorious Skyline Parkway, with Duluth and the endless lake, suddenly steel blue in courageous sun, and the distant pine-stubbly hills all spread out, I loved it all, and wanted to stay.....for a while.

You have never seen the real Northland--it does not start till N of Minneapolis, nor have you been far enough North in Maine. BUT when you leave Mpls, going NE to Duluth, it does start within a few miles of the city....Swamps and scrub oak, a flat land that could be depressing to lots of people but that I find rather free and bracing. Bogs. Muskrat houses. Forests of birch and poplar (called "popple" here) replacing cut or burned pine forests of old. Marshy lakes. Then, in an hour, pines and the stumps left as relics of forest fires. Log cabins and tarpaper shacks in small clearings. Finns and Co-operative Stores. Blackbirds on reeds in slews. Miles, then, of woodland without a house. The vast elevators and boat works (building corvettes) in Superior, Wis. Then Duluth and the greal lake--and the wind howling at the hotel windows.

end of letter carbon

Temperature Thursday at Duluth, max, 36, 6:30 AM; minimum, 34, noon. In Minneapolis, Max, 58; min, 58.

fol. 116

beginning of carbon copy of part of a letter to Marcella Powers

May 20--Saturday 1944

2601 East Second Street
Duluth
Hemlock 6817

that is my proud new address. Downtownbusiness though the street sounds, it is way out in the Best Residential Section as you go from Duluth toward the North Shore and Canada.

It is a kind of English manor house; brick; enter a little courtyard; big drawing room, panelled library, furniture rather shabby but most comfortable; five masters' bedrooms with three baths; couple servants' rooms; in the basement, a jolly foolish miniature bowling alley, and a game room opening right out through French doors on a secluded lawn--wonderful for a summertime buffet supper. There's a fine terrace with a view on one side to the great open lake and on the other out to piney hills to the East (Duluth runs East and West, not North and South, as it somehow should). It's all so quiet, with enough grounds to walk about in....and third story, an unfinished vast attic which is the "ballroom" of the newspaper story enclosed....and outside it, a balcony begging to be sun-bathed in......I think I shall love my manorial splendor.

I am also looking into matters of a shack that can be rented at some one of the 4 or 5 lakes within 10 to 20 miles from here--Superior is too cold to bathe in--so you can have swimmings; and a rentable car; and boats, small yachts, hired by the day, that go up the magnificent hill-and-rock-bound and Indian-haunted St. Louis River.

And the chess I discoursed of on the phone: three games today with Old Mr. Frank Crassweller, 88 years old, born in Londonengland, lived for years as a kid in the Canadian woods, has practised law in Duluth for over 50 years....and has played chess, fairly regularly, for SEVENTY-SEVEN YEARS!....He looks only seventy or so; his age shows, really, only in his stoop when he walks. Last years he did have a bout of pneumonia and amemia combined with the chronic diabetes he has had for years, and was, he says, a little "down," but naturally, no lasting effects....Hell, he's only 65 years older than you are.

And so, for a contrast, yesterday I played, AND WON, with Bob Ridder, son and nephew of the various Ridders owning the newspapers here and in St. Paul (and Journal of Commerce and, I think, Staats-Zeitung in NY); himself starting in the newspaper game; 24 yrs old and very much like my Wells in a lot of ways; nice wife, a nice kid; a Freshman in

Harvard when Wells was a senior. I beathim I beathim I beathim--the only one besides Johnny Baxter, whom I taught, that I have been able to beat here!!! Licked by two professors, one obstetrician, and one 88-yr-old lawyer--that's the kind of Capablanca I am.

end of letter carbon

fol. 117

May 1944--Duluth

Fri. May 19. Wake to heavy rain and fog almost hiding lake, but streams of ore and wheat boats are going thru the canal that leads to inner harbor. Max 39, min 33; noon, 35; 3 PM, 36. Mpls, 62-45....As predicted, this Nor'easter has lasted three days. Afternoon, rain quits but chilly, gray, autumnal strong wind. Spray on rocks on lake shore thrown fifteen or twenty feet high.

Sat. 20. Nor'easter still continues. It's gray, cool, bracing, not raining. The lake is more tender-colored. A little sun in the PM. 51-40; noon, 44; 6:30, 48....Mpls, 74-48.

Temperature maximum & minimum hereafter without the "max" & "min"

Sunday 21. AM gray then rainy. Lake a mysterious blur in fog. No surf. Then clear a bit and lake a (daytime!) nocturn in silver and pale green - distant dark line of Wisconsin shore....Women's voices in Duluth usually shrill, harsh, brassy--distressing when they're meaning to be so amiable.....Seen no sea-gulls here yet......51-39; noon, 42. Mpls, 72-60.

Monday 22. 64-43; noon, 48; 6:30, 60. Mpls 81-59. Sunrise (WST) 5:22, sunset, 8:46.....I understand why Duluthians, after being cold ever since last October, are mocking when I say I like this gray weather; when (after too hot in New York and Winona) I like rising to another day of fog, rain and chill, with steamers on lake fretfully hooting. M would mock with them.

Tue 23. 57-43. Mpls 84-60. This time of year, Duluth runs 20 degrees colder than Mpls-St.P. Rise to thin sunshine on lake - almost first sunshine since arr last Wedn. Sun gone by ten: fog. Out again at 11:30 and fine day. Spring in Duluth at least 3 weeks behind Mpls, which means 5 or 6 weeks behind NY--this yr, at least. I get 3 springs this year. Thus Housman's Shropshire who fretted because he would have only 60 springs could have trebled them--by coming to Duluth--if he had been willing to pay that much.....Evening: steamers, lighted aft, coming to white lighthouse and green lights at opening to Aerial Bridge Canal. Lighthouse and line of lights on Wisconsin shore--maybe 4 miles away. Steamer is beauty against moving water.

Wedn 24. 64-46. Mpls 82-64. AM, sun thru light fog on lake. PM delicious, just cool enough.

Thur 25. 58-44, noon 53. Mpls 83-65. Sunrise WST 5:20; set 8:49. AM gray and fog again, dark and disagreeable till late PM. Evening, fog dripping and fog horn wailing.

Fri 26. 77-46. Noon 74, 6:30 77. Mpls 78-57....Am, shyly clear and sunny across blue-silver lake. PM, suddenly hot - 75 at four. Should bring out the leaves, now only ½ out. At 9:30 PM, still a pale green light over hills SW.

fol. 118

beginning of carbon copy of part of a letter to Marcella Powers

June the first

I am enclosing some carbon copies of pages of my Minnesota Diary which you may want just to glance through--it's not meant to be at all personal, but just a record of weather and the like--you know, just as if I were a fussy author that, he dunno why, keeps careful track of unimportant things----

This is really a gorgeous house. When you walk on the terrace and look down at the lake, then turn and look up at the Tudor fascade of the house, with limestone edged bay-windows like a very small Oxford college, you will be impressed; and when you walk on lawn and in garden, you will yelp with distress that it hasn't been better kept up.

It's amazing how much happier I am here than in Hollywood, a year ago, with all its Kate Hepburns and Cedric Hardwickes and Romanoff Restaurants. It's because, really working on the novel, I feel justified, tinily triumphant, in life; out there, doing the piffling work on the childish scenario, I felt guilty and irritably bored.

I'm just getting acquainted with an amusing variety of people--the variety that I always kicked about lacking in NY (and that Connie so handsomely corrected by those many doctors he always almost brought around): John Malick, the extremely intelligent Unitarian minister and his really attractive quiet wife, both from Cambridge (the Unitarians, you ignorant papist, are the leftwing among Protestants); Judge Mark Nolan, district judge, a big cheerful Mick from the Iron Range--I go often to his court; young Bob Ridder & wife from NY; old Mr. Crassweller of the 77 yrs of chess; Richard Singer, a very handsome 25-year-old Rabbi from the great Hebrew Union Theological School of Cincinnatti; Ray and Kitty Sicard--he the intense nervous city editor of the Herald here; Kenneth Cant, real estate, full of bluff but most likeable; Elsa Anneke, widow who plays piano and chums with the Finnish conductor of the Duluth Symphony Orchestra--whom I'm to meet at her house tomorrow night--he's supposed to be good, and his name is spelled either Hainikainen or Hainnikkainnenn or, as above, Cincinatti or Cinncinnati or possibly Jones.

Did I, in haste of Mpls-Winona-Mpls-Duluth, tell you the one high spot of luxury in handsome millionaire country house on Mississippi (or Hainenkainen) bluffs--sofa pillows covered with MINK? I must have.....I told this to Dorothy Lewis and Mary Baxter as the height of acme of capitalistic horror and they looked dreamily at each other and breathed, "My, what a wonnerful idea!"

Women, thy name is--women; and unless I hear from you soon, I shall call your tribe something even worse.

end of letter carbon

fol. 119

1944 - Duluth

MAY

Sat. 27. Move to Williams-Webber house, 2601 East 2nd St. (Built 1914±) Day starts warm, sun-thru-mist. Hot afternoon. Max 82, min. 56. Mpls 81-53. Still a little light, enough to make way aby lawn, at 9:30 (W.S.T.)-- i.e., 8:30 God's Time. (or CWT—Central War Time

Sun. 28. Bright, clear, hot. 84-60. 3 PM, 81. Mpls. 86-57. Great golden cliffs, with clear crevasses, of cumulus cloud over lake in P.M.

Mon. 29. Flowering almond, plum, lilac in bloom. Trees out nearly full. Lots of swallows fly high and chirp toward evening. 85-61. Noon, 66, 6:30, 80. Mpls 89-68.

Tuesday, 30. 90-63. Wedn paper says: Hottest day in Duluth in two years; in 1942, hottest during whole year was 89; in 1943, 87....Mpls. 88-69.....Late afternoon, heavy thunder shower, lake lost in fog, fog horn like menancholy and calfless cow. Still hot after the rain.....Sunrise, 5:17, sunset, 8:54. Or so the paper claims!

Wedn. 31. Awaken to light mist over wastes of birch, poplar, pine and the glittering lake. Fresh and beautiful to look at, but air hot and woolly to breathe. At noon, gray and suddenly much cooler. Evening, so cool shut windows. When sky gray, the smooth lake was pure silver; evening, after sunset, it was rose-silver....Lake with its irregular points sticking out more beautiful than a too-regular seacoast like that at Miami. 79-64; Mpls 88-66

Top of blue spruce, w. red buds, like bl Xmas tree.

JUNE

Thursday, June 1. Awake to chill rain ans thick fog in which the green birch leaves nestle, and woodland spaces look mysterious. Mist blows before the wind. At 6 PM, rain, sky threatening and lowering except over lake, where long silver streak. Dark in the house....On the lake, steamers were anchored in the fog from 7 PM Wedn to 8 AM Thursday....53-44. Mpls, 88-70, with heavy thunder showers--2 inches in four hours.

Fri 2. 60-46, noon 56. Mpls 87-66. AM, fog and cool. Sun coming thru fog at 9 and breeze tastes fresh....Trees about this house include elms, maples, mountain ash, balsam....Industries in Duluth include meat-packing, fish-packing, rugs from flax fibres, mfr of ice (non-elec) refrigerators, steel mill.

Evening, chill and heavy rain--Nor'easter started again. Lights out for a while from lightning while at Hannikainen's--see next page.

fol. 120

Sat June 3 Duluth--1944

beginning of carbon copy of part of a letter to Marcella Powers

That was a pleasant party, last evening--one with Mr. Hannikainen, the Duluth Symphony Conductor--yes, that seems to be the real way to spell his name. He proves to be a solid, likeable, somewhat impressive man of circa 40; he looks like the broad-faced ruddy golf-playing Englishman--looks, in fact, like pictures I remember of Lord Northcliff, the gt English newspaper-owner, when he was young. His wife, part Russian and part Finn, looks completely the Frenchwoman, and very much to be fallen-for if it were not that they leave for summer in Boston next week. (He has guest-conducted Boston Symph).

They have a small house in what ought to be the most and is one of the least popular places in Duluth, right <u>on</u> the shore of Lake Superior. (My place, though it overlooks the lake wonderfully, is probably ¼ mile from it). The waves--another driving Nor'easter started yesterday--rode right up to the foundations of the house, and while I listened to the music, I looked out at the turbulent steel-gray water, with far-off steamers rolling, till it got dark--and then there was lightning spearing the lake.

Hannin (see above for spelling) played cello, with extremely good local female pianist and violinist--the latter looking about 24, and the mother of 5 kids--she must have bowed them in--Mrs. H. They played a wonderful trio of Schumann which I had never heard; then, just cello and piano, a Finnish folk song, and Sibelius's "Song of my Heart."

The room belonged to the music--white plaster walls, good prints, and very lofty studio-like windows giving on the lake.

There were maybe a dozen people--Mrs. Anneke, the pianist, you may meet in Duluth; the violinist wife of an eye-ear-throat surgeon, which is the jewel-work of all surgery; a fine old Finn who was once in Congress, a lawyer tho born in Finland, looks like a movie senior-diplomat--Larson; a lovely old boy who looks abt 80, a piano teacher who actually studied with Liszt (who died 1886!)--Ernst Lachmann; a pretty dull photographer--Dworshak, so on. Kind people, travelled, not too arty. It was good.

end of letter carbon

Sat 3d - weather: cold, rain, continued offnon all day, night. 37-35. (Normal for the day is 53.) Mpls, 86-73. NY, 84-69. With the fog, winds up to 40 mph, which held ships in docks; caused one of them, abt to enter Superior canal, to turn & ride out storm at-lake...Another Nor'easter, & I like it.

Sun 4; again awake to fog, chill. Even I, the Finn, could get tired of this weather...Fog all day, with several heavy rains; creeks swollen, water in places over Route 1. Ships tied up by fog after 7 PM////Flowering almonds now faded, cherry blossoms and mountain laurel in bloom; lilacs out but damaged by Saturday wind. Rome falls to British-American troops... 50-36, noon 41. Mpls 82-61.

Monday 5th. At 7 this AM, sun breaks through, first time in days, but light rain again at 10:30. PM gray but no fog or rain, and warmer. 57-50. Mpls 55-52! NY 67-51!!

fol. 121

June 1944--Duluth

Tuesday 6. Invasion Day! Troops land in France. Talk here of nothing else--relief. Even if on radio there was a "spontaneous prayer-meeting in a rustic church in Ohio" which had evidently been thoroughly prepared long ago, this very efficiency in emotion may have some virtue. Glad Wells is in Italy, not this big invasion. (My just-come last letter from him dated May 19.) Temp: 63-41, noon 55, 6:30, 61. Mpls 65-44. NY 77-60. Sun out early AM. PM sunny and just pleasantly cool, with gt cumulus clouds....Lake Superior has a tide of 3 inches....9:30, the moon, invisible last few evenings, is full, with great rippled path of gold over lake....Twigs across face of moon.....Midnite, too high for moonpath--high and silver--the whole lake was a calm, radiant plain with yellow lights in Wisconsin gentle across the water, and lights from a slow gliding ship--the whole tender and inviting.

Wedn 7. Sun out most of the day, bright and cool. 71-40. Mpls 72-49.....Evening, clouds hid moon till ten, when it came up through a vast rift of dark clouds, gilding the rough edges of the vast lofty oval with splendor before it crept up into sight, a gold coin.

Thur 8, the first really Perfect Minnesota Day--p.d.--since I've arrived. At six radiant but cool, air delicious with all the dampness gone out of it, lilacs and new green leaves shining, birds exultant--and a little gray cat, another Ben Trovato come to call. Beautiful all day. 68-50

Fri 9. 68-50; Mpls 70-55. AM sunny, but thru strato-cirrus veil. With Kenneth Cant to Pike Lake, Grandview, Jay Cooke Park, Fond du Lac, the "Lost Valley" two or three miles s of F du Lac on #23. Astor Trading Post built at Fond du Lac in 1817. A squarehead named something like Oscar Peterson had it as a log barn, logs 2 ft square, and tore it down.

Sat 10. 73-45. Hot morning, sun thru fog, then developing into a real p.d.

Sun 11. Damp gray fog all day, with light sprinkle. 65-54. Mpls 67-59. For Sunday evening, see PAGE after NEXT.

fol. 122

beginning of carbon copy of part of a letter to Marcella Powers

Duluth--Sat June 10 1944

I told you, I'm afraid, that you take the Milwaukee railroad from Chicago to Duluth. I was wrong; my God, how pitifully and tragically wrong. It's the NORTHWESTERN railroad you take Chi to D.

I asked you on the phone if you had met Margaret Banning's boyfrien' with her and you said Yes, and then your letter shows that it was Victor Johnston, the Stassen-booster, that you met. No, no, no, no, no. Margaret's sweetheart, whom she may yet contrive to marry, even though she is a good Catholic and though she does have an ex-husband living--I believe it's done with annulments and mirrors--is Roy Salsich, that round, amiable, shrewd Dodsworth-like gent, very important in Minnesota, who is president of the Oliver Mining Company, the iron-mine dept of the Steel Trust, and probably the most powerful single iron-mining company in the world. You'll meet him here.

Victor J is head of the State Tourist Bureau, and we may be glad that he does want to see us both, we two lil darlings, in Minnesota, because he can open up state forests, bears and mooses, water-falls and wondersofnature to us--including state cars with gasoline.

I think Margaret is dead wrong in predicting a gay social whirl for you here, and you wrong in planning to bring all of Heddy Lamarr's wardrobe with you consequently. Margaret loves her Duluth--and stays here as little as possible. Except for Malick, Unitarian pastor, and his darling wife, and the young Ridders--none of whom Margaret really knows, I have found the people here kind, friendly, and about as ponderously dull and unkittenish as any I have ever known outside of the pages of that gt masterpiece "Babbitt." She sees them with the roseate eyes of unforgotten youth--about the way you see a horde of heels, actors, Stacys, ballet-dancers, Lord Russells or Lords Russell, and like trash. As to young people--meaning anybody under 38--either there just aren't any here, or I have to meet them.

Maybe I shall, when Margaret gets back here, but unless I am converted to Duluth's prankishness and jinks, don't brimg that wardrobe--bring slackses.

The 2 worst female voices that I have heard in Duluth, real corroded brass, belong (1) to a woman born in Idaho or Montana and (2) to the daughter of a well-to-do St. Louis, Mo., brewer.

The plans I am making for you--trying to keep them flexible and varied enough for you to make choices, run somewhat as follows: (1) I quit work entirely, except to keep up my chess--do you play that interesting game?--while you are here. (2) We--meaning Povah the Pooh and you and I--spend three or four days in Duluth, mildly seeing it and some people. (3) We go out, taking Lilian the Cook, to a lovely lake near here, one on which I <u>think</u> I'm going to be able to rent a commojus and comfortable cottage for a week or so, for another three or four or five days, and just loaf, sleep, swim, canoe, read, talk, play c-e-s-s. (4) we go, without too much motoring--I think I can manage the car and gas all right--up to the glorious North Shore of Lake Superior, and into the deep woods, say along the delightfully named Gunflint Trail,

end of letter carbon

fol. 123

beginning of carbon copy of part of a letter to Marcella Powers

Duluth Monday, June 12, 1944

And the garden is so lovely now, with lawn, great bushes of white lilacs and the purple French lilacs, cherry blossoms, white-blossoming mountain laurel which later will have red berries, elms and maples and so many kinds of conifer: white pine and balsam and spruce.

I suppose every city of over 40,000 has its Greenwich Village, its Bohemia. The other night I saw one part of Duluth's in the music at Hannakainen's; last evening a humbler but livelier and rather sweeter part--differing from a NY Greenwich Vge party not so much in talent as in a humble, almost-unalcoholic and non-posing friendliness. (beer only)

Clara Stocker, spinster of maybe 37, daughter of a prosperous Duluth doctor, now dead, has that eternal artistic longing which with her shows itself in writing symphony-orchestra notes, in adoring music, in having wandered about Europe, especially Finland, a lot, and in preferring to live alone and like it rather than manage to marry another grain-commission man with a brick house on the hill. She has a tiny--four-room--white cottage out on Minnesota Point, a long flat arm of land which divides the ocean-like Lake from the Harbor, i.e. St. Louis Bay.

It is right on the water of the harbor. When the Malicks (Unitarian) and I arrived, there was fog, and the bay was magic, low green islands, anchored sail boats, the water rippling silk under the grayness, and little puttering amateur boatyards along the shore....Inside, believe it or not, that empty wicker-covered Chianti bottle that used to be the sign and adornment of Hobohemia a generation ago. But also, comfortable chairs, and a couple pretty good original paintings--one by David Erickson, The local artist, now 70--I have still to meet him.

Presents besides Malicks and me: old Juho Rissanen, refugee Finnish artist--really of some, though not large, standing in Europe. Clara showed us a volume about him, printed in Finland, and solemnly, with that magnificent artistic egotism which I really lack and thus can never aspire to the greatness of a Faith Baldwin or a Philipvandorenstern<u>stern</u>, he showed us what seemed like a million photographs of his paintings--Finn peasant women braiding each other's hair, hairy gents with axes or fishing boats--and of his designs for stained glass windows.

He looked like Sibelius: a huge solid chunk of head with slit mouth, solid and solemn. But then he began to sing Finnish folk sounds--they sounded dirty to me--and you loved him; you saw him in every Paris atelier any time from 1800 to 1939. He is here because there are about 40,000 Finns in Minnesota--most of them farmers or iron-miners on the Mesabe Range, but between 3000 and 10000 here in Duluth--and they have cimmissioned him to paint, for the State Historical Society, a panel about pioneer Finn farming.

(2) Dr. Allane, a really charming Finnish scholar and uplifter, a jolly old cigar-smoking egg, half student and half business-man, who has been in America for years, and who runs the Minnesota co-operatives, which were founded largely by the Finns.

fol. 124

Duluth Mon June 12 cont.

(3) An immensely comic and rather endearing little man, a round and curly little man with a round little face and a curly little mustache, actually wearing, with a huge linen wing-collar, the first ascot tie I've seen in years. He is a music teacher, has a Studio of his own over in Superior, Wisconsin--which is really part of the port of Duluth, the state line running at the St. Louis River; himself teaches piano there, and in the season, with no wars about, teaches History of Music in the Superior State Teachers' College/ His name is something like Brousseau, spelled something like Browsough, and he--who looks more European and cafe-on-the-lesser-boulevards than six Elliot Pauls put together--was born in some Sauk Centre or other in America, worked as a railroad fireman while studying music, and has wandered a lot abroad. He claims to speak French, Italian, and German--I know he does speak the last excellently.....He talked, not too pretentiously, about the philology of Max Müller and the amiable dirt of Celleni.

(4) Miss Stocker herself, and another gal piano-teacher, from Duluth teachers' college but now going into the Red Cross. And they two together, on recorders--you know that Elizabethan musical instrument?--a kind of vertical flute?--played some of the Finnish airs which Stocker had heard from Rissanen and written down. Rather sweet and gay, and altogether unpretentious.....and you felt, all the while, how tragically lonely the old (at least 70) Finnish exile artist must be here, after a life in Finland, Denmark, Paris, Italy.

And the Malicks and I came out of the little white house, and the fog was gone, and across the water, the lights stared out from the hills of Duluth, which rise 500 feet from the water, but seemed to rise a thousand.

Yes, it was better than Greenwich Village; better than your buddies Johnny and Jay and Quenty and Franky, the hairy-chested hero-correspondents, who intrepidly cover the Invasion lands from the perilous heights of Radio City; and ten times better than the couple of dreary parties I've had here in the houses of the pretty-rich, where the expensive women discuss the horrors of Servants and Finns.

end of letter carbon

****

Monday morning; fog again, cool.

fol. 125

Duluth, June 1944

Mon 12 CONT. 60-49; Mpls, 81-61. Gray all day. Night loud with steamers. Evening, with Malicks to Rabbi Richard Singer.

Tue 13. 57-47. Mpls 74-67. Early AM, fog and chill rain. Fog clings so tenderly among thick poplars. Fog all day and dreary rain most.

Wedn 14 - 85-59, Mpls 88-65. WEDN-FRI, North Shore trip with Mark Nolan. SEE NEXT THREE PAGES. Early AM before start, sun had broken through for first time in days. p.d., though PM very hot.

Thur 15, Duluth 85-68, north shore cooler; Mpls 85-67. Outdoors, no moon, cd read watch at 10:15 PM. Fireflies

Fri 16, Duluth 85-60, Mpls 82-66.

Sat 17. Duluth does have the damdest variety of weather. From the hot midsummer of yesterday, with all possible windows open last night, it has leaped back, this morning, to chilly windy March. Another nor'easter. 69-43 (3 PM, 46—nearly 40° colder than 24 hrs before.). Mpls 85-71. Gray, windy, all day. Evening, thunder shower

Sun 18. AM, chill gray mist, and all day--noreaster continues. 41-37--40 under a few days ago. Mpls, 91-58! (Chicago, 94-74. Wash'n DC, 98-72! 57 degrees higher!)

Mon 19. Early AM fog burned away to radiant p.d., not too hot. To Carlton with Judge Ed Kenny. Seen from hill, St. Louis River in Real North setting--pines, birch, poplar, a little ragged, fresh and strong.....Suggested that dark water of St. L, Manitou rivers from iron....Suggested that when work low-grade iron ore, will be, because of extra weight, smelted in Duluth, so population grow.....Swing bridge over rapids of St. Louis r, in Jay Cooke Park--whitewater....74-44; Mp 71-50

Tue 20. p.d. in AM. PM a little hot, and sky filmed--cirro-stratus. Rain, thunder-shower, at 10....76-56. Mpls 77-54. NY 81-68.

Wedn 21. 84-60, Mpls 88-66. At 5:45, low sun makes the slight mist over woods and lake a golden froth over lake, then wash of gold on lake....Rain at 12, sun at 1--is this April? Late PM and evening, first hot steamy weather since been here. Some afterglow still at 10:45 PM.

Thur 22: 63-50, Mpls 85-68. Brilliant with wisps cloud at 6 AM, turned dark and storm-promising by 7; not storm but gray and windy all day, Pastoral Lakewood section - low hills w shorn pastures amid sloping woods, lake seen like ocean between hills, all like Devon--with Victor Ridder.

Fri 23, 77-47, mpls 75-58. gray and drizzle at 6, p.d. PM with one brief rain - explore harbor with Kenny Cant et al. - see later page. June 19-23 incl form "shortest day of year." Hate to see days "draw in" again. Wedn 21, sunrise here in Duluth 5:12, set 9:17 CWT; Fri 23, rise 5:13, set 9:07. Calendar gives for Boston on 23d: rise 4:23, set 7:40, EST = 5:23-8:40 EWT, so day here 37 min longer   Fri: cd read watch at 10:25 PM

fol. 126

beginning of carbon copy of part of a letter to Marcella Powers

June 17 1944—cont

David Erickson, the local artist....Born in Duluth, went to Art Institute in NY, studied under Whistler, lived over 30 years in France and Italy, has come back here at 75, a little deaf, a little lame, his long beloved wife dead, his son, an oil engineer, not very well.....A little round man, in worn blue suit and little black shoes and a little black bow tie and a little round black hat, right out of the Cafe du Dome in Paris.....His face a round comic mask, but his eyes sad. His painting a combination of imitation-Whistler and imitation-Turner with a little broken color thrown in.....The cathedral and the Piazetta at Venice and a festival on the Grand Canal and villages in Brittany, in Normandy....Ceased entirely to be Duluth but never quite became European....One of 10,000 artists--professional, competent, utterly mediocre....Lives now by selling a painting very rarely, and by teaching a class of amateurs.....There's the whole novel; lonely in a boarding house in Duluth; the richer Duluth women almost too pityingly kind to him. The End.

Mrs. Griggs, wife of the banker, who took me to his studio (in a Duluth store building!) is herself a pretty good painter--about as good as her revered master, Erickson! Once she did Street in Chartres, Hill with Ruins; for years now, did sons and daughters and grandchildren; still boyishly handsome, curly-headed, erect, gay. At once a sturdy 20, and a handsome fifty-odd. And so kind to Erickson......You do get all the world in this microcosm.....But as to liking people: my chief delights are Jack and Elizabeth Malick, and Mark and Ann Nolan--as incompatible a quartette as the Bertrand Russells and the Spike Hunts. (Not that Ann is one bit an Emmy.)

....

end of letter carbon

Sun red ball in mist casts only blurred path on water

---

fol. 127

<u>Insert</u>

beginning of carbon copy of part of a letter to Marcella Powers

Duluth, Friday June 16, 1944

A great two days on the North Shore of Lake Superior, where I took Micky two years ago, this time with Judge Mark Nolan.

I think you know that the central character of The Novel is a District Judge in a city somewhat like Duluth crossed with Winona with overtones of Minneapolis. So it is the greatest luck to become so well acquainted with Mark. My man's character will be as different from his as can be, but I do get back stage; come to know how a judge can, or does, drink, read, garden, make love, go fishing, talk to ministers, in private life. With Judge Vince Day of Minneapolis--all gentle uplift where Mark is boisterous drive--and Mark, I now really know something about judges with the make-up off.

Mark is a big Irish Catholic, mildly leonine black hair and blue eyes that could be choleric, fond of liquor and women, called by his first name by almost every one from clerk of court to the man running the beer truck up the North Shore, yet a learned and good judge, graduate of Notre Dame and taught Government there for a year after graduation; from the Iron Range and so looked at doubtfully by some of Duluth's more refained; witty, blasphemous, frightfully on to everything; completely a Good Fellow and, I rather suspect, completely honest and rigidly just.....He handsomely wears dark double-breasted coat and black tie with fine white stripe when he is on the bench (here, unlike Mpls, the judges do not don silk robes) but off it he prefers sports jacket--or just shirt sleeves, with suspenders festively showing--while he finishes his sixth highball--which, next morning, is incredibly NOT going to produce any hangover at all!

And, just to make everything inconsistent, as are all human characters, he is as much of a view-collector as I am; he stops the car for every waterfall, fisherman's cottage, high-colored cumulus cloud, point sticking out into the blue and golden lake.....He is, in fact, almost a fictional Irishman, lovable, a fighter, a dreamer, a hell-raiser--but with it all a stark streak of Anglo-Saxon strictness in his duties as judge.

His pleasant wife Ann, whom you will meet, did not go along; just Mark and I started off by car Wednesday morning, and up to the slightly dirty town of Two Harbors, 30 miles from Duluth and its adjunct in loading iron ore into steamers. To thr Lake County court-house there--theoretically, our trip was for him to hold court; and in the oak-panelled small courtroom, with the damndest echo from a small inside dome which some local architect had been inspired by the devil to use for adornment, We (I as silent assistant judge) heard for hours a dreary case in which a muzzy-faced Mpls lawyer did allege that a Mpls druggist, a North Shore farmer and a Chippewa Indian pinched the materials of a summer cottage which he had torn down.....The farmer's wife was born and has lived all her life in the woods and, from dress, speech, manner, coolness, you would swear that she was the gardening and golfing wife of a prosperous super-commuter on Long Island....Her husband brought the only bright spark; the plaintiff,

fol. 128

Insert Fri 6/16 -2

who was unhappily conducting his own case, demanded, "This letter your wife wrote me about the place--she doesn't take any major action without consulting you, does she?" and the beaming husband grunted, "You'd be surprised!"

I am now, per Mark, a lifelong friend of all the Lake County courthouse attaches: the sheriff, a big Swede who used to be in the motor business; the clerk of court, who used to be a contractor and really had once piled up about $200,000 before his partner got to him and now anxiously inches on in this small job. Most everybody there was Scandinavian. In fact the whole population of the North Shore--they live by deepsea fishing, small farming, and renting tourist cabins for three months of the year--is Scandinavian, and their accented and rather pleasant language is commoner than the pure valiant language of South Orange and Brooklyn.

Mark had there his own reporter, who came up from Duluth--Stanley Gilpin--a short, worried, casual man, who serves as judge's secretary, court jester, and counsellor.

Mark, by the way, is only 42, though he has been on the bench for eight years.

Well, court over, we started scooting up the north shore. He had arranged for us to get a quite decent cabin--indoor toilet, shower bath, good beds--right on the shore of Superior, among the pines and birches. It was one of a cluster touchingly named ELVING'S MIGHTY FINE CABINS.

All the rest of Wednesday, and all Thursday & part of this AM--since there wasn't another case till this morning--we explored the North Shore, Mark, being the perfect politician--but also being a very kind fellow who likes people, almost all people except reformers and Methodist evangelists--stopped at cabin after cabin, and introduced me to Swede women running little roadside restaurants, a Yankee-faced whisky-loving farmer who is county commissioner, the lone Irish wife of a large-scale fisherman, the proprietor of a joint with slot machines, the wife, very nice, of the captain of one of the Great Lakes oar boats, who rents cabins during the summer, a grand old Norwegian who first came to the North Shore in 1886, when, since there wasn't even a horse road, he had to walk in, pack on back and axe slung above it.

And we saw waterfalls and waterfalls--don't sniff, they were quite exciting, choked with the full chocOlate-colored floods of late spring. The smooth, sneering, rather terrifying floods of the Baptism River and the Gooseberry River, suddenly bursting over a rock barrier and dropping fifty feet.

Best was Manitou Falls. We climbed up and up a hill, by a rocky and neglected path, then on the flat, cool among birch trees, then cautiously down broken stairs, foot deep in water, panting in the heat that on

Wednesday had suddenly replaced the stretch of grayness and cold fogs, edging down, hoping not to turn an ankle--and came out on a boiling down-pouring river that must drop seventy feet down into a dark, rock-lined gorge, melodramatically beautiful. Along the lofty

fol. 129

Insert Fri. 6/16 -3

rocks of the gorge, seemingly living without earth at all, cling dizzy little cedars and birches. The gorge is filled with mist flung up by the shattered waters, and through it, casual, so delicate in all this tumult, where Kubla heard ancestral voices broadcast on the war, gaily flittered white butterflies!

The gayest thing we saw was in a little roadside saloon which, with its cement floor and walls, whitewashed, resembling some little backcountry French or Italian trattoria, two Swedes who had spiked their beer were indulging in that rather earnest and lugubrious gaiety, that psalmodic melody, characteristic of the Norlanders. The juke box was playing "Home on the Range" sung in Swedish, believe it or not, and the Swedes were accompanying it in strongly Swedish Americanese. Behind the bar, beaming, were the entirely virtuous female proprietor and a couple of nice farm girls, her wartime assistants.

And then there is Rudolph Illgen, a cherry little Heinie, who came to America as a penniless kid, built and flew an aeroplane in about 1916, and now has a mess of roadside cottages and an almost Hollywood fantasy in the way of an Aztec Temple, which looks just as Aztec as I do and which is, of course, a combination beer-saloon, restaurant, souvenir shoppe......This is, by the way, the only Boston Post Road or Hollywood horror on the North Shore, There are a good many tourist cabins, but they are mostly inoffensive clusters of log cabins, and are quite lost and unnoticeable in the 150-mile stretch of woods and lake, glittering on the reefs, with magnificent bluffs and headlands breaking the coastline.

Then there was Grand Marais, that tiny village between lake and a vast semi-circle of tall hills, and here in the little harbor were two vast lake steamers loading pulp wood--picking up the round yellow logs from a floating raft, yanking them up over an endless chain of hooks, and petulantly spitting them out into the steamer's hold,.....And ashore, a coast guard, a Stetson-hatted Border Patrol man, and a drunk Irish sailor, all out of a movie.

Late evenings, we sat around our little cabin while Mark drank Bourbon (and I the old vintage soda) and he told stories of courts and judges.....And it was Mark who cooked breakfast, Mark who washed the dishes, Mark who loaded and unloaded the car, and it was somehow right in the picture of this profane Wild Irishman that he should be as neat and fussy a housekeeper, as much a cleaner-up and putter-away, as S. M. Povah herself.

Those blue and silver and golden days, waves and streaked currents and bold brown headlands, ducks and sea-gulls, birches and poplar and spruce and pine and balsam and cedar, all flashing in sunshine the more grateful after many days of fog and grayness, the smell of pine logs and sea, and the good gay judge--one is able to live in a romantic novel for a day or two, now and then!

end of letter carbon

waves sparkle coming in shore from under lite mist Sea-gulls—not seen in Duluth—abt fishing vges. One flutters w. broken wing

fol. 130

NORTH SHORE DISTANCES

Center of Duluth	0
French River	12 miles
Sucker "	15
Stony Pt.	16.4
Knife River	18
Two Harbors	26
Silver Ck Cliff	31
Encampment	33

Lafayette Bluff	34
Gooseberry Riv	39
SR Lighthouse	45
Beaver Bay	51
Palisade Head	56
Baptism Riv	58
Illgen	59
Little Marais	68
Manitou Riv	69
Cross River	80
Temperance Riv	80 plus
Tofte	83
Lutsen	91
Cascade Riv	100
Grand Marais	110
Hovland	130
Grand Portage	148 (5 mi on side road)
Pigeon River	150

fol. 134

DULUTH--LAKE NOTES

The ore boats have pilot house in bow, then maybe 500 ft of hatches, then quarters after. Red or black. All day you hear their whistles as approach the Canal--signalling 3 times got the aerial bridge to be lifted. Deep-toned whistle.

When not too windy, smoke lies in long horizontal lines.

Saw a small freighter, stubby, deep well deck. One w 2 booms

Ore boats run 600 & 640 ft long. Average 24 in 24 hrs out of Duluth. Fleet of abt 375 on lake--not all to Duluth.

See steam from whistle bef hear whistle
Lighthouses. Foam on rocks.
Stacks of dif. liners.

Fog horn—yawp & dif one follow
Steamers all anchor for fog 8 PM - 7 AM, May 31
Green light

fol. 135

beginning of carbon copy of a letter to Marcella Powers

Duluth June 24--Saturday

The longest day of the year is--or are, since that day is anywhere from June 19-23, incl.--over, and that always gives me a brief sentimental sadness, to see the days "draw in" again.

Two really noble trips (after work-hours) on Thursday & Friday. First--about Victor Ridder. He is the father of Bob, of whom I have written. With two brothers, he publishes the Staats-Zeitung and Journal of Commerce, in NYC--where he lives, with summers in Duluth, the only two papers in St. Paul, the ditto in Duluth, and a paper in Grand Forks, N. Dak. Important. Though an ardent Republican, he once, at a difficult time, took over the running of the whole WPA in NYCity. Of a good ancestral German family he is, though apparently anti-Hitler with several nephews and I think a son in the service, now being attacked by your bearded and auto-papal (new word just coined) friend Rex Stout as being practically a German agent, which is pretty vicious nonsense. (Whether Rex's running mate Kip Fadiman is also in on this stink, I don't know--I'm afraid so.)

Victor stays out here for the summer with Bob, pretty modestly, except for blowing himself to chauffeur, which is necessary, for he is lame, walks with elaborate pair of metal crutch things, after having had tuberculosis twice and cancer once and having, for latter, breast almost cut away. But he doesn't show it at all; his face--he must be 55-60 - is curiously young and eager, with a soft touch of Peter Loree (when playing Nize People, not Villains), of some European strangeness about it. He knows Europe bassackwards, but so does he such assorted sections of America as the Catskills, Vermont, Colorado. A really clever man--and, like myself (that other clever man, you know--the one you met) he is a Collector of Views; goes up, like me, to a hillscape or an ocean, takes a delicate pinch, smells it, and says, "Johannisberger Cabinet, 1917--very fine brand."

When I first met him, I thought him dictatorial, a man who, like Dorothy and Geo Jean Nathan, never listens to anybody else. But I have come to like him immensely, and so will you, when you meet him here.

And he has become my chief chess-mate--he plays maybe a little better than Herb Mayes, not quite so well as old Frank Crassweller.....Well, Thursday, he drives me out behind this rim of hills to Lakewood, some complete charming, un-Northern-Minnesota country NE of Duluth--pastures and little hills, with little upland meadows, and between and beyond the hills, the great arc of ocean that is Lake Superior. We might have been in Devonshire.....So we go to the Northland Country Club, and play chess, and look out at the oldish (but many of them were oldish at 28) women chattering in pretty lounge, and have dinner with kolossal roast beef....and play chess....and I get licked three several games. (You still have not explained, whether done on boards or in the mind, whether in yr three-dimensional chess you move on one board after another, through the eight, or play eight players at once, or WHAT--or don't your bright young innovators know?)

fol. 136

June 24 -2

Then yesterday I had another of the trips which are beginning to make me love Duluth--as I do a number of places in New England and England and Italy; far more that I ever did Minneapolis.

I went out from 3:30 in the afternoon till 11 in a motor cruiser exploring the Duluth-Superior Harbor, and it's glorious--starting with big industry and in a few miles becoming forest and wilderness--with every known kind of waters in between.

The dividing line between Wisconsin--Superior, and Minnesota--Duluth is the St. Louis River, a fine large stream full of rapids and Indian

History (oh yes, both visible) and the current down through the habor which is formed by the course of that river. The harbor is protected by an immensely long thin neck of land called Minnesota Point, with one opening cut through it at the Minn end and one at the Wis end. Through these stream all day long the innumerable long low steamers which come in loaded with coal (to be distributedfrom here as far west as Dakota and Montana and Saskatchewan, and to be edifyingly sent down also to Mpls-St.Paul) and go out jammed with wheat or iron ore. The passage at the Minn end has a bridge whose whole center portion suddenly alarmingly leaps up into the air when a steamer wants to go through--the Aerial Bridge, we call this.

I tell you all this not only so that you may inspect with informed eyes when you arrive, but also so that you can report to the Henry George League, to Jay Allan and to tht Mme Mojeska (spelled Hedy Lamarr) who makes the lovely red chairs.

So we depart from a lovely old Southern-mansion sort of boat house--which was, before the damn automobile came in to steal all the excitement away from boating, some 30 years ago, the center of all that was young and brave and terpsichorean in Duluth--and slide down the harbor, passing 640-ft ore boats, vast skinny coal cranes that bite up a ton at a time out of a steamer's hold, the vast smokiness of the Zenith Furnace Company, the Carbide Company, the American Steel and Wire Company. We wriggle through a channel, almost sticking on a sand bar, and are in a bay which, though the steel mill is visible across a mile of river, might be on a Northern Lake 400 miles from any city. Bluffa crowned with basswood and spruce and maple and cedar. And on these we visited two summer houses solidly built in the days when a well-to-do Duluthian went places by boat instead of by the automobile that has changed all the American social habits. Spirit Lake. Spirit Island—Indians thought haunted—& Big Island, w. farm

You remember--the French and Sullivan families?--Mr. Sullivan married Mrs. French after (presumably not before) Mr. F died? Two big, solid, uncomfortable, quite ugly summer houses of 40 years ago. The screens have all rusted. In one place, the vines had grown right <u>through</u> the screen. We went in and here were old kitchen stove, rockers, fireplaces all untouched. In one were several magazines dated

fol. 137

June 24 -3

1938--probably the last time anybody had been in there. The elaborate grounds were all overgrown with brush and saplings, and what had been a bridge over a ravine between the two houses was broken.....Here, young people had danced and swum and laughed, and now all silent--though if you had wedged your way through the undergrowth, you would have seen, across 2 miles of water,—1 mile?, the Steel Plant that wasn't there when they were built.

We made our way into Pokegama Bay, on the shore of which, and East for a hundred miles, there is almost nothing but unbroken second-growth woods, gone back into wilderness since the lumbermen were here. We had supper, and a good one--cold roast beef, salad, Lucullan huckleberry pie, while The Boys had a great many Bourbon and sodas and poor Mr. Lewis drank ginger ale, and everybody told informative anecdotes about travelling men and sexual intercourse. A little storm came up--you could see it travelling from the hills behind Duluth, miles away, with long lances of rain--but when it hit us, the anchored boat just rocked comfortable, and Charlie Liscomb said, "Say, have you heard the one about the boy that wrote his father if he would send him $500, he knew a fellow that would teach their dog to talk?"

We came back into the main harbor and now, weather cleared, a vast sunset roared over the hills, showered down across the water. Again we passed industry--cement elevatora like Pan-pipes 200 ft high, fantastic coal cranes, more ore docks, at Allouez, where the Jesuit of that name founded the first Indian mission in these parts, his name known now no longer for the tinkle of his little mass bell, but only for the G.N. Ore Loading Docks. A fable of civilization.

Following one of the vast ore boats, looking up at cheerful sailors on deck at their stern quarters, we went out through the Wisconsin channel to the open lake--open ocean--as it was now calm....with maybe not more than a 40 % chance of a squall, of a fog that would hold us all night, and that to these Duluth men, who serve 2 or 3 nights a week in the Coast Guard reserve, was no more than it would be to a professional Vikingess like you....So for six miles we clicked along toward the main portion of Duluth, with a faint quiet afterglow in the skies even till 11. The hills were at first just a dark bulky haze, then little by little you saw--well, anyway, I mean I saw--the street lights arching up the hill, past the crinkled plane of waters....My God, I did love the place then. Marcella, with her damn Minneapolis and her birthplace, Winona, has nothing like this, I said to The Boys.

Said Boys were seven men all from 40 to 55--Kenneth Cant, the real estate man who got me this house, big and kindly and somehow touching and lonely, Lou Castle, the banker, Fred Buck and John Hoff and Winton Brown, all real estate--the first always running charity drives and war loan drives and getting out of it for himself nothing but satisfaction, Arthur Miller the banker, Charlie Liscomb the insurance broker.....They all are prosperous, they all have wives and children, sons in the war, they are all good members of a

fol. 138

Duluth June 24, 1944 -4

June 24 -4

Protestant Church and of the Chamber of Commerce, they all hate Roosevelt (and especially Eleanor Roosevelt) and the Farmeers' Co-operatives, they all love golf a little and duck-hunting passionately, most of them are college graduates, none of them are dull, really, but they do repeat over and over the same little family-like joke--about Charlie having been born in the village of Aitkin and Lou in Heron Lake--not very good jokes--not MUCH better, really, than one of Geo Macy's.....Snd all so wonderfully kind to the outsider, so eager to duck down into the cramped little four-berth cabin of the cruiser to bring him up coffee and more salad.....and more damn ginger ale.

These men are halfway between a Babbitt and a Dodsworth: not so drearily illiterate as Babbitt, not so executive and powerful as Dodsworth.....They are Upper Middle Class America, and I think that if one lived among them ten years, one would like them rather better than all our War Correspondents.

They love their sons in the war....They have illusions abt their sexual prowess and when they go to Minneapolis, they try to pick up what they call, generically, Blondes.....They are proud of their city....They are good outdoor men....I think they are peculiar to America, and in Babbitt I just began to paint them. You, alas, will probably see almost none of them, when you come, and you'll go back to NY ignorantly supposing that Duluth is inhabited solely by New Yorkers like Margaret Banning and 62 Ridders, where as, in the rich possession of these Babbitworths, it's really far more interesting than that, Comrade--

end of letter carbon

Sat. 24. 73-57, Mpls 86-62. Gray, fairly cool, AM. 2:10, rain storm, have to close windows, turn on lights, thunder, then torrent and hail. Sun out shyly in 15 minutes. 2:50, rain again, and at 3:50, terrific thunder-lightning, kind when you say, "That hit the house"--1st I remember since Minnetonka, 2 yrs ago. And did hit wires in alley by house, and lights off. Over, and sun out again at 4:20. No wonder I complained in Calif of monotony of weather.

Sun 25: Not been so many p.d.'s as at Minnetonka, but not so many hot here, either--fine for work. 60-47; Mpls. 96-67! K.C. 97-72; Omaha, 100-73. But NY 72-62. AM, chilly, gray, lake a black and silver waste. PM bright, slightly chill, almost p.d., tho fog on the lake.

Mon 26, 79-50; Mpls 95-73. Cool, bright, absolutely clear AM, real p.d. at last. 5:20, sun was up full, red and hearty, with garland of little gold clouds like riotous cherubs. p.d till evening--then rain.

Tue. 27. 85-56 (6:30 PM, 84). Mpls 91-78. NY, 88-58. AM, gray, lake a wash of silver. Fog, over lake and land, & drizzle at 9. PM p.d., then turns hot. Could, tho just barely, read watch outdoors at 10:25 P.M.--just heavy dusk then.

Wedn 28. AM chill, very windy, gray sky w sun coming thru. PM, clear, bright, cool, wind just a liveliness in branches & clouds. 66-55; Mp, 74-56; Chicago (Dewey nominated today) 98-75; Cincinnati and Cleveland, top of 100.

fol. 139

74-52; Mpls 75-58; NY, 92-73

beginning of carbon copy of part of a letter to Marcella Powers

Duluth, Thursday, June 29, 1944

What a day--the first in Duluth this year completely of the type known to meteorologists as a p.d., or "absolutely perfect day"--cool, the air sweet, sky ringing blue except for lovely lazy clouds, as idyllic and indolent as a Grecian glade, yet full of energy for people from Chicago. The grass in my lawn here softly green; dusky shadows among the shrubs with fleur de lis set in front of them. The lake a mirror of many kinds of blue and gray glass, some sleek, some delicately wrinkled. The robins on the lawn full of optimism, and a song-sparrow reciting with a gaiety unknown on ordinary days.

I don't know any place, not even New England, that has quite such perfect days--and if one did come there, I think it would be end of May, not end of June....This is a Minnesota day, to be extremely scientific; in the southern part of the state, we suffer the horrors of the tropics; up here, we go about with icicles on our red beards; but after such torments, we are all rewarded and made singularly blessed by such a day as this.

end of letter carbon

9 AM, whole lake suave and rose-colored, with quiet steamer trailing smoke....A p.d. is crystal, emerald and sapphire.

Fri 30, 78-57; Mp, 83-58...6 AM, hot sun behind curtains of light mist, and the lawn seems sprinkled with gold dust....Noon, rain threat; PM, warm, beautiful. To American Steel & Wire plant with John McConnaughy. Dark plant with St. Louis River shining among isles on one side, dark-ravined hills rising to Bardon's Peak on the other, Smacking wire to make nails. Metalurgist who thot 14 hrs a day work fine for health of men.

JULY

Sat. July 1st. 76-59; Mpls 82-62. I hate to lose another June--in Northern US it is that month, not April or May, that is beyond all precious. 7 AM, warm, half-gray, soon much cooler, and p.d. afternoon. Evening, with Margaret and young Dr. Mary Banning to Roy Salsich's for dinner. Vast peonies, many fleur de lis in gardens

Sun. 2: Early, storm is promised; clouds half-dark, half-silver, marshalled as for battle. But PM bright, with cirrus. 67-53 (67 at 3 PM). Mpls 82-62. All day, with lunch of fish planked before fireplace at Fred & Gladys Buck's cottage, Schultz Lake: Kenny & May Cant, Chas & Mrs. Liscombe...The peonies now are as lavish and fleshy as Rubens ladies. Many particolored daisies, too.....Rice and Sunshine Lakes nr Schultz...Flicker of rhythmic light waves on side of a boat, on under side of screened summer house. "Sleep cabins" of canvas with wood floors.

fol. 140

July 1944--Duluth

Mon. 3: 81-60. Mpls 84-63. AM gray, one gash of burning gold on lake from early sun.

Tue 4: 6:30 AM, drizzling, foggy, hot, humid--worst type of seashore day, and 1st since I've been here. No wind, breathless, hard to work. By 10, rain quits, sun beginning to struggle out. Fog horn first sounds like plaintive calf, then like furniture being dragged across a floor, PM, gray, fog on lake. Heavy fog creeps up from lake, stealing like detectives among shrubs. Evening, no fog, but chill.....73-56. Mpls 89-69.

Wedn 5: 61-53. Mpls 86-71. Cincin 96-59. NY 91-67. Early AM, fog, chill drizzle. But exciting, at 6:15 AM coffee, to look across wet terrace, through cement balusters and wet mountain ash trees, down into the fog-filled valley with the thought of the hidden lake 250 feet below, whence fog horn and steamer's anxious whistle. Nothing prairie-flat here! Very thick fog all day everywhere, and cool till 6, when sun suddenly out.

Thur 6: 78-51, Mp 80-63. NY 94-74. AM, drizzle, light fog, cool. Dark beauty of early-morning fog....7:30, Fog and Thunder--a title..Lights on in house till 9 AM. What is this? Iceland? But I like such weather. Sun out abt 11. Dark again at 2, rain again at 6.

Fri 7: 81-63. Mpls 86-64. NY 90-70....8 AM, sun breaks thru, warm, steamy, irritable. Hard to start work, not bad when get going...All AM, thin sunshine, fog on lake. PM, sun out, hot. 11 PM, thunder storm, heavy rain.

Sat. 8: 71-61. Mpls 73-66. NY 94-68. Early AM, radiant, lots of cirrus, which clears from sky, and most of PM and evening, p.d., bright, cool, light breeze, lingering carress of golden light in early evening, with sweet smell of bare earth and meadows beyond F. du Lac. Lake glittering all PM. With Kenneth Cant & Ellen Gibson to Rest View, past Buffalo Bill's abandoned house but not seeing it, Mission Creek, (Bardon's Peak), Fond du Lac, ski jump, Swedish meat balls, Lost Valley 2 miles beyond F d L on Route 23, across rough cut-over country, itching with ore-rr tracks, to Superior and cribs on old 3d Street--was it Indian Sadie, ½ Mex, ½ Indian?...Duluth full of ripe fleshy peonies now: pink, white, wh with red splashes. They prefer North climate.

Sun 9: MARCELLA TWO WEEKS FROM TODAY!
64-51 Mpls: 79-59; NY 91-74. Early AM, gray, but lake a glory of grays, silvery, rough and dull, sleek, frowning dark to E on horizon. PM and even, p.d Buffet supper at Helen Bede's on Minnesota Point--Malicks,

Flynn, a county commissioner, Wassings, refugees, he plays cello in Duluth orchestra but has to earn living as Hotel Duluth porter (Austrian Jews), she teaches French-German, A. E. Rich, State Inspector of municipal budgets (probably once Riccio) and lover of canoe-trips with Supreme Ct Justice Magney who weighs 350--even in a canoe!. Mrs. Fred Buck's bro, a photog. Conversation at least better than the boozy kiddings of Griggs, Salsich, et al.--labor unions afraid to back school-teachers' demands. Place glorious: front door on long sea beach, driftwood and damp edge with wave tracks and birds and all. Look out on glittering lake to 3 steamers, seeming so tall on horizon, then going golden in late lite out under cumulus, eastward bound! To left, crouching hills of Duluth & spires

fol. 141

Duluth, July 1944

Mon 10: 68-50; Mpls 79-62; NY 90-72. Gray most of the day. In garden now besides peonies: fleur de lis, painted daisies, single roses, tiger lilies, delphinium.

Tue 11: 61-54; Mpls 74-66; NY 91-74. All day, thick fog right up to the houses; steady drizzle all PM till mid-evening. Northern Land!

Weds 12: 75-54; Mpls 77-58; NY 88-74. p.d.--for which abt 75 seems to be ideal temperature; cool, golden, serene, yet vigorous breezes in late PM.

Thur 13: 76-51; Mpls 85-60; NY 87-72. Early, light fog with sun trying to struggle thru. Fog horn gets on nerves. By PM, p.d. ashore, though Lake still milky with low fog, which goes in late PM, then everywhere p.d.

Fri 14: 75-61; Mpls 77-64.....6 AM, out over lake, magnificent dark thunder clouds, with a vast fissure edged with polished copper. Rain, but only a few minutes, at 6:30. All morning, battle of clouds, like that going on at St. Lo in Normandy just now. Sometimes a narrow bright glare at the horizon edge on an otherwise dark lake; or a bright trusting cloud amid the black celestial mob. Gets darker; lights on in the house; suddenly, at 3:30, sun out and rather warm.

Sat 15: 77-58; Mpls 79-61; NY 85-65. Day starts grandiosely with sun on a wine-dark sea, bold red on Eastern horizon with fragment of old moon bright above it. p.d. all PM. To Oneota Cemetery and memorial slab to Geo R. Stuntz.

Sun 16: M arrive week from today......81-55, Mp 85-59; NY 84-72. Sea afire with sunrise at 5 AM and still the little wafer of the courageous old moon...Clear all day.

Mon 17: 68-59; Mpls 78-63. Early, thin sunshine with promise of rain. Clear by 10:30 and real p.d. Chilly clear evening. Tweed Hall and County Historical and satin wall cloths and tall green marble fireplaces--old Cotton house.

Tue 18: 80-55 (but seemed less hot), Mpls 82-64; NY 86-65. Early, gray mackerel sky. PM p.d.

Wedn 19: Rain threat all day but no rain; sooty underside of shining cumulus.

Thur. 20. The best day, the most unquestionable p.d. this summer; so bright, the air so cool and sweet and enlivening, rolling clouds, and the lake very blue--which it is rarely. 73-44; Mpls 72-55; NY 82-68.

Fri 21: 78-54; Mpls 81-53; NY, 99-69!....Almost as beautiful as yesterday. Walking the leafy streets with the Peytons, great sense of a village.

Sat 22: 82-59. Great plum-colored sunrise. Hazy sky in the morning, gray all afternoon, rain starts at 6 & keeps up all evening, with terrific thunder shower at 4 A.M. Sunday.

fol. 142

Duluth, July 1944

Sun July 23: Marcella and her mother arrive from NY--fog in morning looked unco-operative, but PM cleared. Drive to Fond du Lac. Col.

Cody's house with staggering porch. Whiteside the other name for Big Island. 78-62; Mpls 81-65; NY 90-71.

Mon 24: 82-53; Mpls 86-60; NY 90-74. p.d.

Tue 25-Sat 29 incl. Asa Lyons, driver. North Shore of Lake Superior, to Fort William and Port Arthur, Canada; staying at Lutsen's and Jesse & Mrs. Gapen's Gateway Lodge at Hungry Jack Lodge--see 1942......Sat 29: 74-56; Mpls 78-57; NY 85-72. Lakes reached from Hungry Jack: Bearskin, Duncan, Rose (with steps portage).

Wild sorrell in long grass....Double red poppies in Rudolph Illgen's garden.....Lyle Oreck and Thelma and Dr. Jumer.....Place names: Gunflint Trail, Grand Marais, Thunder Bay (Canada - P. Arthur).....Mrs. McNeal at Grand Portage....Bob Pack's and Dr. Curtiss's shore houses.

Fish: northern pike, lake trout, walleyed pike, land-locked salmon, bass, crappie, brook trout (herring in Superior)......Thimbleberry leaves fill opening of portage on old trail at G. Portage.

Conifers: spruce, Norway & white & Jack (or yellow) pine, balsam, arbor vitae, cedar.....Larch.

Sun 30: 81-56; Mpls 85-57; NY 90-71. p.d., most beautiful day so far this summer. Lake in the afternoon a mosaic in gray--riffled streaks between mirror patches, and couple sail boats out, not common; after sunset, lake all rose, with quarter moon.....New of Hal. Eveng, last of the Ridders.

Mon 31: 79-60; Mpls 85-65; NY 89-74. Gray. Rain in the evening, after tea at Carly Heimbach's, makes us shift intended at-Enger-Park picnic with Mark & Ann Nolan to basement here and bowling.

AUGUST

Tue August 1: 74-60; Mp 92-69; NY 80-75. Early AM, heavy fog; sun thru at 8:15. To park on Minnesota Point with Malicks. Evening, big party with music, bowling, too much Bourbon: Margaret Banning, very corrective, with Mary and Leroy Salsich; Marvin Orecks, she Australian actress; Malicks, Nolans, 3 Peytons, 3 Anneckes incl CharlOHtte Galvan, Barbara Griggs, Kenny Cants, Otto & Florence Lachmund, John & Mrs. McConnaughys, Saltuses, Harvaliks, Ellen Gibson, Lew Castle.

Late July, meeting of the Duluth Kiwanis: C. Elmer Hammer presided vice Harry C. Applequist, and Miss Dorothy Tart sang, accompanied by Jackson K. Ehlert. The worst names I ever invented--as I must have.

fol. 143

Duluth, August 1944

Wedn August 2: 80-60; Mp 92-69; NY 80-75. Hazy PM. Klearflax factory.

Thur 3: 84-64 (but PM seemed hotter than 84); Mp 94-75; NY 82-70. Brule River all PM and evening with Bannings, Lew Castle, his daughter Francis, and Jane Coulter, Jean Peyton sr, Marshall and Margaret Alworth, Lachmunds, Dr. Frank Hirschboeck....Cedar Island Lodge (Henry Clay Pierce to Jack Ordway), 4000 acres and a bear pit and Coolidge. Roy's place on the Brule, Rainbow Bend. Drive back with Lew through thunder storm as reach Itasca on edge of Superior.

Fri 4: 84-64. Heatwave thru nation; tops in other cities: Mp 84, NY 99, KC 101, Phila 97, F. Worth 102, Detroit 98, Madison 96, Phoenix 113--but Bismarck and Des Moines 76.

p.d. Marcella and her mother lv for New York. Party at Elsa Anneke's, incl Jean Nelson, John and Efith Hoff, Forrest Graham of Little Theater....Full moon rioting through mackerel sky over the lake, with a lighted steamer on the moon-glossy sea. But thunder storn late in the night.

Sat 5: State Historical Society at Two Harbors with Hirschboeck, Dick and Cornelia Bardon. Gray day, radiant moon-blazing evening, moon over the ripples on Agate and Burlington Bays. 73-62; Mp 82-68; NY 99-79; Phila top 97, F Worth 102, Chi 91, Detroit 92.

Sun 6: Early, gray and chilly. Sun thru at 10, and a cool p.d. Harvalik, chess. Even, Julius Barnes and his book, maybe "Business Is Exciting." 67-59. Mp, 85-63. NY 87-77/ Bismarck & Des Moines, which behaved so well on the 4th, had highs of 90 & 85.

Mon 7: 67-54. Mp, 86-83, NY 79-72. Mountain ask berries are reddening for autumn now; already are yellow and orange. From this house, not only incredibly beautiful prospect, soft brilliance of the demure hills, radiance of the lake, trees hiding the houses below, but also delightful sounds: train whistle, deep demand of the steamers, rustle of leaves, idle dogs not too close.

Starts as p.d. but by noon, gray and chilly; 3 on, drizzle. Tom and Kitty Gibson come in with Peytons, evening.

Tue 8: The damndest day; AM mild rain, then, rain over, gray and chilly. Very gray in PM, with fog on lake, the SS Moronic laboring out thru it, and sticky-warm, as in evening, plus light rain......Speaking of Moronic, libel of my saying Duluth women "delightful morons." 82-59; Mp 90-69; NY 82-68.

fol. 144

Duluth, August 1944

Wed 9: Early PM, p.d. on land, haze on lake. Late PM, too hot. 84-63; Mp 94-69; NY 87-65. Sunrise, 5:57 CWT, set 8:30....Cocktails at Sigrud Mitchell's: Hope & Genevieve Washburn, Sassoons, Mrs. Gudger, Mrs. Blair, Sharline Heimhach....Henry Gilbert, photog, brother Mrs. Buck, gives life up hill....Evening, chess lesson to Jean Anneke Nelson and Sis Scanlon.

Thur 10: Hottest day so far this summer--indeed only one uncomfortably hot: 88 (90 at airport)-72; Mp 94-81; NY 95-68. Highs: Washn 97, F Worth 102, Chi 90, Cin 95, Cleveland 97, Detroit 98, KC 101, Omaha 100. AM, small drizzle, very warm & humid, poor day for work. At 10, sun out and too hot. To modernist house on Lake View Avenue, looking down across rough wild woods of Congdon Park to lake, of the architect, Harold St. Clair Starin. Glass brick, double windows. First really hot evening: to Jim and Peggie Nye's for din: Frank Mannheimer, pianist; Mrs. Hugo, Hope Washburn. Home and bright young people not unpleasantly intrude: Bernard (a speechless lump) and Mary Killorin; Rena (Mrs. Jack) Campbell.

Fri 11: The perfect day so far this summer, from sunrise till to bed with stars half autumnally bright. 78-66, but seemed cooler, in light breeze. Early AM, blaze of sun glory on shadowy woods, purple sea. The air delicious and alive, softly cool and brisk, and a radiance on leaves, grass, stones, tree-trunks, even the dull blue spruce and balsam shining, with just the right number of small cumulus clouds in brightly, not hotly, blue sky. By noon, the lake for once a deep true blue, with purple streaks and small white caps. Later, lake a flawed blue-gray....Steamer smoke on far horizon somehow poignant--people sailing to strange ports, even on these lakes. (Rem: in fine weather, inside passage behind islands from Port Arthur here).

Evening: to Marvin and Margot Orreck's for dinner--Marvin cooked the goulash--Fred the Lewellyn setter....Alice King, who runs Woodruff Lumber Company (whence the oak panels in this house, probably) for her brother, in the service....To completely "modernistic" Starin house of Roy (wife:) Halverson, who invented and monopolized the silver-dipped Xmas tree. A new kind of human being; almost no books but all electricity: color-changing vapor lights over d.r. table, haut parler by which can hear and answer departing guests, master burglar-light-in-every-room switch, music piped to all bedrooms to put them to sleep and awaken at definite hour, vast cooler filled with foods kept frozen, and food cupboard with electric opening and phony brass doorknob, walls of Tecco metallic papering and structural glass in kitchen & bathrooms, bar with such signs as "Men Drinking," air conditioning so windows nev open so air stale - it is worked by time clock coming on and off certain hrs of day; phone plugs every rm, But fundamental thing of stairs: too steep.....Roy, in Bahamas, undersea color photography, diving helmet, barracuda mooing around. Our 78-66 not shared by other cities; Mp 83, NY 100, Chi & Cin and Cleve 96, St. Louis 101, D Moines 92, Phoenix 111!

fol. 145

August 1944 - Duluth

Sat 12: Beautiful AM; sunrise gold-brown blaze above blazing dark-blue dawn sea. But PM a little too warm, with cirro-stratus haze. Herbert Sorenson, prest Duluth State Teachers' College, in with wife Mable, daughter Barbara, 13. Evening, Jewish discussion society, which has been going for 30 yrs, house of Wiener, asst supt schools--his own paintings, windows with vases on glass shelves, view of harbor & aerial bridge. His daughters, Judy & Louise, Harry Davis, Jewish attorney with competent uplift wife. Paper on propaganda by Ruth Slonim, Teachers' Cge instr, daughter Sig Slonim, J. atty. 81-54; Mp 89-57; NY 97-77; Cin-Detroit 96.

Sun 13: 82-66; Mp 90-70; NY 92-77. p.d. In my garden now, hydrangeas, yellow day lilies. With Jean Peyton sr & jr, house of Francis W. (Isabel) Sullivan (ex Mrs. French); Georgian with terrace, formal garden, summer house; all satinwood and flowers and tooled leather.

Mon 14: 74-57; Mp 88-67; heat wave in East: NY 96, Chi & Cleve 97, Cin 93, Det 99. Blazing sunrise (6:04 today) across lake, high triangle of bright gold clouds; shore plum-colored. Almost p.d., but a little hazy....Dick Lawrence of KDAL, chess. Margaret Mitchell, sister in law of Sigrid.

Tue 15. Day starts with stormy sunrise - magnificent long splash of crimson admid dark clouds - then heavy rain, which quits at noon, sun out and p.d. by 4....Rabbi Richard Singer, chess.....69-58; Mp 79-65; NY 91-76; Det-Cleve 96, St. Louis 98. Chicago 98-72, 12th day out of 15 so far this month over 90 in Chi.

Wed 16: These sunrises over the lake a riot; water mostly dark blue-silver; clouds every shade, fast changing, and in a ball or long streaks. This AM, long horizontal bands of pink--usually a washy color, but this time sparkling. p.d. till six, then rainy. On a mirror sea, three steamers each beneath an apparently unmoving black smoke pall....Slums (see next sheet): Greek family, woman dark but classic in house in center block, half shed; dirty, smiling, still pretty S. Dak. 28-yr-old Swede wife & five kids, gathering kindling....Evening, dinner with Dick Griggs, who never stopped talking. Add financial potentates: Gerald Sellwood, Hartleys, Francis Sullivan (selig). In 1st Natl: Geo Tweed chairman, Willis Wyard. 71-54; Mp 76-59; NY 95-78

Thur 17: 71-52; Mp 75-57; NY 94-71. p.d. Sunrise a surprising contrast of horizontal deep-gold sky with blue water....From Snively Boulevard extension, look down on Lester River valley, full of poplars, silver-green leaves...Hollister Farm (seen from my house high on hill to East), empty house and concrete board-like barn, reached by road past Lester Park municipal golf course; best view back over city...Also Seven Bridges rpad by the Lester....Evening, Tom McQueen, Congo pastor, Rabbi Singer; Jean Peyton Erickson being new-thoughtist and exhibitionistically eager.

fol. 146

From Relief org

Packingham - 316½ W. 4th Street.
Husband and wife were brought up in rural districts in South Dakota. They had always lived on a marginal income. They came to Minnesota in the fall of 1942, locating first in Lincoln County, and more recently moving into St. Louis County were jobs were more plentiful. Husband became ill and was found to have tuberculosis. The family was considered to be a Federal transient family and Mr. P. was not eligible for admission to the Sanatorium in St. Louis County and was sent elsewhere. Mrs. P. and the five children continue to live here. Mrs. P. is desirous of moving into better living quarters.

Solon - 618½ W. 3rd St.
Mr. and Mrs. S. were born in Greece. Mr. S. has been disabled for approximately 12 years and the family has been receiving Public Assistance during that time. There are five children. The oldest son joined the U. S. Navy this summer and is no longer in the home.

fol. 147

ANNEKE, PEYTON, LEWIS & CO., INC. SATURDAY, AUGUST 26

		Party Aug. 26 1944
Annekes	3	
Peytons	3	
Lewis	1	
Margaret-Roy	2 ✓ no	
Sig, Margaret Mitch	2 ✓ yes	
Lachmunds	2 no	
Malicks	2 ✓ yes	
Marvin Orecks	2 ✓ yes	Heimbach
Barbara Griggs	1 ✓ yes	Hem 4818
Lew Castle	1 ? no	
Diehls	2 ✓ yes	
Nyes	2 ✓ yes	
Heimbachs	2 ✓ yes	
Fred Bucks	2 ✓ no	
Cants	2 ✓ yes	
Jane Coulter	1 ✓ yes	
Dick Bardons	2 ✓ yes	
Hirschboeck	1 ✓ no	
Fran McGiffert	1 ✓ yes	
Salyards	2 ✓ yes	
T-K Gibson	2 yes	
Hoffs	2 ✓ yes	
Frybergers	2 no	
Davis Bradleys	2 yes	
Brad Heffelfinger	1 ?	
Adam Thompson	1 no	
Dancers (& Helen)	3 yes	
Mary Scanlon	1 yes	
Dick-Neva	2 ✓ no	
Gerald & Mrs. Sellwood	✓ yes	

Singers ?

Mon—plan food & order—w plates, napkins

fol. 148

August 1944 - Duluth

Fri 18: 69-48 (note how low the low); Mp 81-51 (note the range); NY 86-73. p.d. Air through window, as work in morning looking out on green pine plain of Congdon barony, so softly cool, so caressing. PM, Margaret Ann Hubbard in with historic Duluth MS. To Sigrid Mitchell's: Sybil Malo, Virginia Sellwood.

Sat 19: 79-54; Mp 85-60; NY 78-62 (1st time this summer that NY cooler). Rain till mid-afternoon. Evening, to Rustic Inn with Jean Erickson, Tom and Katie Gibson, Ted and Mrs. Wohl, whose says that some of his best friends are Jews. The point, last up lake seen from my house, proves to be Stony Point, Johnson white barn & cottages, 16½ miles from center Duluth, between Sucker and Knife Rivers.

Sun 20: p.d.! 79-62; Mp 81-69; NY 81-60.

Mon 21: 6:30, just after sunrise: dark galley of oreboat sliding over wine-dark sea--the Aegean with diff. p.d. August seems to be the month to be in Duluth. 78-56; Mp 84-60; NY 85-67.

Tue 22: Overwhelming sunrise over the lake, which changes amethyst - silver - blue, p.d. 73-52. Mountain ash berries now all red. Evening, pretty cool: Jewish party at Harry Davis's, Irwin Oreck (whom I mistook for a Protestant minister; Anti-Defamatn League and North Shore), Zolt, scrap iron, O. G. Larson, Finnish ex-congressman.

Wedn 23: 70-52 Early this morning, which is clearing for what looks like p.d., mass of dark clouds, one ray through made sparkling sunny circle on lake, behind that, in dark mystery on the lake, two steamers piratically stealing. So ends up my very good Duluth summer. I leave for

New York next Monday, August 28, after a wind-up Saturday evening party, given with Jean Erickson and Elsa Anneke, which will presumably include: Annekes, Peytons, Margaret & Roy, Sig & Marg Mitchell, Malicks, Barbara Griggs, Lew Castle, Diehls, Nyes, Heimbachs, Cants, Jane Coulter, Dick Bardons, Frannie McGiffert, Salyards, T & K Gibson, Hoffs, Dancers, Mary Scanlon ("Sis," Jean Anneke Nelson's friend), Sellwoods, Singer, David Bradleys. Unabl acct: Lachmunds, Fred Bucks, Dick & Neva Griggs, Adam Thompson, Dr: Frank Hirschboeck, Frybergers. Bradd Heffelfinger was expected here for annual carnival of hay-fever, but she is out kissing babies to become a state representative.....NY!--Connie, Carl, Macys.

Fri. 25—67-48 (note low) In Alworth garden: petunias, dahlias, begonias..Golden rod in fields.

Sat. 26: 68-55. All cloudy

Sun. 27: 64-53. Gray, some rain

Mon. 28: p.d. Sunrise, 6:22—set 7:56 To NY. 8:15 P.M.

fol. 149

1945 N.Y.
winter notes.

Jan: rising sun in murk a crimson ball above Reservoir, frozen—frosty silver.

Snow storm in fog—air looks mildly sulphurous

Jan. 25 Sunglow on frosted panes... In frost pattern, long thin lines—& crissX like fallen timber in forest

Jan 28—Reservoir—ice in damascened waves—like steel

Feb. 1—moonlite gloss on snowless ice

Feb. Snow here wh. makes far-spread checkerboard of roads so pretty, melting & dirty in 2 days—never deep enough

2/22 Rain & driving thick fog

2/24—Ice ½ gone in reservoir

fol. 152

Weather 1945

April	New York		Duluth		St. Paul & Mpls.	
4	52	43	29	23	31	26
8	67	44	44	33	69	40
	Shrubs all out in Central Park; trees almost					
10	72	50	42	27	75	54
11	fog in NY, very humid, full spring					
13	79	58	43	34	50	44
30			Duluth; daffodils out			

May	DULUTH ONLY		
5	72	41	(year ago, 33 24)
6	73	53	(year ago, 48 23)
8	38	25	(all day, alternate snowing & bright sun & fog. At night, 25--coldest May 8 on record)

.24 Spring suddenly full, Jap flowering almond in bloom.

24 40 70

26-7 Two days fog.

May 31 thru June 2: Noreaster, driving rain. June 2, 7 AM, 34 and light snowing, wh continued off and on all day, melting as fell. First June snow in 60 years, and at 34, coldest June 2 in 75 years. But also in New York, at 56-44, coldest June 1 on record.

June DULUTH —1945

8: 57-45

14: Lilacs just coming out. Daily rain

18: 74-46

Long Grasses by road pushed back by wind from passage of car—agitate, brighten

Yard vista now w. honeysuckle, fleur de lis, lilacs, phlox, full trees; valley & lake beyond

22 to 85°

26—lilacs & honeysuckle still full; mt laurel in bloom; ivy nearly all out

27 AM 50° & rainy—fog all day—high, 61°

28—55-48; rain or fog all day

29—PD—

fol. 153

WEATHER DULUTH--JULY 1945

1: 62-50 Dark clouds most of day. Some rain. Lilacs, honeysuckle gone. Poppies in bloom.
2: 72-50
16: 65-53
23: 93-63
24: 89-70
26: 69-58
27: 58-55
29: 74-50 (typical of Duluth summer)
End of month, delphinium and hollyhocks full. Hannakainen says since winter only 14 p.d.'s

August 1-4, trip to Sauk Centre, Inspiratn Peak

How may fancy farm houses with front doors left without steps.

Little Falls to Sauk Centre, prairie & woods; enticing dipping road always promising a beyond. Lots of oats--pale to deep gold now, and being harvested. Hay being cut. Corn poor.

Natural park on valley edges due west of Long Prairie.

Dark green of corn beside tawny gold of oats.

Facing sun near setting, black top road turns purple bef you. Another, facing sun almost down, telegraph wires--and, at station, tracks--become intricate silver spider web....At Battle Lake, many planes in elevator, for painter.

Plump, demure field-hills, few fences, Alexandria to Fergus. Sunset on lonely prairie slews.

From a distance, tell a gt deal abt character of driver of car ahead, when can see only his shoulder.

Chippewas at Mille Lacs, dark as negroes. (Baskets, canoes for sale of birch bark; loll or work beside summer lodge, conical roofs.

fol. 154

1945 Weather Duluth 1946

DULUTH--August
No blossoms or berries on mountain ash this year. Too wet? Max temperature, Aug 1-13: 60 to 80. Mostly 65-75. MUGHA PINE in yard.

NEW YORK
September-October. Almost all hot and very humid. Few days cool. Not cold till Nov 4, when 47-44, with spring warmth again 11/7-10.

DLUTH
Light snow in Duluth in October.

DULUTH WINTER

12/13 Zero. 12/15, 8 below. Dark before 5, not very light till 7:30 AM. 12/17, 6 AM, 10 below. 12/22, 8 AM, 12 below. 12/23, all of St. Louis Bay and parts of open lake been frozen, but on this date lake 1st completely frozen over. 12/24, up to 24 above zero; later in week up to 30 above; mostly zero to 10 above.

Windows dimmed by frost, with ingenious littlr inserts of glass left clear....Moon beautiful on frosted panes.....When light is dying, 4 to 5 December afternoons, the snow stretches out between trees seems whiter than ever, on gloomy days. When sun, with rich late light, the birch trees fairly burn against the snow.

Before it froze, the whole lake surface smoked. A strong land in winter; dark brown of tree trunks and branches, green of pines, wide white of snow, gray of open lake whether frozen or not....Looking down on little lights in valley; but some mornings murk of snow mist, can't see them....Symphonies of light in winter, on snow, trees.....Xmas, trees by front windows; a few out in yard strung with lights; Paul Van Hooven's big creche with sparkle board magi and camels and palms.

Dec. More winter fog in morning than remembered. Xmas--Marcella here nine days--plane to Mpls, drive here at 17 below, back by train--missing bag and cat's stocking; the end of Lillian.

Dec. 29: Evening, driving snow in the forecourt lighted from bracket light over entrance; wreath on the glass door against that sparkling spume--that is Xmas!

1946

Normal January weather in Duluth runs from ten below to twenty above.....A whole landscape <u>fuzzy</u> with fallen snow.....Snow on ground <u>drags</u> at feet when walk.

Late January afternoon; dark by five. Yellow lights of the smallish houses, the curtains not drawn, so cheerful beyond the wide spaces of snowy yards; tree trunks vs the lights. Houses about here just high enough to shut out the winter night; not high enough to feel imprisoning, like walls of city apartment houses

fol. 155

January 1946--Duluth

Along with strength, winter scene has more <u>delicacy</u> than the bawdy colors of summer. Sun on snow, gold and every color except white--gray toward twilight. Sun shyly out after day of murk delicately picks out snow patches - tender amid encircling gl-oo-oom.

January up to 4th: temperature zero to 30 above. 1/5: Raining! Roads hell for skidding. Up to about 35 for 2 days. Fear of rain freezing on roads.

1/8 AM, sun a low furnace glare on horizon in otherwise dun sky, light across the gray ice like a calm sea, with one dark blotch of open water. Two mornings, below zero, sun up thru cold cloud-banks a red ball.

Jan 9, on train to Mpls: Cold blue snow on hills just before dark, and the brush ragged. Stumps show up as they don't in summer, against the snow. Mid-Jan. from 8 below to 30 above in 2 days. Morning after morning, the full red sun appears after 8, crawling up thru murk; the cloud bank edged with ochre.

January 19 to Sauk Centre, Fred's funeral; starts snowing at noon, when roads been absolutely clear of snow, ice (that is, high-roads)...... Ads of Christ, tourist cabins, and Burma shave the chief rural adornments....Farms seem asleep. Ghosts of corn in the snow....Snow fences on every slight rise....Roads had been clear before this snow, and across their blacktop, snow flows like wavering streamlets, like smoke whiffs....Locomotive smokem by road, pressed low....Later, files of snowflakes drive straight at the windshield.

1/22, Mpls to Duluth, seven below at start, car cozy with its heater but get out by road into wind---! White blanket of unchanging snow broken by brown clumps of brush or of trees about houses; some p,aces, corn stalks and stubble thru snow. Grand View is above Elde's Corner, on #61.

This side Forest Lake: Grindstone and Moosehorn rivers. 1/23, Duluth: curtains of thick snowing cut off all valley, hills, the lake; shuts one in amid a circle of pines--nothing else in a blanked out world but a luminous gray void.

The most brilliant thing: morning after day of snow; early sun on snowy pine boughs. Jan. 26: 24 below. Sun comes up burly and red faces thru feminine chiffons, then the day shamelessly flaunts blue and silver and gold...Sunset not grandiose but gay with many little varicolored bright clouds and a tender glow on the hills; the ice-coated twigs seem of glass, against light sky; the icy lake is part open....1/26, 8 AM, 24 below; 1/27, 8 AM, 15 above--forty degrees difference in 24 hrs. (literally thirty-nine.) 1/30 Snowing all day; some wind; hard to walk down past Eve Glendenning's with flakes blowing right into eyes. Take shelter behind a tree.

fol. 156

February 1946--Duluth

2/2: Rose and crystal and sparks of fire of frosted windows against red rising sun. 15 below at 8 AM....Late PM, sky to North of palest gold....Spectacle of the unending stretch of the frozen lake Superior: no steppes flat like that; rough, speckles, dark stripes; all of it turning lavender in low late sun.

2/3: Before sun-up, window a valentine all in silver, with the frost borders, and black pines below a sparkling gray sky. Then, sup up, vast purple curtains along the horizon, the crimson disk of the sun thru it, and above it, gold from deepest to faint.

2/5, 7:30 AM. 28 above. Thick fog, and the scene lovely in 3 shades of gray: snowfield lightest, then sky, then dark beautiful masses of pines, with the light from Glendenning cottake a reassuring yellow square..... Noon, thirty above, and icy rain in heavy waves before wind. All twigs coated. In increasing wind, gaunt elms writhe, throw their arms abt in agony....Strange to hear rain beat on window in Feb in Duluth!....Deep snow covered with thin ice sheathing--like glaze on cake--crackles as step thru....At dark, low fog seems not beautiful now, but dirty. Sky flashes from trolley contact with icy wires. (Today, at Fairmont, Minn, lightning and thunder.)

2/6: 8:30 AM, 15 above and a heavy snow starts. Then, at 11 AM, a mild sun out--bunched birch boughs faintly bright in it.

2/9: Before sunrise, dull silver plane of icy lake; above it a nameless ochre-ish red. Dark pines in silhouette. Sun up a terrible crimson sphere--probably end of the world by this PM, but I'll have these notes copied from scrawled memoes, anyway. Sun up, lake all lavender, pines become golden.

2/9 After sunny day, in late PM lake ice for once not lavender but gray with streaks of blue steel, and glare-ice prismatic. Wonderful sweep of snow-pine-hill view from Moose Mountain (Hollister farm) to clearly-seen Rocky Point.

2/10: An hour before sunrise: Lower half of branches of spruce, and its trunk, blended & lost in dark mass of woods; upper part silhouettes against a streaked a faintly luminous gray sky that prmises clear sun...Evening: Northern lights in waves....Mougha pine the shapliest - fine vs sunrise.

2/11: Bright sun, strong shadows of trees on snow. Dangerous walking for weeks--when light snow, slip on ice under it.

2/12: Snow thick on spruce branches in early AM all falls off by night. So many trees in Duluth that looking down on Lakeview, prevailing color brown, not white with snow.

	Moon full	Moon rise	Sun rise	Sun set
Jan 1946:	17th	5:1	7:26	4:55
June '46:	14th	7:47	4:22	7:38

fol. 157

February 1946--Duluth. Begin March

2/14: 10 P.M., ten below zero, full clear moon; inky tree shadows on new-fallen snow; lights from little houses in valley twinkle clear; sounds from it audible--a door closing, a sleepy dog, a car. All perfect Kitsch and very satisfying. Moon was up at 5 P.M.

(On trip home from Mpls in January: Ragged Northern Minnesota village or hamlet snowbound. Calfskin coats, mackinaws, ear-muffs, flopping overshoes. Burnt-over country of birch, poplar, brush; rather flat. A few white pines remaining. One-story stores; the cement-block garage the center of mirth.)

2/16: When rising sun clears clouds, a streak of gold across the ice as across water. Light now from about 6:45 AM to 6 PM--in November in Miss, dark at 5, and 6 seems vast gain.....A great, one-day-after-full, rather alarming polished-brass moon with path across ice; it rose at 6:07. The glaze of ice on snow in yard shines.

2/18: Sunrise with trails of light seemed to turn frozen Lake Superior back into open water. First light on Eastern horizon now at six AM. By 6:10: at top. darkish sky, then pale blue strip against which are pine silhouettes with streak of apricot below. The pale blue turns into luminous gray; the apricot to purple robes. Neighbor: "The back of the winter ought to be broken by now."

2/19: 11 A.M., 45 below....2/20: With the first red in the sky, more lights appear down in the valley. Then radiance, and the smoke from the houses is bright...Birch trunks now, with no veil of leaves, are piercing white in the winter sun. Many sunny days now.

2/24: Day been sunny, about 20 above; toward dusk, the hills and woods and lake and gray, silent--yet waiting. Northland.

2/26: Rich late-afternoon light is bright gold on the birch trunks, pink on the lake and Hollister upland.

MARCH 1946

3/1: PM, sun and fifty above! Marcia Ann Nolan, slipping on ice as every one been doing here, has fracture of upper arm, has to carry a 50-lb weight 6 or 8 weeks.

3/4: Columns of smoke from houses in valley, early morning, in sun, are so cheerful.

3/6: After several days of 20 to 40 above and melting, in early morning sleet and rain; continuous little lightning from trolley 'bus wire-connections. Then snow! The world of trees turns from brown to crystal as rain freezes. And, 3/7, the twigs make a glittering glass forest as sun comes up. Afternoon, surface of rotted snow is covered with crystal corpses of ice tubes fallen from the twigs.....Grasses in snow make straight-line tracings as well as circular. Brief glory of winter morning just after sunrise; so wide and bright (with lake plain) that it does not seem cold or confining.

fol. 158

March 1946 - Duluth

3/11: 40 above at 5 P.M. Have been days as warm, recently, but this the first day that feels like spring...Snow going, revealing some grass that is still half green, but ice is caked on walks beside roads ever since last mid-November; too sullen to melt....Superior St now seems meagre, ill-constructed and -assorted; a small town--the First Natl Bank's proud bldg just a huddle of assorted brick boxes.

3/14: 9 AM, 55 above. Snow nearly all melted; quite a little green grass. Valley an all-brown mass now, no snowfields anywhere. And, 3/18. first p.d., temp. 48 at 8 A.M., and snow all gone but banks in shade, with flecks of ice still clinging.

Plan to leave for New York on March 21, in car, with Asa Lyons, jr.; the house, which I have loved but sold to Jay Markle, because it is time to wander again, will be turned over to him on May 1st. Meantime I look for a house in New England for the summer. Then: buy a house there?--England, Ireland, Italy, Africa? Or California? Or the Root River Valley in Southern Minnesota?

fol. 159

Nicolet—not Nicollet, the Italian—landed at Green Bay, Wis., in 1634, in the days of Louis XIII & Richlieu

See State Historical Society, at St. Paul

Trinity chapel, Excelsior, founded 1854, prest church 1862—fortified.

Notes

ANNOTATIONS INCLUDE IDENTIFICATIONS of people, facts about Lewis related to the diary, Lewis's sources, translations of foreign language material, and clarifications.

The annotations are selective, not exhaustive. They are designed to serve the text where the text cannot readily serve itself in the hands of an able reader. Hence annotations do not identify people who are already well identified in the text or who are already well identified in *The New Columbia Encyclopedia* (1975), *The Oxford Companion to American Literature* (1983), or *Webster's New Biographical Dictionary* (1983), unless such people have particular connections to Lewis. Also excluded are most place names, which can be easily located by the reader on a map of Minnesota. Notes are not offered in cases where research has not produced reasonably certain identification. Nor are notes offered that fail to do much more than confirm what the text already reveals. Finally, Lewis's extensive lists of grave-marker names have not been annotated.

Because the available sources for identifying people living in the 1940s (obituaries, city directories, regional biographical indexes, library clippings files) give more facts about men than women, men are for the most part more precisely identified than their wives. Notes on people's jobs refer to what they were doing up to the time of the diary, not later, unless so specified.

Locations in the text are specified by page and line number in this edition and key words—all in **bold.** For example, **37.18 McNally** means the McNally who is mentioned on page 37, line 18.

The following abbreviations are used for bibliographic aids:

Blegen — Blegen, Theodore C. *Minnesota: A History of the State.* Minneapolis: University of Minnesota Press, 1963.

Koblas — Koblas, John J. *Sinclair Lewis: Home at Last.* Bloomington, Minn.: Voyageur Press, 1981.

Schorer — Schorer, Mark. *Sinclair Lewis: An American Life*. New York: McGraw-Hill, 1961.

WPA Guide — *Minnesota: A State Guide*. New York: Viking, 1938; reprint as *The WPA Guide to Minnesota*. St. Paul: Minnesota Historical Society Press, 1985.

37.18 McNally. William J. McNally. 1892–1967. Vice-president Minneapolis Star Journal and Tribune Company. Journalist, novelist, playwright, friend of SL. Wife Lois.
38.1 Asher Howard. 1877–1945. Mpls grain dealer, lawyer, one-time state legislator, 1916–21.
39.6 Virginia. Virginia (Ginny) Lewis. Of the two Virginia Lewises in the diary, this one is SL's niece, 1912–1986, daughter of brother Dr. Claude Lewis. She often visited SL summer 1942.
39.14 the hollow from which Jude scared the rooks. Lonely field, newly seeded, in Thomas Hardy's *Jude the Obscure,* where young Jude is employed to scare away birds.
39.21–23 Ruhe . . . 1907. Rest in peace. Greta Braun, born Schmidt, died 1907.
41.4 Claude's house. Claude Bernard Lewis. 1878–1957. St. Cloud, MN physician and SL's much admired older brother. Wife Wilhelmina (Mary), d. 1949. The house: 724 Fourth Avenue South, St. Cloud, built 1929.
41.12 Grace Davis. Grace Kaercher Davis. 1887–1965. First woman elected to a constitutional office in MN. Clerk MN Supreme Court, 1922–34, 1938–54.
41.12–13 Judge Royal Stone. Royal Augustus Stone. 1875–1942. MN Supreme Court associate justice.
41.17 Charles Lane Harris. b. 1889. Mpls president furniture retail company. Lived part 1942 at 2112 Pillsbury Avenue, then moved 1820 Girard Avenue South. Wife Ida B. Landlord of suburban house on Lake Minnetonka, outside Excelsior, 26710 Edgewood Road, where SL lived summer 1942.
41.26 Confer. Ogden A. Confer. 1886–1962 (not as old as SL thought). Head Mpls real estate agency that found SL the house at 1500 Mt. Curve Avenue where SL lived fall 1942.
42.1 Joseph. Joseph Hardrick. SL's black driver-butler-cook from New Orleans, fall 1939 to fall 1948. See Schorer 653, 772.
42.20 Schiek's and Charlie's Exceptionale. Well-known Mpls restaurants.
43.3 W. B. RILEY. William Bell Riley. 1861–1947. Founder Northwestern Bible Missionary School. At Riley's request, Billy Graham succeeded him as head of school 1947–51.
44.5 Addison Lewis. 1889–1971. Owner Mpls advertising agency. Friend, not relative, of SL, who called Addison cousin anyway. Had thoroughbred horses at suburban Long Lake residence. Wife Dorothy, d. 1972, aged 78.
44.21 BURMA SHAVE ROAD SIGNS. Celebrated advertisements for a brushless shaving cream produced by the Mpls Burma-Vita Company, owned by Clinton Odell and sons Allan and Leonard. The signs were rhyming lines set at intervals beside a highway.

The Odells pioneered the signs in 1925, distributed them eventually throughout the United States, and removed them after the sale of the company in 1963.

47.7 Jay Hormel. Jay Catherwood Hormel. 1892–1954. Hormel meat-packing company president, Austin, MN.

47.8 Cream of Wheat. First produced in Grand Forks, ND, 1893, Cream of Wheat moved to Mpls 1897, sold out to Nabisco 1967.

48.15 dayton's. Prominent Mpls department store, founded 1902 by George Draper Dayton, 1857–1938.

49.19 Brenda Ueland. 1891–1985. Writer, free-lancing for *Saturday Evening Post, Harper's, Ladies' Home Journal,* and *Collier's.* Wrote daily column *Minneapolis Times* 1941–48. Member prominent Mpls family, her mother Clara Hampson Ueland, 1860–1927, a noted suffragist, her father Andreas Ueland, a judge and banker. Brothers Arnulf, Sigurd, Rolf.

49.19–20 Le Roy and Mrs. Arnold. LeRoy Arnold. 1881–1958. English professor Hamline U in StP. Wife Kate.

49.25 Jim Hart. James S. Hart. SL's research assistant and traveling companion, winter 1941 to spring 1942. Former secretary Rhode Island Governor William H. Vanderbilt. Wife Gladys.

53.10 Joseph Meighen. Joseph Felix Meighen. b. 1901. Preston, MN farm manager, bank president, insurance agent.

54.1–2 Townsend Club signs, proclaiming that plan would be needed, and would conquer, after this war. The Townsend Plan was proposed 1934 by American physician Francis Everett Townsend, an old-age revolving pension of up to $200 per month based on a national two percent sales tax.

55.20 Jos and Dagmar Beach. Joseph Warren Beach. 1880–1957. Noted professor of English at U of MN. Second wife Dagmar.

55.20–21 Dotty Bennett. Dorothy Bennett. Friend of niece Virginia Lewis and employee U of MN.

55.21 Starke and Mrs. Hathaway. Starke R. Hathaway. 1903–1984. Professor Elliot Memorial Hospital Mpls. Clinical psychologist, co-developer Minnesota Multiphasic Personality Inventory (MMPI). Wife Virginia.

55.21 Eddie and Marie Ford. Edwin H. Ford. 1891–1964. U of MN journalism professor. Wife Marie.

55.23 Carleton Miles. Carlton Wright Miles. 1884–1954. American writer and journalist. Drama critic for *Minneapolis Journal* 1907–28. Visited SL in England 1921.

55.24 George Jean Nathan. The noted writer. Long-time friend of SL.

55.26 Marcella. Marcella Powers. 1921–1985. SL's young girlfriend in the 1940s. The diary shows that SL worked hard to attract her to Duluth—for example, see 3 June 1944, fol. 120. See Schorer 646–770.

57.4 John Cowles. 1898–1983. President Minneapolis Star Journal and Tribune Company. Wife Elizabeth (Betty).

57.4–5 brother of. John Cowles's brother was Gardner Cowles, Jr., 1903–1985. Publisher. Raised *Des Moines Register* to national prominence. The two brothers founded *Look* magazine.

57.9–10 A. M. and Mrs. Wilson. Alfred Mayo Wilson. b. 1903. Assistant to president Minneapolis-Honeywell Regulator Company. Wife Josepha (Fefa) W. Suburban (Excelsior) friends of SL 1942.

57.10 Mrs., (Rufus) Rand. Helen Starkweather Chase Rand. d. 1965, aged 70. Mpls civic leader. Husband Rufus R. Rand Jr., Mpls businessman, president Rand Company, investments.

57.15 Oliver Dennett Grover. 1861–1927. American artist.

57.17 GSB. Perhaps mistake for GBS, George Bernard Shaw.

57.30 Pace. Charles Nelson Pace. 1877–1954. Methodist minister and president Hamline U in StP, 1934–47.

58.4 Cowling. Donald John Cowling. 1880–1965. President Carleton College, 1909–45.

58.12 Oscar Kalman. Charles Oscar Kalman. 1872–1956. President StP investment banking firm, Kalman & Company, 1929–39. Wife Alexandra (Xandra).

58.14 W. S. Cooper. William Skinner Cooper. b. 1884. Botany professor U of MN, 1915–51. Wife Dorothy.

58.23 Camilla Wing. Mrs. Daniel Holland Bessesen (not Bessenen). Known as Camilla Wing, author milling-company-sponsored children's books on grain. Widow Excelsior physician, d. 1926, aged 79.

59.2 Marcus Goodrich. Marcus Aurelius Goodrich. b. 1897. American journalist, screenwriter, novelist. Novel *Delilah* (1941) based on his experience on destroyer in Asiatic fleet WWI.

59.13–14 19-rm granite castle of Joseph R. Brown. Joseph Renshaw Brown. 1805–1870. Fur trader, Indian agent, politician, soldier, second editor StP's first newspaper *Minnesota Pioneer.* Known for partial success inventing steam-powered automobile. The nineteen-room house was built 1861, then destroyed in 1862 Sioux uprising, Mrs. Brown and children being taken captive. See *WPA Guide* 394, Blegen 137, 277.

60.12 Harry Piper. Harry C. Piper. 1889–1968. Partner Mpls investment firm Piper Jaffray & Hopwood. Wife Louise G.

60.13 Charles Swett. Charles B. Sweatt. 1894–1977. Executive Minneapolis-Honeywell Regulator Company. Brother of Harold W. Sweatt.

61.1 MAY TEN, Sunday. Five-year anniversary. Not the five-year anniversary of knowing Marcella Powers, whom he met in summer 1939, nor is it precisely the five-year anniversary of breaking up with Dorothy Thompson. SL walked out of Bronxville house 28 April 1937, and the divorce decree was 2 January 1942. The best guess is a five-year anniversary of breaking his ribs or of a subsequent vow to stay off liquor. Not many days after leaving Thompson on 28 April 1937, SL was found with broken ribs, having bout with delirium tremens. Thompson helped to get him to a sanitarium where he could dry out. See Schorer 629, 630, 684, and John Hersey, "First Job," *The Yale Review* 76 (winter 1987): 184–97. There was another drinking binge after this, winter 1941, requiring the help of Thompson, Dr. Traeger, and a strait jacket to get SL to a hospital. He thought Marcella had betrayed him. See Schorer 673–74.

62.15 Fred. Fred K. Lewis. 1875–1946. SL's eldest brother. Sauk-Centre flour miller. Wife Winnie.

62.21 John Lewis. 1815–1884. SL's grandfather. 1849 California gold-rusher, developer of Pennsylvania match factory that failed, and Elysian, MN farmer. Wife Emeline Johnson Lewis, 1817–1886.

63.5 E. J. Lewis. Edwin J. Lewis. 1848–1926. SL's stern physician father in Sauk Centre, MN. First wife Emma Kermott Lewis, 1849–1891, who died of tuberculosis when SL was six. Second wife Isabel Warner Lewis, 1849–1921, stepmother who raised SL.

64.9 great Sioux Massacre. Major uprising of August–September 1862 in Minnesota River Valley, bringing death to about 500 whites, civilian and military, ending in mass hanging of 38 convicted Indians 26 December at Mankato and expulsion of Sioux from state. See Blegen 259–84, *WPA Guide* 55.

64.23 Mencken. H. L. Mencken. One of SL's few lifelong friends.

65.14–18 English colony . . . riding hurdles. Started in 1873, the colorful colony of English farming gentlemen eventually failed. A novel on the colony was written already: Maud and Delos Lovelace, *Gentlemen from England* (New York: Macmillan, 1937). One source for SL almost certainly the *WPA Guide* 414–15. See also Blegen 306.

65.18 Ward, bank prest. Albert Luke Ward. 1842–1931. Fairmont, MN banker, farmer, publisher. Owned 8,000 acres in Martin County. Born in New York State, he came to MN 1864 and homesteaded.

66.9 Model T Fords. The last were made in 1927.

66.25–26 marble log-cabin momument of Moses Sailor in Blue Earth. According to *WPA Guide* 414, this is a 2½-by-4-foot cemetery marker honoring first settler Moses Sailor.

69.25 BOTTUM FOR GOVERNOR. Probably Joseph Henry Bottum. b. 1903. SD director of taxation, 1937–43.

69.26 Herbert Agar. Herbert Sebastian Agar. 1897–1980. Historian, London correspondent, editor *Louisville Courier-Journal* and *Louisville Times.* Winner 1933 Pulitzer Prize for American History.

70.14 Harvey Dunn. 1884–1952. American painter, magazine illustrator from SD. Did some 250-odd pieces for *Saturday Evening Post,* 1908–39.

71.1 H. C. Dale, "The Ashley-Smith Expeditions." Harrison Clifford Dale, ed., *The Ashley-Smith Explorations and the Discovery of a Central Route to the Pacific, 1822–1829* (Cleveland: Arthur H. Clark, 1918).

73.20 Gracie. Grace Hegger. d. 1981, aged 93. SL's first wife, married 1914, divorced 1928. The marriage produced one son, Wells Lewis, born 26 July 1917. Gracie was in part the prototype of Carol Kennicott in *Main Street* and Fran Dodsworth in *Dodsworth.* See Schorer 286–87. The cross-country Model T Ford trip in 1916 provided material for the novel *Free Air* (New York: Harcourt, Brace, 1919).

74.1 John Moses. 1885–1945. Norwegian-born governor ND, 1939–45. Elected U.S. Senate 1944. First Democrat ever to represent ND in Congress.

74.9–14 Marquis de Mores . . . Duc de Vallombrosa. Antoine de Vallombrosa, Marquis de Mores, 1858–1896. French nobleman adventurer. Tried to found transcontinental meat-packing empire in ND, 1883–86, financed by New York and Paris banker father-in-law L. A. von Hoffman. Wife Medora.

76.9 Elmer E. Adams, Prest, 2/6. 1861–1950. Fergus Falls bank president, editor *Fergus Falls Daily Journal,* and MN state politician. The fraction seems to mean the percent of ownership of the newspaper.

76.18 Judge Himsl. Joseph B. Himsl. 1872–1950. Austrian-born district court judge St. Cloud, MN.

79.9 Ed and Chuck Rathe. Ed L. Rathe was editor, son Charles associate editor, of *Sauk Centre Herald.*

79.13 Dave and Hattie Caughren. David Byron Caughren. 1885–1965. Sauk Centre bank president. Mother Hattie A. Caughren, 1858–1947. Wife Harriet Lockhead Caughren.

79.14 Harry C. Harry J. Caughren of Osakis, brother of David.

79.14 Laurel and Laura (Thompson) Kells. Laurel Lucas Kells. 1883–1958. Sauk Centre lawyer. Wife Laura Ann Thomason Kells, 1884–1970.

79.14 Ben. Benjamin Faville DuBois. 1885–1981. Sauk Centre bank president and SL's childhood contemporary. His father Julian A. DuBois, medical competitor of Dr. Edwin Lewis in Sauk Centre. Wife Cecile, 1885–1974. See Schorer 32.

79.14 Julian DuBois. Julian F. DuBois. 1887–1963. Sauk Centre physician. Brother of Ben DuBois. Wife Katherine, 1890–1991.

79.15 Lynn Whitson. Lynn W. Whitson. 1887–1961. Sauk Centre salesman for grocery wholesaler.

79.15 Doc and Mrs. Monahan. Andrew Francis Moynihan. 1873–1945. Sauk Centre physician. Wife Emma.

79.16 Carl and his wife; Bobbie. Nephews of SL, sons of brother Fred. Carl H. Lewis, 1910–1965. Wife Helen, 1911–1991. Robert C. Lewis, 1914–1996.

79.16 Pat Costello. Patrick Henry Costello. 1897–1971. Sauk Centre native. Had career as pharmacist and mayor in Cooperstown, ND.

79.17 Rydholm. Henry G. Rydholm. 1886–1964. Sauk Centre photographer.

79.17 Billy Parker. William M. Parker. 1879–1962. Sauk Centre businessman—insurance and real estate. Municipal judge, 1940–56.

79.17 Nelly Hanson. Nelfield S. Hansen. 1885–1971. Part-owner with siblings of Sauk Centre clothing store The Model.

80.17 Farmer Labor Party. MN's liberal third party, arising out of A. C. Townley's Nonpartisan League 1918, peaking 1930s, and merging with Democrats 1944 to form the DFL.

81.12 ELMER ANDERSON. Clyde Elmer Anderson. 1912–1998. Brainerd, MN newsdealer. MN lieutenant governor, 1939–42, 45–51. MN governor, 1951–55.

81.15 Freeman. Freeman Lewis. 1908–1976. SL's nephew, Dr. Claude Lewis's son.

81.16 Knutson. Harold Knutson. 1880–1953. Norwegian-born U.S. congressman, 1916–48, from St. Cloud, MN.

81.23 Kensington Rune Stone. A stone found near Kensington, MN in 1898 with runic inscription bearing date 1362, as if from Vikings. Thought a hoax but has generated much discussion. See Theodore C. Blegen, *The Kensington Rune Stone: New Light on an Old Riddle* (StP: Minnesota Historical Society, 1968).

83.9 Boratko. Andre Boratko. 1912–1990. Czechoslovakian-born artist, raised and educated in StP.

83.17 Fruits of Schnectady. Schenectady, New York, home of General Electric Company, established there 1886.

83.19 Hinckley Fire. SL's source must have been *WPA Guide* 295: "the raging forest fire of 1894, in which more than 400 persons lost their lives. The hero of the disaster was Northern Pacific's engineer, Jim Root, who backed his train through a wall of flames and on over the burning Grindstone Creek bridge all the way to Duluth. He saved 350 lives, but his hands were burned fast to the throttle." For more reliable account, see Stewart H. Holbrook, *Burning An Empire: The Story of American Forest Fires* (New York: Macmillan, 1943), 13–30, or Richard F. Snow, "The Hinckley Fire," *American Heritage,* 28 (August 1977): 90–96. Root was a hero, but his train did not reach Duluth.

85.6 Paul de Kruif. 1890–1971. American bacteriologist and popular science writer. Science consultant for SL's novel *Arrowsmith* (New York: Harcourt, Brace, 1925).

85.13 Log Cabin Theater. Old Log Theater, founded 1939, in Excelsior at 5175 Meadville. According to Koblas 116–17, it never produced a SL play; SL was annoyed when managing director Robert Aden wanted to produce *Dodsworth* instead of *Angela Is Twenty-Two.*

85.16 Elaine Norden. Elaine R. Norden. Worked for Mpls advertising company Campbell-Mithun Inc.

85.25 His and Dorothy's daughters. Five daughters as follows: Dana Lewis Atkinson married to Harold M. (Addy) Atkinson II, b. 1914, who was a department manager at Harold Inc., Mpls ladies' clothing store; Virginia (Ginny) Lewis, d. 1988, aged 65, about to marry on 8 August 1942 Harry C. Piper, Jr., 1917–1990; Charlotte Lewis; Gretchen Lewis; and Carol Lewis.

85.30–31 John and Bernice Dalrymple. John S. Dalrymple. 1873–1958. Mpls businessman with 30,000-acre farm operation in North Dakota. Wife Bernice B. Dalrymple, 1889–1980, civic activist.

86.20 Luther Weaver. d. 1963, aged 78. Owner StP advertising agency.

87.7 X is born to be a secretary. May refer to research assistant James Hart, with whom SL had falling out evening of same day; see 28 May 1942, fol. 43. More likely, though, is that this is rare instance of SL assessing Marcella Powers, who was studying shorthand in New York spring 1942. SL tried to be helpful in letters to her. In Lewis to Powers, 18 March 1942, he wrote, "Do you want me, when you type your letters, to criticize the typing and spelling, as part of your present training?" Then he added copy-editing notes. More copy notes appear in Lewis to Powers, 24 April 1942 and 3 May 1942, Marcella Powers Correspondence, St. Cloud State University Archive.

88.21 Dewey O'Gara. W. Dewey O'Gara. 1898–1981. Ran Sauk Centre Chevrolet and Pontiac garage, succeeding father George O'Gara, 1871–1951.

88.28 Mayor Steve Schwartzbauer. Stephen Gregory Schwarzbauer. 1880–1959. Austrian-born Sauk Centre grocer and mayor.

89.1 Borgmann. Ed Borgmann. 1905–1977. Sauk Centre John Deere implement dealer.

89.14–15 Asa, John and Judson Hutchinson. SL's source very likely *WPA Guide* 384: "The town was founded in 1855 by the brothers Asa, Judson, and John Hutchinson, members of a family of singers, who gave concerts of popular and abolitionist songs throughout the United States from 1841 until the close of the Civil War."

89.23 the Whites and railroad man in The Happy Man. According to Schorer 802, SL wrote a long narrative poem titled "The Happy Man" years later in Europe, winter-spring 1950.

89.25 Carol Kennicott. Protagonist of SL's famous 1920 novel *Main Street.*

91.14 unerhört. Unbelievable, outrageous.

92.2–3 "Main Street Goes to War." SL sent script to Treasury Department. In March 1943 he wrote to find out whether it had been produced. The Treasury Department had no record of the script. Yale now lists a typescript and a carbon in its collection. See Schorer 687.

92.13–14 F. Peavey Heffelfinger. 1897–1979. Mpls grain executive. Vice-president F. H. Peavey & Company, later president and chair of board. Grandson of company founder Frank Peavey.

92.24 Dahlberg's. Summer estate of Swedish-born Chicago Celotex manufacturer B. G. Dahlberg on private island in Rainy Lake. SL was there August 1926 working on *Elmer Gantry* (New York: Harcourt, Brace, 1927) when his father died. See Schorer 461, Koblas 104–5.

92.24 Gott soll behüten. Figuratively, God is my witness.

92.34 Brad Heffelfinger. Elizabeth E. Bradley (Brad) Heffelfinger. 1900–1981. Mpls civic leader, prominent Republican, ran for legislature 1948. Husband F. Peavey Heffelfinger.

93.1 Robert McClure. Robert Emerson McClure. b. 1896. American author.

93.1–2 Mr. and Dorothy Bauman. John S. Bauman. b. 1894. Mpls investment counselor. Wife Dorothy.

93.2 Mrs. Philip Pillsbury. Eleanor Bellows Pillsbury. 1913–1971. Mpls civic leader. Husband Philip Winston Pillsbury, 1903–1984, president Pillsbury Flour Mills Company, 1940–52. Probably the daughter of H. B. mentioned above on fol. 45. Mentioned again fol. 104 as "the unlikable Eleanor Pillsbury." H. B. is Henry Adams Bellows, 1885–1939, Mpls music critic, translator, radio executive.

93.3 Mr. Tierce(?). Possibly Harold H. Tearse, Jr. 1894–1972. Vice-president Searle Grain Company. Wife Katharine.

93.7 Robt. J. FLANAGAN. 1899–1974. Mpls lawyer living in suburban Long Lake.

94.13 her mother. Mrs. Powers, Marcella's mother, widow from South Orange, New Jersey, who later kept SL company as sort of guest-housekeeper for longer periods of time in Duluth than Marcella.

94.28 Innisfree. Allusion to William Butler Yeats's idyllic poem "The Lake Isle of Innisfree," about small lake near Sligo in west of Ireland.

95.2 Gabby. Gabriel (Gabby) Ueland. Daughter of Brenda Ueland.

95.2 Sandra. Sandra Ueland. Brenda Ueland's niece, daughter of Sigurd Ueland.

95.17 WPA Writers' Project. WPA effort to produce a guide for each state. In MN involved 120 writers. Director of MN Federal Writers' Project was Mabel S. Ulrich. See result, the *WPA Guide,* on which SL relied for information for this diary. See fol. 75.

95.20 Peg o' My Heart. Successful comedy by J. Hartley Manners (1912), written as vehicle for actress wife Laurette Taylor.

96.15 Russell Plimpton. b. 1891. Director Minneapolis Institute of Arts for thirty-five years, retiring 1956.

96.16 Alan Priest. Alan Reed Priest. b. 1898. Curator Department of Far Eastern Art in Metropolitan Museum of Art in New York.

98.14 Robert & Ruth Pack. Robert F. Pack. 1874–1961. English-born Twin Cities electric utility chairman of board, Northern States Power Company. Second wife Ruth, 1893–1958.

98.15 Charley Nelson. 1863–1948. Swedish-born Lake Superior north shore pioneer, founder Lutsen's resort 1885, from Duluth ninety miles up shore.

99.6–7 Carmel, Calif. Writers' colony where SL spent six months as fledgling writer 1909.

101.5 Ritters. Three Ridder brothers building newspaper chain including *St. Paul Pioneer Press, St. Paul Dispatch, Grand Forks Herald,* and in New York *Staats-Zeitung* and *Journal of Commerce.* They purchased *Duluth News-Tribune* and *Duluth Herald* 1936. The merger creating Knight-Ridder occurred 1974. The brother known best to SL was Victor Ridder, 1886–1963, publisher of the Duluth papers, 1941–52, wife Ruth. He was SL's chess companion in Duluth 1944 until SL felt slighted. See Schorer 719, Koblas 129.

101.5–6 Nathan--Nate--Cohen. d. 1962, aged 56. Arts writer *Duluth News-Tribune* until 1944. Editor film magazine *Boxoffice* Kansas City 1945–62.

101.6 Stewart. James Alexander Stuart. b. 1875. Executive editor *Duluth News-Tribune* and *Herald* starting 1941.

101.13–15 part of town rebuilt . . . great hole. Oliver Mining Company, mining arm of U.S. Steel, moved the village of North Hibbing, starting 1921, to mine ore underneath. This not without controversy. See *Iron Range Country: A Historical Travelogue of Minnesota's Iron Ranges* (Eveleth, MN: Iron Range Resources and Rehabilitation Board, 1979).

101.31 Dean Dreacher. Henry Adolph Drescher. b. 1889. Dean of Hibbing Junior College, 1929– .

105.29–30 Willard's Folly. Probably refers to E. Victor Willard. b. 1880. Engineer MN State Drainage Commission, 1913– . Commissioner Department of Drainage and Waters, 1919–31. Commissioner Conservation Commission, 1933– .

106.24 Fritz Kreisler. 1875–1962. Austrian-born American violinist. The coach was Herbert Orin (Fritz) Crisler, 1899–1982, head football coach U of MN 1930–32, Princeton 1932–38, U of Mich 1939–48.

108.15 Mary down from St. Cloud. Sister-in-law Mary, brother Claude's wife.

108.16 Harold & Mrs. Swett. Harold W. Sweatt. 1891–1980. President Minneapolis-Honeywell Regulator Company. Wife Mary Buchanan Sweatt, civic leader, d. 1966, aged 74.

108.16 Woods. Perhaps Hugh McKinnon Wood, Mpls lawyer, and wife Catherine.

108.22 "Planish." The novel *Gideon Planish,* published April 1943.

109.3 SHORTEST DAY OF THE YEAR. Mistake for longest day or shortest night.

109.24 Bert Blase. Burton Blase. Sales manager Confer Brothers Realtors of Mpls. Along with boss Ogden A. Confer, helped SL find house at 1500 Mt. Curve Avenue, where SL lived fall 1942.
109.24 Edmund Burke house. 1500 Mt. Curve Avenue, Mpls. Edmund Burke, former occupant, Mpls businessman, died 1941, aged 56.
109.24–25 Geist & Miller on River Road. Perhaps Geist was Augusta O. Geist, widow of Emil S. Geist, 2904 West River Road, Mpls.
109.26 Dr. Everett MacGibbon. Everett E. MacGibbon. d. 1966, aged 76. Mpls dentist. His father John MacGibbon of Sauk Centre.
109.28 Reuben Latz. Rubin Latz. 1886–1948. Lithuanian-born Mpls trade unionist. Business agent Laundry Workers and Cleaners Union Local.
109.29 Finkelstein. Michael L. Finkelstein. Mpls manager International Ladies Garment Workers Union.
111.2 George Leonard. 1872–1956. Russian-born Mpls labor attorney. U of MN Regent 1937–39.
111.10 P. Wheeler. Frederick P. Wheeler. Mpls grain elevator president.
111.13 John & Mary Baxter. John (Johnny) Baxter. 1903–1948. Mpls insurance executive. Friend and chess partner of SL fall 1942. Neighbors at 1779 Girard Avenue South. Wife Mary kept in touch with SL several years. See Roger K. Blakely, "Sinclair Lewis and the Baxters: The History of a Friendship," *Minnesota History* 49.5 (1985): 166–78.
111.13 Helen Baxter. John Baxter's sister.
111.14 Brenda. Brenda Ueland.
111.19 Farmer-Labor Party convention. SL had long intended to write a labor novel. He also had interest in radical politics, having belonged to Socialist Party as young man 1911–1912 and having greatly admired famed American socialist Eugene V. Debs. See Schorer 178, 281, 338, 341, 779.
111.19 Elmer Benson. 1895–1985. Second and last Farmer-Labor governor in MN, 1937–39, before merger of Farmer-Labor with Democrats 1944. Known for radicalism to the end of his life.
111.20 Susie Stagelberg. Susie Stageberg. 1877–1961. MN Farmer-Labor Party leader. Ran for MN Secretary of State 1922, 1924, 1928, and for Congress 1932. Promoted women's suffrage and temperance. Called "mother of Farmer-Labor Party." Opposed merger with Democrats in 1940s.
111.22 F. H. Shoemaker. d. 1958, aged 69. Farmer-Labor U.S. congressman at-large from MN 1933–35. Known to press as "Fighting Frank." Having addressed a banker on an envelope as "robber of widows and orphans," he was convicted for sending defamatory material through the mails, served nine months at Leavenworth 1931, then pardoned by Roosevelt 1933. This may be the story SL had in mind when saying Shoemaker did time for being a "conchy" [conscientious objector to military service].
112.31–113.1 "Blondie's Happy Event." *Blondie's Blessed Event*, 1942, one of series of Columbia films about comic strip characters Blondie and Dagwood Bumstead.
113.21 August Lindbergh. d. 1893 at age 85. Swedish immigrant grandfather of Charles Lindbergh.

114.23 Chancy . . . Whiting. Chauncey Whiting. 1819–1902. Member Mormon colony from Iowa settling Clitherall, MN 1865.
116.21 O'Meara's. Edward V. O'Meara. b. 1890. Irish-born department store owner in Fergus Falls.
117.22 Minnesota Man was found in 1932. *WPA Guide* 28, 447, discusses this find by road builders near Pelican Rapids, of fossilized remains of teenage girl thought to be 20,000 years old.
118.18 Dr. Lindley. Stanley B. Lindley. b. 1906. Psychiatrist, hospital administrator. Physician Fergus Falls State Hospital, 1939–43.
119.1 Jean Piccard. Jean Felix Piccard. 1884–1963. Swiss-born U of MN professor of aeronautical engineering, known for high-altitude balloon development. Twin brother of Auguste Piccard, 1884–1962, Belgian physicist, also known for high-altitude balloon work.
119.11–12 John MacGibbon. 1859–1939. Canadian-born Sauk Centre utilities supervisor, once mayor, amateur poet.
120.15 Edelkitsch. Means grandly pretentious kitsch.
121.6 "bijou." Means jewel, a charming thing.
121.10 "White Cargo." 1923 play by Leon Gordon, 1895–1960; a 1920s hit.
121.27 Lewis Browne. 1897–1949. Rabbi, popular writer on theology, long-time friend of SL, with whom he did national debating tour November 1941 to January 1942, October to December 1943, and November 1944, on topics like Country Versus City, Machines Versus No Machines, Can Fascism Happen Here?, and The Modern Woman. See Schorer 682–84, 707–8, 722.
122.5 Chas Bolles Rogers. b. 1884. Mpls grain company executive.
122.8 Alfred and Mrs. Pillsbury. Alfred Fiske Pillsbury. 1869–1950. Powerful member Mpls Pillsbury flour family. Son of John Sargent Pillsbury, 1828–1901, governor of MN 1875–81, who was known for nurturing the early U of MN. Wife Eleanor (Gretchen), civic leader, d. 1946.
122.10 Bruce Douglas. Edward Bruce Douglas. 1886–1946. Sculptor. Stepson of Mahala Douglas, "Duchess of Deephaven," and son of Mpls financier Walter D. Douglas, 1861–1912.
122.12 Newells. Maybe Louis Blodgett Newell. 1871–1966. President Mpls wholesale grocers Winston & Newell Company. Wife Helen, d. 1968, aged 90.
123.11 John MacMillan. Probably John H. MacMillan, Jr. 1895–1960. President large Mpls grain company Cargill Inc. Wife Marion Dickson MacMillan.
123.12 Harold Sweats. Mr. and Mrs. Harold W. Sweatt.
123.13 Sumner MacKnight. Sumner Thomas McKnight. 1884–1959. President Mpls real estate company. State legislator, 1921–29.
123.25 Johnny Green. 1908–1989. American arranger, composer, conductor, pianist.
124.2 Dodsworth. SL's novel (New York: Harcourt, Brace, 1929), rewritten for stage by SL and Sidney Howard, produced successfully in New York 1934.
124.8 Mrs. Mac Washburn--Rube. Ruby F. Washburn. Widow Abbott McConnell Washburn, 1887–1939, Mpls banker-lawyer, son of Duluth lawyer Jed L. Washburn, 1856–1931, whose other son, Claude, who died 1926 at age 43, was novelist friend of SL.

124.11 Mr. Atkinson. May be Dana Lewis's husband Harold M. Atkinson or his father Harold E. Atkinson, president ladies' clothing store Harold Inc.

125.25 Folwell's Hiatory of Minnesota. William Watts Folwell. 1833–1929. First president U of MN, 1869–84. Wrote *A History of Minnesota*, 4 vols. (StP: Minnesota Historical Society, 1921–30).

125.26–27 "Ah, Wilderness." 1933 play by Eugene O'Neill.

126.27 Arnulf. Arnulf Ueland. b. 1895. Mpls bank president, Midland National Bank & Trust. Siblings Brenda, Rolf, Sigurd.

126.28 Chas Schoerer(?). Might be David Shearer, 1894–1957, Mpls lawyer, wife Henrietta, or his brother Alan M. Shearer, writer. See Koblas 62.

127.5 Douglases--Mahala. Suburban widow of Walter D. Douglas, 1861–1912, Mpls financier with interests in grain, linseed oil, and Canadian land.

128.11 I. D., BOFlower, Pingree, Richard Ely. Respectively Ignatius Donnelly 1831–1901, Benjamin Orange Flower 1858–1918, Detroit's reform mayor Hazen Stuart Pingree 1840–1901, and Richard Theodore Ely 1854–1943. See Alden Whitman, ed., *American Reformers* (New York: H. W. Wilson, 1985).

129.2 Fort Beauharnais, built 1727. According to *WPA Guide* 110, the first Christian mission on MN soil was begun at Fort Beauharnois, 1727.

131.11–12 Johnny Gunther. Later visited friend SL in Duluth summer 1945 while researching *Inside U.S.A.* (New York: Harper, 1947). See Schorer 735–36.

132.4 Palmer House. Hotel in Sauk Centre where SL worked two weeks in summer 1902 at age 17, then again summer 1903. See Schorer 33, Koblas 9.

132.5–6 Edgar Wesley's book Owatonna. Edgar Bruce Wesley. b. 1891. U of MN professor of education. Wrote *Owatonna—the Social Development of a Minnesota Community* (Mpls: University of MN Press, 1938).

132.29 Clinchy's "The Mask of Sanity." Probably Hervey Milton Cleckley, *The Mask of Sanity: An Attempt to Reinterpret the So-Called Psychopathic Personality* (St. Louis: C. V. Mosby, 1941).

133.2 John Crosbys. John Crosby. 1867–1962. Mpls miller, attorney, banker, a builder of General Mills. Headed Washburn-Crosby Milling Company, one of the companies merging to form General Mills 1928. Wife Margaret Hastings Crosby, d. 1964, aged 93.

133.3 Mr. and Mrs. Albert Crosby. Albert Hastings Crosby. 1900–1946. Mpls bank executive. Son of John Crosby. Wife Esther.

133.3 Mrs. Bovey. Margaret Bovey. d. 1972, aged 84. Widow of Mpls businessman John Alden Bovey, 1867–1938.

133.25 Katherine Overstreet. Kathryn Overstreet. d. 1963, aged 49. Mpls-area concert pianist.

135.12 Walpole, Galsworthy, Drinkwater. SL was proud of knowing these English writers himself. See Schorer 326.

135.13 Wilhemus (sic) Bryan. Wilhelmus Bogart Bryan, Jr. b. 1898. Presbyterian minister, educator. Administrator Blake School in Hopkins, MN 1939–46. Became a dean Macalester College in StP, 1946.

135.14 Dr. and Mrs. Zierold. Arthur A. Zierold. 1888–1976. Professor of surgery U of MN. Wife Marian.

135.14–15 Clarke Fletcher. Perhaps Clark R. Fletcher. 1885–1943. Mpls attorney.

135.15 Weaver Dobsons. Eben Wever Dobson. 1893–1948. Mpls lumber company executive. Wife Marguerite.

135.24 Carl Jones. 1887–1957. Mpls publisher, history enthusiast, writer of books on magic. Publisher of *Minneapolis Journal* 1928–39.

135.25 Gideon Seymour. 1901–54. Editorial writer and editor *Minneapolis Star Journal.*

135.25 Dana Macmillan. Putnam Dana McMillan. 1881–1961. Vice-president General Mills. Member management team founding General Mills, 1928.

135.29–30 "The Long Boats Passing," by Havighurst. Walter Havighurst, *The Long Ships Passing, the Story of the Great Lakes* (New York: Macmillan, 1942).

135.32 Miss Godfrey. Harriet Bezada Godfrey. 1849–1943. Termed first white child born in Mpls. Interviewed by William McNally for newspaper story 30 May 1942. SL clipped story, pasted in diary, fol. 44.

137.18 Rolf. Rolf Ueland. 1899–1973. Mpls lawyer of Ueland & Ueland. Siblings Brenda, Arnulf, Sigurd.

138.7 Micky. Michael Lewis. 1930–1975. Second of SL's two sons, born to second wife Dorothy Thompson. Had career in New York as an actor.

139.26–27 movie "Mrs. Minniver." Melodramatic 1942 Academy Award–winning film by MGM about English housewife surviving WWII.

139.29 Sigurd Arne of World Wide eatures. Sigrid Arne. b. 1900. Washington correspondent for Associated Press in 1945, wrote *United Nations Primer* (New York: Farrar & Rinehart, 1945).

139.29–30 Bart Heffelfinger. Mistake for Elizabeth (Brad) Heffelfinger.

140.31 Blegen. Theodore Christian Blegen. 1891–1969. Prominent MN historian, sometimes called "Mr. Minnesota History." Dean U of MN Graduate School 1940–60. Wrote *Building Minnesota* (Boston: Heath, 1938) and several other books.

141.3 "All Wives Are Angels." Published *The Cosmopolitan,* February 1943, 28–31, 132–33.

143.31 Rufus King. 1893–1966. American mystery writer. *Murder by Latitude* (Garden City, NY: Doubleday, Doran, 1930).

144.12 Gapon. Jesse Gapen. Started Gateway-Hungry Jack Lodge, 1924. See Koblas 121–22.

144.24–25 "For God's sake" . . ."drop the other shoe." Must be version of joke about one-legged man in boardinghouse. The roomer below, hearing a shoe fall, cannot get to sleep, waiting for second shoe to drop.

144.26 Allan Updegraff. 1883–1965. Novelist and writer. SL's classmate at Yale and long-time friend. Married to Edith Summers, once sweetheart of SL. The incident with two "pick-up phone girls" Schorer considers a one-time event in SL's college experience. Schorer 91, 95, 120–21, 406.

145.19–20 high-grade iron ore . . . low-grade. High-grade iron ore was depleted after WWII, but new process to concentrate iron from low-grade ore, taconite, was implemented in 1950s, so Iron Range kept producing.

146.2 Babbitt. Mining village on eastern end of Mesabi Range, developed 1920 when Mesabi Iron Company built processing plant there, named after Judge K. R. Babbitt. SL's failure to comment further here may mean he was unaware of the town name when naming his novel *Babbitt* (New York: Harcourt, Brace, 1922).

148.4 Hartwell. Arthur Mowry Hartwell. 1890–1969. Vice-president General Mills. SL's Mpls neighbor fall 1942.

148.5 Allison. Robert Glenn Allison. b. 1887. Mpls radiologist. Wife Helen Bullitt Lowry Allison.

148.5 Luyten. William Jacob Luyten. b. 1899. Dutch-educated professor of astronomy U of MN.

149.2 Dr. Arey. Stuart Lane Arey. b. 1908. Suburban Mpls (Excelsior) physician. Wife Evelyn.

149.9–10 Congressman Dick Gale. 1900–1973. U.S. congressman from MN's Third District, 1941–45. Farmer (starting 1923) and state legislator, 1939–40. Grandson of Gov. John S. Pillsbury. Wife Isobel.

149.10 Earle Brown. d. 1963, aged 83. Hennepin County sheriff, starting 1920. First chief MN Highway Patrol, appointed 1929. Republican nominee for governor 1932, lost to Farmer-Labor incumbent Floyd B. Olson.

149.14 Wells. Wells Lewis. 1917–1944. Older of SL's two sons, born to first wife Grace Hegger. Showed promise as a writer, publishing a novel *They Still Say No* (New York: Farrar & Rinehart, 1939) at age 21. Died as a soldier in Europe, 29 October 1944.

149.26 "Quiet Wedding." 1938 British stage comedy by Esther McCracken, made into a film 1940.

150.21 Dean Thomas. Joseph M. Thomas. 1876–1962. U of MN English professor and an assistant dean.

150.21 Robt Penn Warren. The famous writer. Professor U of MN 1942–50, between stints at LSU 1934–42, and Yale 1950–73.

150.21 Tremaine McDowell. d. 1959, aged 65. U of MN professor.

150.24–25 Maritta Wolf's "Night Shift." (New York: Random House, 1942).

151.5 Mr. Tyner. Frederick D. Tyner. 1877–1959. Pastor St. Luke's Episcopal Mpls. Known as a chaplain to sports.

151.26 Grace Flandrau. 1889–1971. StP author, known for writing about StP's upper crust and life in other countries. Widow of W. Blair Flandrau, son of Judge Charles Eugene Flandrau.

151.29 old Judge. Charles Eugene Flandrau. 1828–1903. Remembered for heroism during Sioux conflict of 1862. MN Supreme Court judge 1857–64.

151.29–30 son Charles. Charles Macomb Flandrau. 1871–1938. StP writer known for stories about life at Harvard. Son of Judge Charles Eugene Flandrau.

152.23 President Coffey. Walter Castella Coffey. 1876–1956. President U of MN 1941–45. Dean U of MN Department of Agriculture 1921–41.

152.24 Castell. Alburey Castell. b. 1904. Philosophy professor U of MN.

152.24 Morgan. Possibly George Wagner Morgan. 1884–1957. StP lawyer from prominent law firm.

152.25 Arthur Upson. 1877–1908. MN poet, idol of SL's youth. When Upson, aged 31, drowned at Lake Bemidji in 1908, SL eulogized him as if the victim were another Keats. See Schorer 63, 142.

152.25 Mrs. Harding. Margaret Snodgrass Harding. 1885–1976. Original head U of MN Press, 1927–53. Widow historian Samuel B. Harding, 1866–1927.

154.27 Abbott Deutsch. Alcuin Deutsch. 1877–1951. Abbot St. John's Benedictine Abbey and president St. John's U, Collegeville, MN.

156.8 John Sherman. 1898–1969. Music and drama critic and editor for Mpls newspapers.

156.9 Dr. Mecklenburg. George Mecklenburg. 1881–1965. Minister Wesley Methodist Church Mpls, starting 1928.

157.6 Bill Stidger. 1885–1949. Kansas City Methodist minister in 1925, prototype for SL's unflattering portrait of the evangelical preacher in *Elmer Gantry.* See Schorer 441–42.

157.24 Candida. Play by George Bernard Shaw, 1898.

158.4 Love Cruickshank. Student U of MN, received BA 1943. Later a newspaper writer in Albert Lea, MN.

158.6–7 Lily MJ. Lillian MacGibbon Jacobson. Daughter of John MacGibbon of Sauk Centre and wife of retired Alexandria, MN, banker-investor Tollef Jacobson, 1869–1948.

159.9 Sigurd Ueland. 1893–1975. Mpls lawyer. Siblings Brenda, Arnulf, Rolf.

159.10–11 Ginny, Faubion Bowers, Tom Sakamoto & Mrs. Tsukahira. Niece Virginia Lewis and her friends. See Koblas 118.

159.23 Pat Brueckner. One of the children of U of MN professor Leo J. Brueckner, d. 1967, aged 77.

160.5 Ralph Casey. 1890–1977. Director U of MN School of Journalism and Mass Communication 1930–58.

160.24 Dick Brueckner. Brother of Pat and son of professor Leo J. Brueckner.

160.25 Meridel Le Sueur. 1900–1996. MN writer, actress, political radical, called "Minnesota's Proletariat Laureate."

161.9 Miss Jackson. Elizabeth Jackson. 1892–1968. English professor U of MN.

161.11 Allen Tate. Taught at U of MN 1951–68.

161.20 Backus. Edward Wellington Backus. 1860–1934. Mpls industrialist, known for lumber, pulp, paper interests in International Falls.

161.20 Stanley Hawks. 1895–1971. Executive Minneapolis Star and Tribune Company. The huge house was 2201 East Lake of the Isles Boulevard.

161.21 Steve Benet. Stephen Vincent Benet. SL was friend of Benet family in California 1909 where he first met Stephen, aged 10. See Schorer 152–53.

161.30 Mitropoulos. Conductor Minneapolis Symphony Orchestra 1937–49.

161.30 Bird. Charles Bird. 1893–1957. U of MN professor of psychology.

161.32 V for victory with fingers end of --- --. The rhythm of first four notes in Beethoven's Fifth Symphony was associated during WWII with three dots and a dash, Morse code for V, symbol of victory.

162.10 Fred Sweet. b. 1903. Associate Curator of Paintings, Art Institute of Chicago 1939–52.

162.11 Marjorie Sirich. Assistant to Director Minneapolis Institute of Arts. Husband Edward Hinman Sirich, 1884–1963, professor of French U of MN.

162.16 Follrath. Darwin Follrath. b. 1909. Artist, won a first prize award in oils at Minneapolis Institute of Arts 1942.

162.17 Forrest and Mrs. Spencer. Perhaps DeForest Spencer. Officer in charge U.S. Department of Agriculture Marketing Administration, Mpls. Wife Cornelia.

162.18 Miles and Alice McNally. Miles H. McNally. Vice-president Mpls insurance company. Wife Alice, d. 1948, lecturer Minneapolis Institute of Arts.

162.18–19 Dr. Strachauer. Arthur C. Strachauer. 1883–1957. Mpls surgeon.

162.24–25 stone Rogers castle. Formidable stone house at 1415 Mt. Curve Ave., diagonally across T-intersection and up hill from SL's house. Vacant in 1942, it had been residence of lumber company president Arthur R. Rogers.

162.25 Eddie Ruben. President Welworth Enterprises, theater operators. SL's neighbor, residing 1505 Mt. Curve Ave.

163.6 Dorothy. Dorothy Thompson. 1894–1961. Nationally prominent newspaper columnist and SL's second wife. They married in London 1928 and divorced January 1942. One child, Michael Lewis, b. 20 June 1930.

163.8 Ben Ritter. Perhaps Bernard H. Ridder, Sr. 1883–1975. Publisher *St. Paul Dispatch* and *Pioneer Press* 1938–45. Brothers Bernard, Victor, and Joseph ran the Ridder newspaper chain.

163.16 Anson Jackson. Anson B. Jackson, Jr. b. 1885. StP lawyer.

164.1–2 Hildred Howe Smith. Mpls widow of William H. Smith. Former officer Zephyr Oil Company. Lewis to Powers, 4 November 1942, St. Cloud State University Archive, reveals that Lillian MacGibbon Jacobson (fol. 96), Hildred Howe Smith, and Kit McNiece were all Sauk Centre girls about SL's age, living in the Twin Cities, married to businessmen. At this dinner they brought out photo showing SL at high school graduation.

164.2 Kit McNiece (Mrs. Roy Hoople). Katherine Hoople. Husband Roy Nelson Hoople, b. 1873, Mpls grain executive, Cargill Inc.

164.11 Dorothy Atkinson. Dorothy Bridgman Atkinson. 1890–1965. Twin Cities cultural leader, connected to Atkinson Milling Company. First husband Frederick G. Atkinson, 1864–1940, pioneer Mpls miller. Her father Methodist minister Dr. George H. Bridgman, president Hamline U 1885–1911.

164.11 Pierce Butlers. Pierce Butler, Jr. 1893–1957. StP lawyer of prominent family. Wife Hilda. His father Pierce Butler Sr., 1866–1939, was associate justice U.S. Supreme Court 1923–39.

164.12 Mme Silvercruys. Suzanne Silvercruys. 1898–1973. Belgian-born aristocrat sculptress and lecturer living in Connecticut. Second husband Edward Ford Stevenson.

164.19 Charley McCarthy. Puppet operated by American comedian and ventriloquist Edgar Bergen, 1903–1978.

164.31 Dr. Lewis & Hannah Daniel. Mpls physician Lewis Daniel, 1894–1943, was cousin of John and Helen Baxter. Wife Hannah.

165.13 Sidonie Gruenberg. 1881–1974. Austrian-born American writer-lecturer on child-family issues. Lived 418 Central Park West, New York.

165.14 Grauben. Nicolai Graudan. First cellist Minneapolis Symphony Orchestra 1939–44. Graduate St. Petersburg Imperial Conservatory, cello soloist for Berlin Philharmonic nine years. Wife pianist Hansi Freudberg.

165.18–19 John & Mrs. Pillsbury. John Sargent Pillsbury. 1878–1968. Board chairman Pillsbury Flour Mills Company. His namesake the governor was his great uncle. Wife Eleanor Jerusha Pillsbury.

165.19 "Mike" (Richard) Elliott. Richard Maurice Elliot. 1887–1969. Founder psychology department U of MN. Wife Mathilde.

165.20–21 Swedish Consul Hellstrom. Carl F. Hellstrom. Royal Consul of Sweden in Mpls.

166.2 De Laittres. Prominent Mpls banking family.

166.18 Lippincotts. Perhaps Benjamin E. Lippincott. b. 1902. Political science professor U of MN. Wife Gertrude L.

166.18 Mr. and Mrs. Close. Winston A. and Elizabeth Close. Mpls architects, a husband-wife team. Winston died 1997, aged 91.

168.2 Ormandy. Conductor Minneapolis Symphony 1931–36.

168.7 Carl Van Doren. One of SL's few enduring friends. See Schorer 721, 803–4.

168.15 Stock. Probably short for Leopold Stokowski.

168.28 Kit Cann. Isadore Blumenfeld (Kid Cann). 1901–1981. Mpls underworld figure considered a bootlegger boss during Prohibition, later known as "the closest thing Minnesota had to a godfather."

171.13 Feb <u>1943</u>. SL's movements in 1943 show usual degree of busyness. He engaged lavish penthouse apartment at 300 Central Park West in New York at end of January. With Marcella Powers, who helped him decorate, he referred to it humorously as "Big Intolerable" or "Intolerable Towers." At end of February he spent week in StP preparing for article about Governor Stassen. He made two-week trip again to MN in May, spent some of early June in Williamstown, Massachusetts, and left New York for Hollywood June 23 to collaborate with Dore Schary (1905–1980) on screenplay *Storm in the West*. They finished script in time for SL to return to New York September 7, but the sponsoring studio, MGM, decided not to make the movie. From early October to mid-December, SL was on national debating tour with friend Lewis Browne. Posh apartment at 300 Central Park West in New York was maintained until April 1945, when SL made "permanent" move to Duluth. See Schorer 699–708, 725–28.

172.22 Ed Thye. 1896–1969. Governor of MN 1943–46. U.S. senator 1947–58. Farmer.

172.27 "Sibley Tea House." Henry Hastings Sibley, first governor state of MN 1858. According to *WPA Guide* 373, tea house was built of brick on hill above Sibley's house by his secretary Hypolite Du Puis in 1854, was remodeled by D.A.R. and opened to public for meals about 1930.

172.28 Alex Ramsey. Alexander Ramsey. 1815–1903. First territorial governor of MN 1849. Second governor state of MN 1860–63. U.S. senator 1863–75. U.S. secretary of war under Hayes 1879–81.

173.1 Mrs. Furness. Anna Ramsey Furness. 1876–1964. Granddaughter of Alexander Ramsey.

173.2 Hector Dousman. Hercules Louis Dousman. d. 1868. Wisconsin fur trader, land speculator, contemporary of Sibley and Ramsey.

174.3 Ward and Frances (Prenny) Lucas, and Jack. Ward Lucas. 1892–1961. Winona, MN lumber company president. Wife Frances Prentiss Lucas, 1894–1983. Jack may be son John Samuel Lucas.

174.4 Mr. and Mrs. Tearse. Prominent Winona, MN manufacturing family, associated with Dr. Ward's Medical Company.

174.5 Geo and Mrs. Little. George R. Little. 1883–1953. Winona, MN lumber company president. Wife Edith.

174.6 Gretchen (Grata) Lamberton. Gretchen Leicht Lamberton. 1895–1965. Winona, MN newspaperwoman. Husband Henry McClelland Lamberton, Jr., 1893–1962, Winona lawyer of prominent family.

174.8 Mrs. Choate. Adele Choate. Husband Charles A. Choate, b. 1894, of the Winona, MN department store H. Choate & Company.

174.10 Mr. King. Ernest King, Sr. Winona, MN bank president and president J. R. Watkins medicine company. Wife Grace Watkins King.

177.7 Arrive Minneapolis May 6, 1944. After spending winter in New York, SL returned to MN in May, bent on establishing residence in Duluth. See Schorer 710, 713.

177.16 Dr. Roy Swanson. 1890–1963. Mpls obstetrician-gynecologist.

178.3 Luke Rader. 1890–1952. Fiery Mpls evangelist at River-Lake Gospel Tabernacle, which he founded 1928. Son and successor Paul Rader closed it 1968.

179.21 Margaret Banning. Margaret Culkin Banning. 1891–1982. Duluth-bred American writer of popular fiction. On 15 November 1944 she married second husband LeRoy Salsich, 1879–1957, president Oliver Mining Company 1930–46, iron mining arm of U.S. Steel. Her relationship with SL in Duluth was characterized by neighborliness and rivalry. See Schorer 716–20, 735–36, 745.

180.18 Finns and Co-operative Stores. The consumer cooperative movement of the teens, twenties, and thirties was strong in MN, promoted especially by Finnish immigrants. See Blegen 399.

181.30 Bob Ridder. Robert Blair Ridder. b. 1919. Young promotion manager Ridder newspapers in Duluth, later to head Ridder radio-TV interests in Twin Cities. Wife Kathleen, interviewed by phone 1994. Father Victor.

183.6 Housman's Shropshire. The twenty-year-old narrator in "Loveliest of Trees, the Cherry Now" thinks he has fifty more springs to live, not sixty.

184.4–5 Romanoff Restaurant. The glamorous Romanoff Restaurant, eventually a chain, was owned by American con artist Mike Romanoff (Harry Gerguson), who, until 1958, pretended to be Russian prince.

184.9 Connie. Cornelius Traeger. Dorothy Thompson's doctor in New York, who became good friends with SL, treated him during alcoholic debauches, and befriended SL and Marcella Powers in 1941 so much that SL suspected him of being a rival for her. See Schorer 538, 613, 674.

184.11 John Malick. d. 1961, aged 85. Minister First Unitarian Duluth 1942–48. Liberal activist. Wife Elizabeth.

184.13 Mark Nolan. 1901–1967. Notre-Dame-educated Irish-American District Court judge in Duluth 1937–67. Prototype for protagonist of *Cass Timberlane* 1945, the first of SL's Duluth novels. Admired by SL for his heartiness. Wife Ann, interviewed 1990. Daughter Marcia Ann.

184.18–19 Kenneth Cant. d. 1973, aged 83. Duluth real estate agent who found SL the house at 2601 East Second Street. Wife May.

184.19 Elsa Anneke. 1896–1995. Concert pianist and one of SL's best friends in Duluth. During her career, she soloed with St. Louis, Duluth, Mpls, Chicago, and Columbia (CBS Radio) symphonies. Husband Victor died 1937. Reported in interviews 1987 that SL had little ear for music, despite much interest and good intentions.

184.22 Hainikainen. Tauno Hannikainen. d. Finland 1968, aged 72. Finnish conductor Duluth Symphony Orchestra 1942–47, later of Helsinki Symphony.

185.4 Williams-Webber house. John G. Williams, 1855–1937, Welsh-born Duluth lawyer-banker, investor in farming and mining, had the house built at 2601 East Second Street in 1912 and lived there until he died. SL acquired it from family of E. E. Webber, Duluth physician, first by renting it May 1944, then buying it 1 January 1945. SL lived in it May through August 1944, had it redecorated spring 1945 as if to move in permanently, lived there May through August 1945, then again December 1945 through March 1946. He sold it January 1946, after returning from brother Fred's funeral in Sauk Centre, and stayed on as tenant through March. See Koblas 123–24, 139, and Schorer 714, 725, 743.

186.23 They have a small house. 5802 London Road, known as "pump house" because it had been a pumping station. Lake Superior just a few feet from southeast side of house.

187.3 Mrs. H. Inez M. Melander Hilding. d. 1986, aged 83. Solo violinist and Duluth Symphony concertmistress. Husband Anderson C. Hilding, 1892–1977, physician-researcher in nose, sinus, lungs. Although Hilding fits SL's description, pianist Anneke asserted in 1987 interview that the violin was played by Myrtle Wolsfeld, principal violist Duluth Symphony, starting 1940, later member of Los Angeles Symphony.

187.11 Larson. Oscar John (O. J., not O. G.) Larson. 1871–1957. Finnish-born Duluth lawyer and U.S. congressman 1921–25. Honorary consul for Finland and promoter St. Lawrence Seaway.

187.13 Ernst Lachmann. Ernest Lachmund. d. 1954, age uncertain. Duluth cellist, pianist, composer. Called "Dean of Duluth's music teachers" in 1940. Before arriving in Duluth 1890, studied in Europe, audited Liszt's piano classes in Weimer, heard Brahms, Tchaikovsky, Mahler conduct their works. *Duluth News-Tribune* (Earl Finburg, "The Lachmund Story," 27 March 1949) reported he had as a prize memento a lock of Liszt's hair.

187.14 Dworshak. Louis Dworshak. b. 1877. Duluth photographer.

188.10 tide of 3 inches. Lake Superior does not have a lunar tide, but it does have a seiche, a short-term variation in water level, induced by atmospheric pressure changes or by wind. The changes can have an almost regular four-hour action.

188.26–27 Astor Trading Post. John Jacob Astor's American Fur Company maintained this trading post on the St. Louis River 1817–42. Immigrant Peter John Peterson, 1824–1873, acquired property in late 1850s, settled down to farm, built a house. According to daughter Hilma Peterson, 1867–1955, "The old John Jacob Astor fur trading post became our barn. We used it for years until my brother, Oscar, who was a logger, tore it down." See Isadore Cohen, "Ex-Teacher Keeps City Home Intact With Past," *Duluth News-Tribune,* 28 November 1954.

189.22 Heddy Lamarr. Hedy Lamarr. b. 1914. Viennese-born brunette film star known for seductress roles.

189.30 Lord Russells or Lords Russell. Possibly Bertrand Russell, elevated to peerage 1931. The third Earl Russell. SL was proud of knowing him. In 1923 election, SL made speeches for Russell's campaign, irritating British press. See Schorer 389.

190.10. Povah. In the Powers letters, SL uses this term of endearment for both Marcella and her mother.

190.12 Lilian. Lillian. SL's black housekeeper and cook in Mpls 1942 at 1500 Mt. Curve Avenue and in Duluth 1944 and 1945 at 2601 East Second Street.

191.2 Clara Stocker. d. 1973. Duluth devotee of French and Finnish culture, daughter of locally distinguished composer Stella Prince Stocker and Dr. H. M. Stocker.

191.7 grain-commission man. Duluth had its own grain exchange, 1881–1972, which operated from 1894 at 301 West First Street. Grain commissioners bought and sold there.

191.15 Hobohemia. SL's coinage, which Schorer portrayed as one of SL's "exasperatingly reiterated terms" (191). It served as title of short story that SL published in *Saturday Evening Post* (7 April 1917) and that he adapted for stage with help of St. Paul Little Theater director Daniel Reed in 1918. The play opened in New York 8 February 1919, got negative reviews, ran eleven weeks. See Schorer 248–55.

191.16 David Erickson. David Ericson. 1869–1946. Swedish-born Duluth-bred artist. Worked New York 1890s, once sharing studio-bedroom with Stephen Crane. Then lived mostly Europe until WWII when returned Duluth.

191.18 Juho Rissanen. 1873–1950. Refugee Finnish artist in Duluth, considered by *Duluth News-Tribune* on 18 July 1943 as "Finland's Greatest Painter."

191.22 Philipvandorensternstern. Philip Van Doren Stern. 1900–1984. American historian, novelist, anthologist.

192.1 Dr. Allane. Vieno Severi Alanne. 1879–1960. Finnish immigrant, leader in cooperative movement, often headquartered in Superior, Wisconsin. Chemical engineer, author of Finnish-English dictionary, journalist.

192.14 Brousseau. Vere G. Brewsaugh. Superior, Wisconsin piano teacher.

193.2 Jay. Probably Jay Cooke Allen, Jr. 1900–1972. American correspondent covering Spanish Civil War and WWII in North Africa and Europe. Held by Gestapo four months in 1941.

194.5 Ed Kenny. 1881–1969. Duluth District Court judge 1924–1960.

195.19 Mrs. Griggs. Neva Griggs. Amateur painter. Husband Duluth banker Richard L. Griggs, whom she married 1911.

195.19 the banker. Richard L. Griggs. 1886–1987. Powerful Duluth banker, a founder of Greyhound Bus Lines, U of MN regent, big-game hunter on five continents starting at age 75. Schorer called him "a bearish old banker and regent" (733). Griggs's verdict on SL is found in a note in his hand inside the front cover of his copy of the Schorer biography, housed at the U of MN in Duluth library: "Chapter IV and V—involving Duluth people (including Griggs) should be read as having much local interest, gossip, Lewis temperament, friendship problems etc. I knew him well, was his Duluth banker, he came frequently to my home to enjoy my lovely wife Neva and 'direct' me in my University activities, forced me to go to Chicago to become 'informed' on the 'right man' for President of the University of Minnesota (We Regents were looking) (to me the 'right man' was the wrong man). But satirically entertaining, —sometimes an egotistical bore. I think I saw thru a certain veneer that made me a bit sorry for him."

195.27 Spike Hunt. Frazier (Spike) Hunt. 1885–1967. Foreign correspondent *Cosmopolitan* and Hearst papers. Became SL's friend in London 1921. Schorer characterized him as "a Midwesterner, a bluff, downright newspaper correspondent" (311).

196.13 Vince Day. 1885–1945. Mpls judge (Hennepin County District Court), one of the prototypes for Cass Timberlane. Had liberal third-party loyalties. As counsel to A. C. Townley, helped draft Nonpartisan legislation in North Dakota. Served as secretary to Minnesota Farmer-Labor governor Floyd B. Olson, 1931–35.

199.9 Kubla. From Samuel Taylor Coleridge's visionary poem "Kubla Khan": "And 'mid this tumult Kubla heard from far / Ancestral voices prophesying war!"

199.21 Rudolph Illgen. d. 1954, aged 68. German-born resort developer on Lake Superior's north shore, Illgen City Resort.

202.19 Rex Stout. Vigorously anti-fascist during WWII. Dorothy Thompson suggested in 1944 that Stout's promotion of a hard peace for Germany might aid Goebbels's propaganda. This bitter debate was later resolved.

202.21 Kip Fadiman. Clifton Fadiman. 1904–1999. American editor, critic, radio-TV host.

203.8 Herb Mayes. b. 1900. American magazine editor. Publisher of SL stories. Found assistant editor job at *Good Housekeeping* for Marcella Powers spring 1943. See Schorer 712, and Lewis to Virginia Lewis, 31 March 1944, *Selected Letters of Sinclair Lewis,* eds. John J. Koblas and Dave Page (Madison, Wis.: Main Street Press, 1985), 84.

204.13–14 Henry George League. SL is kidding Marcella Powers for her admiration of radical-chic people in New York City.

204.16 Southern-mansion sort of boat house. The old Duluth Boat Club at Tenth Street on Minnesota Point, built 1904, served as training center for crews in heyday of Duluth rowing, known also for its natatorium, served to shelter sailboats and motorboats in 1940s. Fire destroyed main house in 1951, including boat belonging to Fred Buck.

204.31 French and Sullivan families. Isabelle E. French Sullivan. Twice-widowed Duluth woman. First husband George A. French, furniture retailer. Second husband Francis W. Sullivan, 1867–1941, lawyer-banker-businessman.

205.21 Charlie Liscomb. 1888–1978. President Duluth insurance agency. Wife Eleanor.

206.11–13 Marcella, with her damn Minneapolis . . . I said to The Boys. This line, written in letter to Marcella Powers, suggests SL kiddingly represented her to Duluth friends as native Minnesotan with urban ambition limited to Mpls and StP only—hence wholesome Midwestern girl, not East Coast starlet.

206.16 Lou Castle. Lewis Castle. 1889–1960. Duluth banker. Later (1954) U.S. chief of St. Lawrence Seaway. Wife Emelyn died 1939. Daughter Frances.

206.16 Fred Buck. 1887–1972. Duluth real estate agent. Wife Gladys.

206.16 John Hoff. d. 1978, aged 76. Duluth real estate company executive. Wife Edith.

206.32 Geo Macy. 1900–1956. American editor. Originator Limited Editions Club 1929. President Heritage Press.

207.15 Babbitworths. That SL was ambivalent about the American businessman is not only shown in the novels *Babbitt* and *Dodsworth* themselves but also in this word he coined, blending the unattractive with the attractive.

209.5–6 John McConnaughy. Professor College of St. Scholastica in Duluth 1944. In 1945–46 professor U of South Carolina in Columbia, where SL visited on trip south to study race prejudice. Wife Anna.

209.14 Dr. Mary Banning. Scientist daughter of Margaret Culkin Banning. *Duluth News-Tribune* featured her in "Duluthian Is One of 200 Women in Country with Ph.D. in Physics," 6 August 1944. Interviewed by phone 1998.

210.23 Ellen Gibson. Duluth bank employee. Friend of Kenneth Cant.

210.23–24 Buffalo Bill's abandoned house. Nellie Cody Wetmore had home in Duluth, paid for by her brother Buffalo Bill in the 1890s. By 1951, this house at 820 North Ash Street was occupied, after undergoing radical remodeling that made the exterior unrecognizable. See Robert Pomeroy, "Buffalo Bill's Buried Treasure?" *Duluth News-Tribune*, 28 October 1951.

210.27 Indian Sadie. Madam of legendary reputation, managing brothel in Superior, Wisconsin.

210.33 Helen Bede. d. 1978, aged 82. English teacher at Duluth Central High School. Daughter of congressman-orator-editorialist J. Adam Bede.

211.1 Flynn. Paul J. Flynn. d. 1966, aged 67. St. Louis County commissioner 1940–49, deep sea diver, marine engineer.

211.1 Wassings. Ernest Wassing. Austrian refugee in Duluth from 1940. Principal cellist Duluth Symphony. Had been solo cellist nine years Berlin Broadcasting Symphony. Wife Gina, musician also.

211.3 A. E. Rich. Anthony E. Rich. d. 1953, aged 54. MN State Public Examiner 1933–44, then comptroller at Nopeming Sanatorium southwest of Duluth.

211.5 Magney. Clarence Reinhold Magney. 1883–1962. Duluth District Court judge 1921–43. MN Supreme Court judge 1943–53. Conservationist.

211.5–6 Mrs. Fred Buck's bro. Henry Gilbert. d. 1972, aged 78. Duluth photographer.

212.4 Geo R. Stuntz. George R. Stuntz. 1820–1902. Duluth's first permanent white settler, opening trading post 1852. Credited with discovering iron ore on Minnesota's Vermilion Range, hence called "maker of millionaires." He died poor, his grave unmarked until 1938.

212.9–10 Tweed Hall and County Historical. The house at 2309 East First Street, built 1906 for Joseph Bell Cotton, general solicitor for Duluth and Iron Range Railroad, was purchased 1942 by George and Alice Tweed and given to Duluth State Teachers College as fine arts and recreation center. The St. Louis County Historical Society moved its offices there too. Sold by U of MN in Duluth 1961.

212.20 Peytons. Jean Peyton. Widow of William R. Peyton, d. 1942, aged 75, of Duluth-Superior pioneer banking family. Schorer suggests SL cultivated her acquaintance because she was pretty (younger than deceased spouse) and had daughter Marcella's age, Jean Peyton Erickson (719).

213.4 Asa Lyons. Asa T. Lyons, Jr. d. ca. 1970, aged 71. Owner Duluth cab company, ambulance service, garage. Friend of SL, who needed driver because of tremor in hands. Lyons drove SL on long trips, including tour of South fall 1945 researching *Kingsblood Royal*. At age 68 in 1967, Lyons reportedly gave "large number of personal papers of Sinclair Lewis" to Sinclair Lewis Foundation in Sauk Centre. See "Lewis Foundation Receives Gift of Author's Papers," *Duluth News-Tribune*, 17 August 1967. Minutes of Foundation record acceptance of offer but do not record delivery of papers.

213.10 Lyle Oreck. 1894–1962. President Oreck's women's apparel store Duluth. Son of Russian immigrant store-founder Gabriel A. Oreck, d. 1956, aged 91. Wife Sara.

213.10 Thelma and Dr. Jumer. J. A. Jumer. Dentist in Two Harbors, MN. Wife Thelma.

213.21 New of Hal. May mean news from Harrison Smith, called Hal, an editor at Harcourt, Brace, friend of both SL and Marcella Powers.

213.21 Eveng, last of the Ridders. SL's terse dismissal of friends. See Schorer 719, Koblas 129.

213.23 Carly Heimbach. Carlisle Max Heimbach. 1890–1976. President Heimbach Lumber Company. Wife Charlene Bagley Heimbach, 1898–1968, active in Duluth jewelry store founded by father Cassius H. Bagley 1920. Heimbach home at 2432 East Second Street had wood shingle roof shaped like thatch, described in *Cass Timberlane* as Scott and Julia Zago house.

213.28 too much Bourbon. Very likely the party discussed by Schorer when Margaret Culkin Banning berated Judge Mark Nolan for heavy drinking and SL angrily defended him (718–19). All three were heavy drinkers. Although the alcoholic SL was trying to stay dry in Duluth so that most witnesses never saw him drinking, he had not achieved total abstinence.

214.1 Marvin Oreck. 1901–1952. Executive Oreck's women's apparel store Duluth. Brother of Erwin and Lyle. Wife Margot.

214.2 3 Anneckes. Elsa Anneke, daughter Jean Anneke Nelson, and sister Charlotte Galvan.

214.3 Barbara Griggs. Daughter-in-law of Richard and Neva Griggs, married to their son H. Warner Griggs.

214.3 Otto & Florence Lachmund. Otto Gray Lachmund. 1895–1968. Partner real estate company. Duluth air service promoter. Son of Ernest. Wife Florence, 1904–1997.

214.4 Saltuses. Charles N. Saltus. Professor of English Duluth State Teachers College 1932–50. Wife Elinor, librarian Lincoln Junior High.

214.4 Harvaliks. Zaboj V. Harvalik. Prague-trained professor of physics Duluth State Teachers College 1942–48. Wife Charlotte.

214.5 C. Elmer Hammer. d. 1966, aged 68. Duluth meat packing company executive.

214.6 Harry C. Applequist. b. 1904. Duluth lawyer.

214.6 Dorothy Tart. 1902–1998. Professor of Voice Duluth State Teachers College in 1940s.

214.7 Jackson K. Ehlert. d. 1982, aged 76. Music faculty Duluth State Teachers College 1934–48.

214.10 Klearflax factory. Duluth rug factory using flax fiber, founded 1909, ceased operation 1950s.

214.12 Brule River. Renowned Lake Superior south-shore trout stream. Enclave there of private lodges owned by wealthy Duluthians. Cedar Island Lodge on Brule was Henry Clay Pierce estate where President Calvin Coolidge summered 1928. By 1944, estate belonged to StP industrialist John Gilman Ordway, 1886–1966, associated with Crane plumbing-heating supplies and Minnesota Mining & Manufacturing.

214.13 Jane Coulter. b. 1919. Friend of Frances Castle. Later to marry Tom Spencer, Duluth banker. Interviewed by phone 1992.

214.13–14 Marshall and Margaret Alworth. Marshall W. Alworth. d. 1980, aged 97. Elder son of one of Duluth's richest iron ore developers, Marshall Henry Alworth. Wife Margaret.

214.14 Frank Hirschboeck. 1887–1969. Physician at Duluth Clinic.

214.21 Marcella . . . lv for New York. Surviving evidence suggests this visit, July 23–August 4, was rocky for SL-Marcella relationship. Letters from SL to Marcella, frequent during May, June, and early July in the Powers Collection, St. Cloud State University Archive, drop to zero from Duluth in August 1944 after visit. Later reminiscing about Duluth while preparing to leave town, he apostrophized the house, "And twice you have blessedly sheltered Marcella; once, not very happily, but the other time in the happiest Christmas I have ever known," SL to Marcella Powers, 16 March 1946. Tension between SL and Marcella during summer 1944 visit may help account for SL's less than gracious comportment in Duluth society, reported by Schorer 718–19. See notes above, **213.21** *Eveng, last of the Ridders* and **213.28** *too much Bourbon.*

214.26–27 Dick and Cornelia Bardon. Richard Bardon. 1897–1968. Duluth physician. Scion of pioneer family. Historian, editing with Grace Lee Nute, *A Winter in the St. Croix Valley: George Nelson's Reminiscences, 1802–03* (StP: MN Historical Society, 1948). Wife Cornelia, d. 1977, aged 78.

215.2 Julius Barnes. 1873–1959. American business leader from Duluth. Grain merchant, shipbuilder, rug manufacturer. Headed U.S. Food Administration Grain Corporation 1917 for distributing grain to Europe. President U.S. Chamber of Commerce 1921–24, chair of the board 1929–31. Author of business-booster and St. Lawrence Seaway–booster tracts.

215.11–12 Tom and Kitty Gibson. Thomas Gibson. Friend, admirer of SL. Alternately laborer, real estate salesman, broker. Wife Katie.

215.21–22 Sigrud Mitchell. Sigrid M. Mitchell. 1896–1977. Duluth arts promoter.

Husband Wildey Hubbell Mitchell, 1897–1987, lawyer, WWI aviator, son of pioneer Duluth lawyer Oscar Mitchell, 1863–1937.

215.22 Hope & Genevieve Washburn. Sisters from prominent Duluth intellectual family. Genevieve, d. 1986, aged 101, bookstore owner Tryon, NC. Hope, d. 1984, aged 91, musician, teacher, founder Tryon Country Day School, NC. Their brother Claude, novelist and friend of SL, died 1926 at age 43. Their father Jed L. Washburn, 1856–1931, pioneer Duluth lawyer. Their niece is present American writer Carol Bly, b. 1930.

215.22 Mrs. Gudger. Perhaps Mabel S. Gujer, d. ca. 1949, widow of Henry.

215.22–23 Mrs. Blair. Miriam Blair. d. 1985, aged 88. Concert pianist and leader Duluth music circles. Husband Cecil, 1862–1960, grain company executive.

215.30 modernist house on Lake View Avenue. 1700 Lakeview Drive (not Avenue), built 1939–40, its original form known for Bauhaus look, designed by Duluth architect Harold St. Clair Starin, d. 1974, aged 80.

216.3 Jim and Peggie Nye. James Nye. d. 1967, aged 75. Duluth lawyer. Wife Margaret.

216.3 Frank Mannheimer. d. 1972. American concert pianist with international career. His regular summer master class in Duluth for young American pianists started 1943.

216.4 Mrs. Hugo. Virginia Hugo. Duluth homemaker. Widow Victor Hugo, engineer, d. 1913, who was son of Trevanion William Hugo (twice mayor of Duluth, d. 1923, aged 74). In phone interviews 1985 and 1990, Virginia's daughter Mary Hugo, d. 1992, recalled SL visiting their home in search of names of representative poor families to interview. SL left notes on these families on fol. 146. Mary Hugo recalled that SL's visit to the poor caused embarrassment for everybody, except maybe SL himself.

216.5 Bernard. Bernard H. Killorin. d. 1987. Employee Duluth hardware wholesaler, Kelley-How-Thomson Company. Son of John F. Killorin, pioneer logger, railroad builder, a founder of Kelley-How-Thomson. Wife Mary, 1916–1998.

216.6 Rena (Mrs. Jack) Campbell. Irene Campbell. Husband John C. Campbell, Jr., d. 1964, aged 65, Duluth lumber producer.

216.19 Alice King. Executive Duluth's Woodruff Lumber Company. Daughter of Arthur W. King, a founder of company. Brother of Arthur W. King, Jr., who ran company from late 1940s to 1971.

216.22 Roy (wife:) Halverson. Roy E. Halvorson. 1903–1994. Duluth's Christmas tree king, shipping boxed, dipped and dyed, three-foot spruce trees, as many as 1.4 million per year, throughout U.S., 1929–1975. Gadget-laden house 2628 Branch Street. Wife Edythe, d. 1988.

217.4–5 Herbert Sorenson. 1898–1995. President Duluth State Teachers College 1938–46. Wife Mabel.

217.7 Wiener. Joseph B. Wiener. d. 1981, aged 85. Assistant Superintendent of Schools Duluth 1934–63.

217.9 Harry Davis. d. 1948, aged 57. Russian-born Jewish lawyer in Duluth. Wife Ida B., d. 1970, aged 74, civic leader.

217.10 Ruth Slonim. b. 1918. Young English instructor Duluth State Teachers College, later to be professor Washington State University. Father Sigmond M. Slonim, Duluth lawyer. Mother Lena E. Slonim.

217.19 Margaret Mitchell. d. 1990, aged 86. Community activist from prominent Duluth family. Interviewed 1988. Daughter of lawyer Oscar Mitchell, 1863–1937.

218.2 Gerald Sellwood. Joseph Gerald Sellwood. 1902–1968. Duluth banker, businessman. Grandson of Cornish-immigrant iron mine developer Captain Joseph Sellwood, 1846–1914. Wife Virginia Fryberger Sellwood, 1902–1996, from prominent Duluth family of attorneys, interviewed 1993.

218.2 Hartleys. Sons of one of the wealthiest Duluth lumber and iron ore developers, Guilford Graham Hartley, 1853–1922: Cavour Hartley, d. 1986, aged 95; Guilford Hartley, 1907–1983, pioneer aviator. Both sons involved in military missions 1944, thus probably not present at Griggs dinner.

218.3 Francis Sullivan (selig). Francis W. Sullivan, deceased (in 1941). His son Francis C. Sullivan, Duluth lawyer, d. 1990, was away in army 1944, interviewed by phone 1990. SL was probably just listing names of "financial potentates," not guests at the Griggs dinner.

218.3 Geo Tweed. 1871–1946. Duluth mining developer, banker, art collector. The U of MN at Duluth now houses his collection in its Tweed Museum. Wife Alice Lyon Tweed.

218.3 Willis Wyard. 1897–1993. Duluth bank president, First & American National Bank 1943–1963.

218.11 Tom McQueen. d. 1966, aged 62. Minister Pilgrim Congregational Church Duluth 1937–45.

218.16 Packingham. Ronayne and Gilma Packingham.

218.26 Solon. George Solon. d. 1962. Greek immigrant. Wife Demitra, aged 83, was still living at 618½ West Third Street in 1990. Son Louis joined Navy 1944. Present evidence suggests this is case where SL's extraordinary talent for observing American life failed. In his prime he would have known that driving up to see poor family, as if in museum, might leave him with inaccurate view. The family was ambitious. Son Sam is MN State Senator since 1972, son Vlasie investment firm executive. Though family was poor in 1940s, they never considered neighborhood a slum, nor do other witnesses from the era. Sons Sam and Vlasie and mother Demitra, in phone interviews 1990, did not recall SL's visit.

219.15 Diehls. Guy E. Diehl. b. 1879. Duluth mining engineer and executive Oliver Mining Company. Wife Florence B., d. 1966.

219.23 Fran McGiffert. Frances Harrison McGiffert. Member of pioneer Duluth family, their home 2525 East Second Street across avenue from SL. Interviewed by phone 1985, 1997, 1998. After SL left, she and engineer husband Rutherford N. McGiffert, d. 1996, aged 89, built house at 2600 East Second Street.

219.24 Salyards. H. Ely Salyards. 1894–1967. Duluth grain broker, head Ely-Salyards Grain Company. Wife Dorothy, d. 1970, aged 75.

219.27 Frybergers. Possibly Herschel B. Fryberger, Jr. 1906–1997. Duluth attorney. Wife Patricia.

219.28 Davis Bradleys. Davis Woodward Bradley. b. 1912. Duluth clothing retailer. Wife Barbara was niece of Neva Griggs.
219.30 Adam Thompson. d. 1955, aged 66. Duluth grain merchant and hardware wholesaler.
219.31 Dancers (& Helen). Herbert Allan Dancer. 1874–1959. SL's lawyer in Duluth and former district court judge. Wife Ruth Scott Dancer, d. 1965, aged 86, amateur poet. Daughter Helen.
220.7 Congdon. Chester Adgate Congdon. 1853–1916. Founder of one of Duluth's largest iron ore family fortunes. Owner at one time large tract north shore property extending east from Duluth. Builder Glensheen mansion 3300 London Road 1905–8. Wife Clara, d. 1950, aged 96.
220.8 Margaret Ann Hubbard. 1909–1992. Duluth author of over twenty children's books and mysteries. The first, *Little Whirlwind* 1940, was about Red River Valley pioneer girl.
220.11 Rustic Inn. Fondly remembered eating place Two Harbors, MN. A survivor of this dinner party, interviewed 1985, recalled that the twenty-minute wait for a table made SL impatient during whole evening, so event was felt a failure.
220.12 Ted and Mrs. Wohl. Probably Theodore L. Wahl. Officer Duluth real estate company. Wife Frances C.
220.22 Irwin Oreck. Erwin Oreck. d. 1974, aged 81. Executive Oreck's women's apparel store Duluth, president after 1948. Brother of Lyle and Marvin.
220.24 Zolt, scrap iron. Louis Z. Zalk. Officer in Zalk-Josephs Company, Duluth wholesale hardware and scrap iron firm.
221.11 Connie, Carl, Macys. Respectively Dr. Cornelius Traeger, Carl Van Doren, George Macy.
221.12 Alworth garden. Possibly at Marshall W. Alworth house, 314 North Hawthorne Road.
222.6 Weather 1945. SL spent summer 1945 in Duluth, but he neglected to make daily entries in diary. Notable events include dispute between SL and interior decorators within month after his April arrival, commencement address plus five lectures June 20 to July 24 at Duluth State Teachers College on "The Craft of Writing (and the Art of Reading)," lecture at Bemidji State College and another at Moorhead State College, completion of series of articles for *Esquire,* visit from son Michael in late June, and visit in August from John Gunther, who was preparing for *Inside U.S.A.* See Schorer 725–37. See also SL's letters to Marcella Powers, summer 1945, St. Cloud State University Archive, for clearest view of chronology.
224.22–23 NEW YORK September-October. Arriving in New York from Duluth September 13, SL stayed until November 15, when he and driver Asa Lyons set out for three-week tour of the South in preparation for *Kingsblood Royal,* returning to Duluth December 9. *Cass Timberlane* was published October 3.
225.1 DULUTH WINTER. Not mentioned in diary is Marjorie Kelley (later Wilkins, d. 1992, aged 69), almost certainly a prototype for Sophie Concord in *Kingsblood Royal,* who appears in Lewis's appointment books (at Yale Collection of American Literature) December 17, 19, and 23. Graduating from St. Mary's Hospital's three-year

nursing diploma program in Duluth 1947, she continued career as pioneer African-American in Duluth health care when she became St. Luke's Hospital's first black nurse anesthetist in 1955. Interviewed by phone 1986, 1991. Photocopies of SL's letters to her after he left town are housed at Northeast Minnesota Historical Center, U of MN in Duluth Library, Duluth, MN. See Schorer 731.

225.17 Paul Van Hooven. Paul H. Vanhoven. 1886–1954. Vice-president Duluth Missabe & Iron Range Railroad. The house: 3431 East First Street.

227.6 Jan. 26. Not mentioned here are two young MN novelists, Ann Chidester, b. 1919, and Frederick Feikema Manfred, 1912–1994, and wife, guests at SL's house from Thursday January 24 to Sunday January 27, as shown by SL's appointment books in Yale Collection of American Literature. See also Lewis to Powers, 26 January 1946, St. Cloud State University Archive.

227.13 Eve Glendenning. d. 1999, aged 89. Kentucky-born, Wellesley-educated, next-door neighbor of SL at 2621 East Second Street, Duluth. Interviewed 1985 and 1990. Husband John.

230.29 Jay Markle. Jay E. Markle. Duluth bank president who retired and moved to Florida 1947.

Textual Record

THIS RECORD REVEALS details about the transition from document to printed edition. See "The Text and Its Treatment" for a description of the kinds of details. **Locations are specified by leaf number (not page) and line number in Lewis's typescript, so that 4.1∠2 means *fol.* 4, *lines* 1∠2.** The advantage of this method is to show the transition from typescript to print leaf by leaf, which is the way it happens, not printed page by printed page. The disadvantage is that line numbers refer to original lineation that is now lost in print. However, because folio numbers are marked in the printed text, the line numbers below will serve to indicate relative location within a leaf, and each lemma will indicate the precise location. In cases where leaves have not been included in the printed text, the reader can easily scan this record for an explanation of what those leaves contain, if anything at all. Note for example the description below of the contents of folios 1–3.

1. *Notes in Lewis's hand on land areas of New England states, Minnesota, and Texas. See Appendix.*

2. *Notes in Lewis's hand on square mile areas of six lakes. See Appendix.*

3. *Blank leaf with grayish tan thumb tab attached at top saying* Diary *in Lewis's hand and* MINN DIARY *typewritten.*

4. MINNESOTA DIARY] *Typed vertically at right, each letter upright, one under the other. April 8 entry has wide right margin to accommodate vertical title.*

4.1–2 (These temperatures . . . Minneapolis only)] *Inserted in Lewis's hand at top of leaf.*

7.4–9 *Vertical line in pencil drawn in left margin as if to mark first paragraph of April 17 entry.*

13.32–40 GOD IS LOVE . . . N. W. Bible Institute] *Inserted in Lewis's hand at bottom of page in two-column format.*

14.18 Blue Earth County: Medo & Little Cobb] *This part of Lewis's handwritten insertion is above the list of towns where he had more space to write than below.*

14.23–24 Brush Creek . . . Vivian] *Inserted in Lewis's hand below the list of towns.*

14.43 3 of eight] *Typeover correction, almost certainly from* or *to* of.

16.22 MAY FIRST,] *Underlined in red crayon.*

16.24 TREES ARE PRACTICALLY ALL OUT NOW] *Underlined in red crayon.*

16.48 dairy] *Probably means diary.*

17.8 Also is a branch . . . Library] *Lewis's handwritten addition marked for insertion after* school. *This edition adds parentheses for clarity.*

21.24–27 From Fred's family Bible. . . . a Mr. Williams.] *Inserted in Lewis's hand in right margin.*

23.2 Typical farmhouse] *Inserted in Lewis's hand in top margin.*

23.13 Brooder houses.] *Followed by rough ⅜-inch-in-diameter hand sketch—a half-square concentric in a half circle like front view of an igloo:* 

23.26 The last was made in ?] *Space left for date to be inserted.*

26.9–13 Small Dakota . . . & Van Kirk.] *Inserted in Lewis's hand at right margin.*

31.3 1 cemetery,] *Lewis may have meant to cancel the 1 for he canceled a letter immediately preceding.*

33.1–4 Alexandria: . . . kobold house.] *Typed as an insert in top margin at right, with some handwritten corrections.*

33.31 no nice] *Must mean* so nice.

37. *This leaf is a six-by-nine-inch blue-construction-paper program for a Delta Phi Lambda gathering at the University of Minnesota in 1942. Three holes have been punched in the construction paper for insertion in ring-binder like other leaves. The recto, which was once the interior of the program folded, has mounted on it the menu and the after-dinner program, mimeographed respectively on two pieces of white paper. The verso, which was the exterior of the folded program, has in white ink* ΔφΛ *and 1942. See Appendix.*

38–39. *These two leaves, once stapled together, are mimeographed copies of words for songs used by the Delta Phi Lambda literary fraternity. The left margin has three punched holes to fit the diary ring-binder. See entry for May 26, fol. 40. See Appendix for contents.*

41.1 with MAY 28] *Inserted in Lewis's hand in top margin at left.*

41.2 USO—local . . . going thru] *Inserted in top margin in Lewis's hand at right.*

41.5–11 Insert] *Inserted vertically in right margin in Lewis's hand, next to first typed paragraph on the leaf. Whether it means to add the handwritten subjects to the typed notes or to insert all the* MAIN STREET WAR *notes in the diary is uncertain.*

41.13 Bankerm nayor] *Probably means* banker mayor.

41.50 w Boy & Girl Scouts] *Inserted in bottom margin in ink in Lewis's hand with line indicating place in text, but see below.*

41.50 Rubber collectn] *Inserted in bottom margin in pencil in Lewis's hand. Place in text not specified clearly. May be a reminder, not an insertion in text. Or may be intended for insertion in text along with the adjacent lower-margin addition, to be put together as follows:* Rubber collectn w Boy & Girl Scouts.

43.26–30 toward dusk: water . . . Dark 9:20 CWT.] *Added in Lewis's hand in 1¼-inch space left between May 28 and May 29, 1942 entries, marked for insertion in second paragraph on leaf.*

44. *Contains two mounted articles clipped from Minneapolis newspaper. The first, with headline missing, is about a storm on Friday and Saturday that produced flooding, power outages, and broken plate glass windows in Minneapolis. The second is William J. McNally's column "More or Less Personal" entitled "The First Minneapolitan." Lewis identifies the clippings only with a handwritten note at the top of the leaf,* From Minneapolis—Saturday May 30, 1942. *He also adds a handwritten note at the bottom of the second article, which reports on McNally's interview with 93-year-old Harriet Godfrey, who had been the first white child born in Minneapolis:* She died Jan. or Feb. 1943.

46.18 Trib:] *Space left after this word, probably intended for temperatures.*

48.39–45 Trib: 8, 71, 12, 80 . . . after rain)] *Typed insertion in right margin with some handwritten additions.*

53.1–3 Duluth Little Theater . . . Gregory Foley.] *Typed note in top margin at right.*

54. *Lined five-hole notebook paper leaf bearing a letter, recto and verso, in pencil in the letter-writer's hand, duplicated by interlinear typing, probably by Lewis. Typed label at top says:* Letter found in logging camp, Red Lake Reservation. *Writer is an ill mother, Mrs. Hardy, asking son for money. See Appendix for text, which follows the typed transcription.*

56.21–23 A literal <u>sigh</u> of contentment at Otter Tail hills.] *Inserted in Lewis's hand in right margin.*

58.5–6 Start actual writing of novel "Planish." Till now, planning.] *Inserted in Lewis's hand, as if to fit in middle of paragraph.*

58.18 SHORTEST DAY OF THE YEAR] *Must mean* shortest night of the year.

60.53 Benson & some union agts. like young mpls bus. men] *Inserted in Lewis's hand in bottom margin, below an arrow pointing to right edge of leaf, as if to indicate continuation.*

63.38 CHANCEY (sic)] *This is indeed the spelling at line 38, even though on line 3, Lewis had typed* Chancy (sic on tombstone).

66.17 In this haze, all hills] *Best guess of intended reading. Lewis canceled* Battle Lakeall *with his normal typeover* M *so that the result looks like* BMMMMMMMMMeall *which must mean* all *not* Beall.

69.14 Porter of War Dept.] *May be* Potter *or* Porter. *Lewis made a typeover correction, almost certainly correcting* t *to* r .

69.43 cool--9 AM, 62] *These last words on leaf are followed by penciled arrow pointing right, as if to indicate continuation.*

70.1–10 JULY 7, CONT. . . a little ground.] *These lines occupy a narrow column on the left to make room for a newspaper clipping mounted beside them on the right. The clipping includes first eight lines plus one word of an article about weather, identified only by Lewis's handwritten note:* Cedric Adams Star-Journal 7/7/42.

70.44 ate] *Must mean* are.

72.9 faint, though they] *Must mean* faint, as though they.

73.9 stort] *Must mean* story.

73.11 Pingree] *Typed addition in right margin. Lewis's normal mark for insertion, a typed slash, comes after* BOFlower. *The present reading* BOFlower, Pingree, Richard Ely *adds a comma after* Pingree *for clarity.*

76.31–32 as the Buckthorn,] *Must mean* at the Buckthorn,.

81.51 World Wide eatures] *Must mean* World Wide Features.

81.52 Bart Heffelfinger] *Must mean* Brad Heffelfinger.

83.1–3 AUGUST 10, Monday . . . HUNGRY JACK LAKE.] *Directly typed heading. Rest of leaf is blue carbon, first of several letter extracts, typed carbon copies, inserted as leaves in the diary. All of these carbon extracts are from letters sent to Marcella Powers.*

85.51 along Mesabi range,] *Last line on leaf followed by hand-drawn arrow pointing right, as if to suggest continuation.*

86.41 Trib: 8, 52; n, 68; 6, 73.] *Inserted in Lewis's hand between end of August 15, 1942 entry and August 16, 1942 entry. Almost certainly belongs to August 16, but could belong to August 15.*

87.47 heat on in house.] *Followed by hand-drawn arrow pointing right, as if to suggest continuation.*

87v.1–5 Lake colors . . . w. gold] *On verso in Lewis's hand.*

88.14–49 *Entries for August 24 to August 29, 1942 all typed with large right margin (extra inch and a half) where Lewis has mounted a clipping regarding cold snap in weather. Lewis's handwritten note at top of clipping says:* Mpls Star-Journal 8/24/42.

88.32 lites across late.] *Must mean* lights across lake.

89.16 *Leaf has only sixteen lines, more than half blank—possibly to leave room for more material from August 30–September 21, 1942, or equally likely, to show break in continuity caused by trip east.*

90.6–8 Sept. Equinox] *Inserted in Lewis's hand in left margin next to paragraph on weather during September 22–26.*

90.6–51 *Entries from* WEATHER SEPT 22-26 *to* Sat. 26th *all typed in narrow column on left, leaving room for two columns of clippings mounted at right. Layout suggests Lewis mounted clippings first, then typed entries. First article headlined "Temperature Hits Low of 33"; Lewis has written on it* Mpls Star 9/24/42. *Second article headlined "Ten Injured as Cars Skid and Crack Up"; Lewis's handwritten label here says only:* 9/26/42. *Third article (part of same clipping as second) headlined "Snow, Rain, Fog, Blanket Minneapolis"; Lewis has written here:* Saturday Trib 9/26/42.

91.25 l3af shapes] *Must mean* leaf shapes.

91.28 coty] *Must mean* city.

93.1–2 OCTOBER 2-3, . . . letter)] *Directly typed heading label.*

93.3–51 At the entrance . . . Columbus,] *Typed carbon copy letter extract on stationery bearing green letterhead:* PAUL PERRAULT / THE MAN THAT SEES TOMORROW / Fergus Falls, Minnesota. *Letterhead design includes a circular emblem bearing signs of the zodiac in each lower corner of leaf.*

94.1 OCT 2-3 CONT.--2] *Directly typed heading label.*

94.2–25 Ohio--and then . . . toys to the stranger/] *Continuation of typed carbon letter extract from fol. 93. This leaf not letterhead.*

94.26 Friday, Saturday; so many newts] *Resumption of direct diary typing.*

94.28–32 SIGNS ALONG ROAD: . . . Minneapolis.] *Typed addition inserted at right side of page beside the paragraph reading:* Return for peaceful evening, Saturday. *Likely location for addition is before this paragraph, though it might also come after.*

95.15 unchanged pipes,] *Must mean* unchanged pines,.

95.35–55 *The last three paragraphs are typed at the bottom of this leaf in two parallel columns, all appended in a stint of writing done after the typing in the upper two-thirds of the page. In order, the three paragraphs are: the one beginning* OCT. 6. Tue. Trib: 8, 49; *the one beginning* Sunday, above, cont:; *and the one beginning* Monday 5th Cont:. *In the present edition, the afterthought paragraphs are presented in the typescript order but without columnizing.*

96.30 gield] *Must mean* field.

97.13 Bergm] *Must mean* Berg,.

101. *Contains only one news clipping mounted in the center, with headline "November Visitor," labeled in Lewis's hand:* Mpls Trib 11/7/42.

103.14 Daniels, Rolf and Mrs. Ueland.] *Final line on leaf. Remaining two-thirds of leaf is blank except for six-inch-long diagonal arrow drawn from end of last line to lower right edge, as if to suggest continuation. The reason to leave blank space is in order to include the excerpted letter carbon (on the next leaf) under the Nov. 22 date before going on to an entry for Nov. 23.*

104.1 NOV 22 CONT (from a letter)] *Directly typed heading label.*

104.2–32 Sunday November 22 and . . . outworn literary brain.] *Carbon copy excerpt of typed letter.*

104.33 NOV 23, Mon. 9:30 AM, frost on roofs] *Resumption of directly typed diary entries.*

104.40 ':15 CWT] *May mean* 8:15 CWT.

105.29 son] *Must mean* sun.

105.38 trying to find in,] *Might mean* trying to find it,.

107. *This leaf all in Lewis's hand—notes which he may have intended to type into smoother form later. He was in Minneapolis for brief visit in late winter 1943.*

107.1 Feb. 1943] *Written large by Lewis in red crayon in upper right corner as label for whole page.*

108.1 May 1943] *Written large by Lewis in red crayon in upper right corner as label for whole page.*

108a. *When the leaves were numbered, this leaf was skipped. For the purposes of this edition, it is designated fol. 108a.*

108a.39 four quarters] *Must mean* four quarts.

109.1 1943] *Inserted in Lewis's hand in black ink in upper right corner, following the labeling practice of fols. 107 and 108.*

109.5 spave] *Must mean* space.

110. *This full leaf of notes is all in Lewis's hand, has yellow thumb tab stapled at top saying* Winter *in Lewis's hand.*

111. *This full leaf of notes is all in Lewis's hand.*

112. *This leaf, with just four lines at top, is all in Lewis's hand.*

113.43 slops] *May mean* slope.

114. *This full leaf of notes is all in Lewis's hand.*

115.1–3 Temp. Wedn . . . min., 39.] *Inserted in Lewis's hand at upper right.*

115.4–55 DULUTH AT LAST! . . . at the hotel windows.] *Letter excerpt, typed carbon copy.*

115.56–58 Temperature Thursday . . . Max, 58; min, 58.] *This last paragraph typed directly, not carbon like most of leaf.*

116. *Another letter excerpt, typed carbon copy.*

116.1 1944] *Added in upper right margin in Lewis's hand.*

117. *Resumption of directly typed daily diary entries.*

117.9–20 Temperature maximum & minimum hereafter without the "max" & "min"] *Inserted in left margin in Lewis's hand, seeming to refer to the May 20 and May 21, 1944 entries.*

118. *Letter extract, typed carbon copy. Note first paragraph, which explains that carbons of diary do double duty as letter material (just as copies of letters do double duty as diary entries).*

119. *Directly typed diary entries.*

119.29–31 Top of blue spruce, w. red buds, like bl Xmas tree.] *Inserted in Lewis's hand in left margin between May and June 1944 entries. This edition puts it with May 31 entry, but it might belong to June 1.*

119.34–49 *Small news clipping about weather mounted at right. Typed lines of diary in first two paragraphs for June are shortened by inch and a half to make room for it. The article is headlined "Minneapolis Starts To Swelter Again." There are two dates handwritten by Lewis:* June 1 *and* 6/1.

120.1 Sat June 3 . . . Duluth--1944] *Directly typed heading label.*

120.2–36 That was a pleasant . . . It was good.] *These first five paragraphs are carbon copy excerpt of typed letter.*

120.23–25 Mrs. H] *Added in Lewis's hand in left margin, next to paragraph beginning* Hannin *that introduces the piano trio. Double hyphen is emendation to clarify connection to text.*

120.32 Larson] *Added in left margin in Lewis's hand. Double hyphen is emendation to clarify connection to text.*

120.34 Ernst Lachmann] *Added in left margin in Lewis's hand. Double hyphen is emendation for clarity.*

120.35 Dworshak] *Added in right margin in Lewis's hand. Double hyphen is emendation for clarity.*

120.37 Sat 3d - weather: cold] *Resumption of directly typed diary entries.*

121.37 see PAGE after NEXT.] *Last words, with one quarter page left blank at bottom, so as not to let daily diary entries get ahead of letter-copy insertions.*

122.2–36 The 2 worst female voices . . . well-to-do St. Louis, Mo., brewer.] *Typed vertically in left margin with no precise insertion point, the only direct typing on the page. The rest of page is a letter extract, carbon copy, written June 10, 1944.*

123. *Letter extract, typed carbon copy, written June 12, 1944.*

123.12 (beer only)] *Added in Lewis's hand at end of paragraph, perhaps intended to follow the words* almost-unalcoholic.

124.1 Duluth Mon June 12 cont.] *Directly typed label on page that is mainly carbon of typed letter extract.*

124.2–40 (3) An immensely . . . Servants and Finns] *Four paragraphs of typed carbon letter excerpt, continued from fol. 123.*

124.41 Monday morning; fog again, cool.] *This and the preceding asterisks are direct typing after end of carbon letter excerpt. In the couple inches of space at bottom of leaf is mounted Juho Rissanen's calling card. See Appendix.*

125.47 "shortest day of year."] *Must mean* "longest day of year."

125.44–50 Fri: cd read watch at 10:25 PM] *Inserted in Lewis's hand in right margin.*

125.50 EWT] *Lewis first typed* SWT, *then overstruck the* S *to make it* CWT, *then corrected it by hand to* EWT.

126.1–30 *Letter extract, typed carbon, occupying slightly more than half the page. The rest is blank space except for one handwritten sentence (lines 31–32):* Sun red ball in mist casts only blurred path on water.

127.1 <u>Insert</u>] *Added in Lewis's hand in upper right corner.*

127.–129. *Typed carbons of part of long letter for June 16, 1944.*

128.1 Insert Fri 6/16] *Added in Lewis's hand at top of leaf.*

129.1 Insert Fri. 6/16] *Added in Lewis's hand at top of leaf.*

129.53–55 waves sparkle coming in shore . . . w. broken wing] *Added in Lewis's hand in bottom margin.*

130.5 Knife River] *Emended from* Knife " . *The ditto marks refer not to* Pt. *but to* River. Stony Pt. *is an addition in Lewis's hand written off to the right, not in the main column. Inserting it in column where indicated by Lewis disrupts sequence of ditto marks.*

131.–132. *These two leaves are a travel brochure, printed on recto and verso, about the Lake Superior north shore, entitled "Air-Conditioned Vacations." Among other things, it lists vacation spots and their distances in miles from Duluth, a map sketch of the north shore, and photos of things like waterfalls and Split Rock Lighthouse. Someone has circled 36.5, the mileage next to Elving's Mighty Fine Cabins. Too lengthy to be included in Appendix.*

133. *Blank leaf on which are mounted three news clippings. The first is labeled in Lewis's hand* Duluth News Trib June 2, 1944 *and has one article with the headline "Ore Shipments Push Ahead of Last Year" and another article with the headline "Mary Pickford, Mate Adopt Another Child." The second is labeled in Lewis's hand* Aug. 16, 1944 D. Herald *and has the headline "Duluth Cool; East Is Hot." The third is labeled in Lewis's hand* 8/20/44 *and has the headline "Experiment Station Visiting Day Is Scheduled Friday."*

134.4 3 times] *Added in Lewis's hand in right margin with line making connection to* signalling.

134.11–17 See steam from whistle . . . Green light] *Added in Lewis's hand below the typed entries. The bottom half of page below these scribbled notes is blank.*

135.–138. *Carbon of typed letter down through third paragraph of 138, including line 30 ending:* than that, Comrade--.

136.1 June 24] *Added in Lewis's hand at top of leaf.*

137.1 June 24] *Added in Lewis's hand at top of leaf.*

137.7 , across 2 miles of water,—1 mile?] *Inserted in Lewis's hand in right margin. This edition adds comma after question mark to ease fit with paragraph.*

138.1 Duluth June 24, 1944 -4] *Typed directly as heading label for this page that continues the typed carbon letter.*

138.2 June 24] *Added in Lewis's hand.*

138.31 Sat. 24. 73-57, Mpls 86-62. Gray, fairly cool] *Resumption of directly typed diary entries.*

139.1–2 74-52; Mpls 75-58; NY, 92-73] *Direct typing.*

139.2 Duluth, Thursday, June 29] *Typed carbon copy with* , 1944 *added by direct typing.*

139.3–20 What a day . . . blessed by such a day as this.] *First two paragraphs are carbon copy of typed letter extract.*

139.21 9 AM, whole lake suave and rose-colored,] *Resumption of directly typed diary entries.*

139.41–55 *July 2, 1944 entry, last paragraph on page, is typed in increasingly narrow column to make room for clippings of untitled, undated news article about weather in June 1944, mounted at right.*

140.44–52 64-51 Mpls: 79-59; NY 91-74.] *Added in left margin in Lewis's hand next to July 9, 1944 paragraph.*

142.7 Asa Lyons, driver.] *Inserted in Lewis's hand between paragraph beginning* Mon 24 *and paragraph beginning* Tue 25.

143.24–43 *The sixth, seventh, and eighth paragraphs are narrowed by inch and a half to leave room for news clipping mounted at right, which is dated in Lewis's hand 8/2/44. The article is about illegal possession of beaver pelts in Ely, Minnesota; has no headline. Lewis has written at the bottom* Minn. still, fur-bearing.

146. *This leaf contains two paragraphs, each on a family in Duluth. Although the typeface seems the same, the format differs from other leaves of the diary in being double-spaced, as if someone other than Lewis did the typing.*

146.1 From Relief org] *Written in Lewis's hand in upper right corner.*

147.2–5 Party Aug. 26 1944] *Added in Lewis's hand in upper right corner.*

147.3–32 *Column of check marks, question marks, and* yes *and* no *words added in Lewis's hand.*

147.10–11 Heimbach Hem 4818] *Added in Lewis's hand.*

147.31–35 Dick-Neva . . . napkins] *Added in Lewis's hand, along with several names and reminders that have been crossed out.*

148.38 David Bradleys.] *Inserted in Lewis's hand above line. Preceding comma an emendation for clarity.*

148.44–50 Fri. 25—67 . . . To NY 8:15 P.M.] *All added in Lewis's hand at bottom of leaf.*

149. *All in Lewis's hand.*

150.–151.20 *Lewis's typed record of temperatures during selected days from December 6, 1944 through April 3, 1945, with parallel column entries for New York, Duluth, and Minneapolis-St. Paul, and with additional notes on record highs and lows. See Appendix.*

151.21 *The bottom two-thirds of this leaf has two mounted news clippings, one with the headline "Hottest March Day On Record Hits 72" bearing the typed label* Duluth 3/23/45 *and the other with the headline "81° Heat a Record for March, Fruit Trees Face Frost Danger" bearing Lewis's handwritten label* H-T NY 3/29/45.

152.1–25 *Continuation of parallel-column temperature records from fols. 150–151, gradually changing to diary entries. Included in present text because of integral connections between records and diary.*

152.25 June DULUTH] *Last typed words on page.*

152.25–40 —1945 . . . 29—PD—] *Remainder of page all in Lewis's hand.*

153. *Has thirty-one lines only, leaving 3.5 inches blank space at foot of leaf.*

157.32 and gray,] *May mean* are gray,.

158. *Has twenty-one lines only, leaving bottom half of page blank.*

159. *Has nine lines only, all in Lewis's hand, with rest of page blank.*

160. *Blank leaf to divide diary from "Minnesota Hills & Valleys," has grayish tan thumb tab attached at top with* VAL *in Lewis's hand.*

Selection of Lewis's Abbreviations

THE LIST BELOW shows the abbreviations that the reader may need to understand the diary. Many locations are specified in order to show the contextual evidence for the meanings and also to distinguish places where different meanings respectively attach to the same abbreviation. Not shown are all the variations in capitalization, punctuation, and pluralization occurring with each abbreviation. Nor is there a listing for highly familiar abbreviations or for abbreviations that occur only in places where the context clearly reveals the sense.

abt	about [fol. 6, 10, 31, 41, 42, 48, 55, 61, 64, 65, 82, 85, 90, 94, 96, 100, 102, 103, 105, 113, 120, 129, 134, 138, 140, 141, 153, 156]
aby	about, *mistyping for* abt [fol. 119]
acc.	according to [fol. 78]
acc to	according to [fol. 26]
adv	advanced [fol. 96]
AF of L	American Federation of Labor [fol. 58]
Amers	Americans [fol. 98]
ann	announced [fol. 95]
anthrop	anthropologist [fol. 53]
app	apparently [fol. 69]
arr	arriving/ed/al [fol. 80, 113, 117]
B correspondent	Bismarck correspondent [fol. 27]
bef	before [fol. 134, 153]
bl	blue [fol. 119]
Bril	brilliant [fol. 106]
bus. men	businessmen [fol. 60]
CAccts	checking accounts, *must mean* savings accounts [fol. 41]

cd	could [fol. 11, 19, 28, 36, 42, 45, 67, 91, 96, 107, 125]
cge	college [fol. 6, 33, 52, 100, 145]
ch	church [fol. 40]
C.I.O.	Congress of Industrial Organization [fol. 45, 81]
Ck	Creek [fol. 130]
Co	company [fol. 51, 75, 86, 102, 105, 108a, 113, 115, 147]
Co	county [fol. 30, 33, 59, 114]
compo	composition [fol. 53]
Congo pastor	Congregational pastor [fol. 145]
Conn.	Connecticut [fol. 21, 69]
corr	correspondent [fol. 104]
C.P.W NYC	Central Park West, New York City [fol. 110]
crissX	crisscross [fol. 149]
CWT	Central War Time [fol. 18, 43, 46, 48, 57, 58, 78, 91, 99, 100, 104, 106, 119, 125, 144]
D	Dorothy Thompson [fol. 99]
Det	Detroit [fol. 145]
dif	different [fol. 134]
dif	difficult [fol. 105]
diff	difference [fol. 148]
diff	difficulty [fol. 65]
din	dinner [fol. 105, 144]
d. r. table	dining room table [fol. 144]
D.T.'s	delirium tremens [fol. 94]
ed	editor [fol. 51, 52, 104]
EG	e. g.—for example [fol. 6]
elab	elaborate [fol. 74]
Eng	English [fol. 90, 100, 114]
even	evening [fol. 41, 77, 88, 92, 99, 104, 105, 140, 143]
eveng	evening [fol. 142]
EWT	Eastern War Time [fol. 125]
exch	exchanged [fol. 69]
FDR	Franklin Delano Roosevelt [fol. 69]
fol	followed [fol. 69]
fr	from [fol. 18, 25]
gals	gallons [fol. 105]
gd	good [fol. 26, 92]
G. N.	Great Northern Railroad [fol. 62, 137]
gt	great [fol. 8, 10, 40, 48, 60, 66, 69, 73, 79, 81, 90, 95, 120, 121, 122, 153]
GT	Greenwich time? [fol. 99, 100]
h. a.	high Anglican? horse's ass? [fol. 98]
h&c	hot and cold water [fol. 86]

hd	head [fol. 99]
H-T	Herald Tribune [fol. 151]
incl	including [fol. 41, 55, 142, 143]
incl	inclusive [fol. 125, 135]
in re	in result of [fol. 15]
instr	instructor [fol. 145]
int al	inter alia—among other things [fol. 52, 108a]
I S p.d.	Indian Summer perfect day [fol. 97, 98, 104]
IWW	Industrial Workers of the World [fol. 91]
J. atty.	Jewish attorney [fol. 145]
Jos	Joseph [fol. 16, 63, 86]
K. C.	Kansas City [fol. 138, 143, 144]
lil	little [fol. 91, 122]
lv	leave [fol. 24, 88, 113, 143]
M	Marcella Powers [fol. 43, 99, 106, 117, 141]
M	Monday [fol. 20]
Marg	Margaret [fol. 148]
mfr	manufacture [fol. 119]
mid	midnight [fol. 88, 90, 91, 92, 95, 97, 99, 100, 108a]
min	minimum [fol. 74, 115, 117, 119]
min	minutes [fol. 47, 125]
Miss	Mississippi [fol. 157]
mos	months [fol. 67]
Mp	Minneapolis [fol. 125, 138, 139, 140, 141, 142, 143, 144, 145, 148]
Mple	Minneapolis [fol. 6]
MS	manuscript [fol. 43, 88, 106, 148]
n	noon [fol. 43, 48, 68, 69, 77, 84, 85, 86, 87, 88, 90, 91, 92, 94, 95, 96, 97, 98, 99, 100, 102, 105, 106, 108, 108a]
n *or* N	north [fol. 32, 42, 76, 95, 115]
nev	never [fol. 144]
nr	near [fol. 8, 12, 19, 20, 21, 23, 24, 66, 68, 80, 139]
NW	northwest [fol. 5, 13, 65]
NY	New York City [fol. 4, 10, 48, 107, 108, 117, 118, 120, 121, 123, 125, 138, 140, 141, 142, 143, 144, 145, 148]
NYMills	New York Mills [fol. 66]
occ	occupied by [fol. 76]
occas	occasional [fol. 69]
offnon	off and on [fol. 120]
opp	opposite [fol. 23, 35]
org	organization [fol. 146]
P. Arthur	Port Arthur, Canada [fol. 142]
Pathet	pathetic [fol. 99]

p. c.	post cibum—after meals [fol. 40]
pd *or* p.d. *or* PD	perfect day [fol. 72, 76, 77, 78, 79, 80, 81, 86, 87, 88, 96, 97, 100, 102, 103, 108a, 121, 125, 138, 139, 140, 141, 142, 143, 144, 145, 148, 152, 153, 158]
perf	perfect [fol. 48, 67]
perfday	perfect day [fol. 19]
photog.	photographer [fol. 140, 144]
Pk	Park [fol. 98]
Pk	Peak [fol. 66]
pop	population [fol. 22, 26, 31, 35, 57, 96]
prest	present [fol. 159]
prest	president [fol. 17, 22, 26, 30, 75, 102, 113, 145]
prop	proprietor [fol. 52, 75]
pt *or* Pt	point [fol. 62, 72, 105, 130]
PWA	Public Works Administration [fol. 40]
q.v.p.	quod vide pagina—which see on the page [fol. 40]
rd	road [fol. 4]
re	regarding [fol. 33, 50, 64, 69, 88, 95]
re	result of, resulting from, from [fol. 15, 33, 51, 58, 61, 68, 69, 92, 95, 102]
recd	received [fol. 8, 91]
rem	remember [fol. 8, 30, 47, 96, 108, 109, 144]
ret	returning [fol. 66]
RR	railroad [fol. 8, 13]
rwy	railway [fol. 13]
s *or* S	south [fol. 6, 20, 76, 113, 121]
S.C.	Sauk Centre [fol. 24, 41]
secy	secretary [fol. 30, 41, 108]
shd	should [fol. 14, 77, 85, 92, 95, 104]
SL	Sinclair Lewis [fol. 93]
S. M.	sergeant major [fol. 129]
So.	Southern [fol. 8, 14, 19, 22, 68, 109]
SR Lighthouse	Split Rock Lighthouse [fol. 130]
SS Moronic	Steamship Moronic [fol. 143]
st *or* St	street [fol. 41, 47, 66, 89, 102, 110, 113, 114, 119, 146, 158]
St. P	St. Paul [fol. 7, 99]
sur.	surrounding [fol. 46]
surr	surrounded [fol. 17]
SW	Southwest [fol. 117]
ther	thermometer [fol. 16, 17]
tht	that [fol. 136]
Trib	Minneapolis Tribune [fol. 36, 40, 45, 46, 47, 48, 55, 57, 58, 60, 64, 66, 68, 69, 70, 71, 72, 74, 75, 76, 77, 78, 79,

	80, 81, 82, 84, 85, 86, 87, 88, 90, 91, 92, 94, 95, 96, 97, 98, 99, 100, 102, 104, 105, 106, 108, 108a]
Unabl acct	unable-to-attend account [fol. 148]
vge	village [fol. 22, 25, 26, 34, 35, 102, 105, 109, 123, 129]
vs	versus, as opposed to, opposed to, against [fol. 20, 25, 67, 68, 85, 154, 156]
vv.	vice versa [fol. 4, 18, 49]
w	with [fol. 28, 41, 57, 69, 87v, 103, 107, 110, 112, 114, 115, 119, 125, 129, 134, 136, 138, 147, 152]
Washn	Washington (Irving) [fol. 18]
Washn	Washington D. C. [fol. 55, 60, 104, 125, 144]
wd	would [fol. 8, 42, 55, 67, 91, 95]
wh	which [fol. 45, 97, 106, 111, 149, 152]
wh	white [fol. 140]
WPA	Work Projects Administration [fol. 28, 34, 42, 47, 75, 135]
WST	War Saving Time [fol. 107, 117, 119—see SL explanation fol. 4]
Xian	Christian [fol. 17, 85]
y	young [fol. 33, 55]
Y men	young men [fol. 26]
yr	year [fol. 18, 33, 45, 56, 68, 78, 99, 107, 116, 117, 118, 138, 145]
yr	your [fol. 58, 135]

Appendix

Miscellaneous Notes and Unpublished Scrapbook Materials in the Diary

fol. 1 in Lewis's hand

State Area (Land & <u>inland</u> waters)

Maine —	33215
N.H. —	9304
Vermont —	9609
Mass —	8257
Conn —	5009
R. I. —	<u>1214</u>
	66,608
Minnesota —	84,068
Texas —	267,339

fol. 2 in Lewis's hand

Lakes of World

	sq mi
Gt. Bear	14,000 (nearly 9,000,000 acres)
Manitoba	1,817
Winnipeg	9,400 (about 6,000,000 acres)
Lake of the Woods	1,500
Gt. Salt	2,560
Nipigon	1,730

fol. 37 layout not preserved, contents only

VICTORY RATIONS: Fruit Cup, Fried Chicken, New Potatoes, New Peas, Green Salad, Mayonnaise, Ice Cream, Coffee, with or without sugar.

ORDER OF THE EVENING: 1. General Sam Russell; 2. Adj. General Klohn; 3. Battles Won; 4. Presentation of Major General Thomas; 5. Secretary of War Lewis cautions, "Stay West, Young Woman." 6. Regimental singing; 7. Mrs. Victoria Janda reports on Ink Invasion; 8. "Lullaby for the Campus Oaks"--vocal with piano; 9. Skit--Literature for the Duration; 10. "Taps"

fols. 38–39

DELTA PHI LAMBDA

1. ("Happy Birthday")
Happy writing to you!
Happy writing to you!
Happy writing, dear writers,
Write creatively, too!

2. ("Love's Old Sweet Song")
Back in the dear, dead days in
English class,
It was a cinch the courses for to pass,
I wrote a term paper, bored the
teacher blue--
He once had written papers,
boring too.
Yet, since the years an afterglow
have cast,
Splendor doth seem to clothe my
work at last!
Just an old term paper, just a
student's toil,
Reeking of the burning of the mid-
night oil;
Not a spark of brilliance, dull
and doubtless true.
Nonetheless I'm startled at all I
knew,
At all I once, once knew.

3. ("Old Gray Bonnet")
Get out your last year's sonnet
With the mothballs upon it,
Read it once again--it might be
worse!
And your class in Folwell
(If you do at all well)
Will praise your refurbished verse!

4. ("Long, Long Ago")
Bring back the days when my
writing was free--
Long, long ago, long, long ago.
Young was I then, full of sim--
plici--tee--
Long, long ago, long ago.
Heavy my hand now, turgid my style;
Structure inhibits--to read me's a
trial.
Critics they scowl, though I once
hoped they'd smile,
Long, long ago, long ago.

5. ("In the Shade of the Old
Apple Tree")
In the shade of the old ivory
tower
It is pleasant to loaf for an
hour.
The winters are bland
And the summers are grand
And a cyclone is only a shower.

You can hear the dull buzz of
the poet;
What he means, you will never
quite know it,
For it's all very quaint;
What you think it is, ain't,
In the shade of the old ivory
tower.

6. ("I've Been Working on the
Railroad")
I've been working on a novel
For ten years more or less:
I've been working on a novel,
But it's not a huge success.
Each year I take it out of
mothballs
To try for a new relationship
For Art and Crass Commercialism-
Result--a rejection slip!

7. ("Annie Laurie")
Folwell Hall is large and
roomy;
There the atmosphere's serene;
And 'tis there that Doctor
Anna
Discourses like a queen.

Be the sky ashine or cloudy,
The theme be real or romance,
Doctor Anna sits in judgment
With Pomp and Circumstance.

With Pomp and Circumstance
And Justice by her side
Our delightful Doctor Anna's
Unaccustomed to be defied.

8. ("The Old Oaken Bucket")
How dear to my heart are the
themes of my childhood,
From weightier writing my mind
they relieve!
For now I must ponder style--
yes, plot and climax,
Oh, how I now suffer effect to
achieve!

The sweet simple writing,
The moss-covered subjects,
The trite, time-tried phrases
of pre-erudite days!

9. "My Bonnie Lies Over the
Ocean")
My muse has gone into hiding,
My muse has seen fit to flee,
My muse hides her face in her
draperies,
Oh, bring back my sweet muse
to me!

Bring Back, bring back, the
swift flow of words to me, to me,
Bring back, bring back, my coy
inspiration to me!

10. ("Daisy Bell")
Writer, writer, give me your
promise true,
No more drivel out of the pen
of you--
You will never be dejected
By manuscripts rejected;
Nor editors will think the worse
Of the silence that comes
from you.

11. ("Oh, Susanna")
Oh, I came to Minnesota with
creation on my mind,
And I made my way to Folwell Hall,
The secret for to find.
But I got nowhere with lit'rature
So I heeded what I heard
And I cast my lot with Fawcett
--to--
Tell ALL--one cent per word!

Oh, Doctor Anna,
Now don't you cry for me
For I've made my fame and fortune
--on--
A True Confessions spree.

13. ("Old Black Joe")
Gone are the days when my heart
was young and gay;
Gone are my friends from Folwell
Hall away;
Still, every week, I haunt that
corridor--
On Monday nights I'm there again,
in 3--0--4.

I'm coming! I'm coming!
Wait till I get down my came.
I'll hobble off to Seminar
Next fall again.

14. ("Silver Threads")
Darling, you are growing punk;
What you write is fearful junk.
Though they buy it, I'm afraid
Public taste has quite decayed.
Once your standards they were
high, were high;
Fame through Art was worth a try.
Sob I now and shed a tear--
"Confidentially---" my dear!

15. ("John Brown's Body")
John Doe's novel lies a-
moldering in the drawer.
He sometimes figures that it
wasn't worth the chore.
And yet in wistful moments, he
reviews its quiet charm,
That only he can see.

Shed a tear for Johnny's fiction,
Bad in structure, worse in
diction,
Worst in character depiction--
As all but John can see.

16. ("Taps")
When I die, 'way up high
Will my name be a flame in the sky?
Will they toast my poor ghost,
When I die?

fol. 54–54v

Letter found in logging camp, Red Lake Reservation

Ah-gwah-Ching Minn.
Feb. 7 - 1942

Dear Son:

Well first of all son I just want to let you no what the Doctor in Red Lake had promised me I really didn't want to come over here but he said if I'm not to get well or very sick that they would take me back to my own home town, I'll write to you if I think that Im not to get well. So you can come after me. Tell your brother to please send me some money as I have it hard here sure wish to have a small spending money I just have to ask or borrow my paper and envelopes and stamps to write. I really do not like to borrow from any one so soon as he send me the money I can return what I borrow. I am poor as ever and I have no comb I do not (?) when I comb my hair, Say please tell him to be sure and send the money so as he can I will be waiting for the money. You can tell Clarence to send me money as that why I am writing this because I am in need. I feel much better since I am here and I want to ask you to get my purce what I left at home get it and send it to me. and send me a comb. I will close hope to hear from you real soon as ever your mother you can also send me a little money. Mrs. Hardy

Ah-gwah-ching
(?) Minn
Excuse all mistakes and poor writing.

fol. 124

calling card

Juho Rissanen

ARTIST

Member of Academy of Fine Arts of Sweden
Member of Academy of Fine Arts of Finland, Charter Member of "de Salon d'automne a Paris." Holder of medal of Paris Exposition. A Knight of the First Class of the White Rose of Finland.

fols. 150–151.20

TEMPERATURE

1944

December	New York		Duluth		Minneapolis, St. Paul	
6	52	39	28	26		
8	55	42	27	21		
12	45	31	23	14		
14	38	24	33	13		
17	40	30	8	-2	11	7
20	33	15	22	-1	30	22
21	37	30	-5	-16	9	-9
(Winter solstice, 12/21 - 7:15 PM)						
23	36	24	12	-11	19	-3
25	41	34	-7	-13	3	-2
28	37	28	10	-8		
29	29	16	21	13		
31	43	32	15	8		

(Heavy rain NY, Xmas and NYEve

1945

January						
1	55	37	-2	-6	-1	-5
2	31	16	0	-18		
5	37	21	-1	-25		
9	37	18	-3	-4	5	-13
10	21	8	18	-2		
(Coldest 1/10 in NY since 1875)						
12	39	21	19	9		
14	31	19	24	18		
16	33	22	24	17		
(NY: heavy snow, sleet)						
17	33	19	20	19		
18	31	11	31	22		
21	35	20	32	25	32	27
24	34	7				
25	18	0	21	0	34	19
(Coldest 1/25 on record, in NY, & high, bitter wind)						
26	21	3	19	11	22	4
30	33	19	5	-7	7	-1
February						
4	36	16	24	11	27	24
7	42	26	17	10		
9	46	28	34	17	36	20
11	45	38	16	-4		
15	43	29	27	24		
21	38	28	25	15	29	23
25	48	35	28	8	33	11
27	57	36	38	-1	30	13
March						
2	51	34	27	15	26	22
4	46	32	22	13		
6	47	39	19	-6	21	-2
9	49	22	37	16		
12	44	33	49	29	49	27
15	65	44	35	32	48	39
(NY: hottest 3/15 on record; damp & thick fog.)						

fol. 151

1945

March (cont)	New York		Duluth		Minneapolis-St.Paul	
16	76	48	35	32	49	37
(NY: another record)						
17	80	54	49	32		
19 (NY: 1st thunder storm)						
20	80	55	44	26	37	34
22	42	33	72	39	71	38
(NY: sudden cold rain; couple of snow flurries)						
24 (NY: leaves budding)						
25	66	47	42	36	62	55
27	73	51	58	49	67	46
28	81	58	45	34		
(NY: record heat for March)						
29	83.7	59	58	33	64	35
(Again break all-time NY heat record for March)						
April						
2	65	53	29	26	43	32
3	74	58	28	25	31	28

Index

Where positive identifications have been made, proper nouns appear in a form confirmed by exterior sources. Otherwise, Lewis's versions are used. References to notes, which begin with the letter **n** and show in **bold**, specify the page and line numbers introducing each note on pages 232–59.